T*SQ Transgender Studies Quarterly

Volume 7 ★ Number 4 ★ November 2020

Trans in a Time of HIV/AIDS

Edited by Eva Hayward and Che Gossett

Trans in a Time of HIV/AIDS

CHE GOSSETT and EVA HAYWARD

COVID-19: Refuse Analogy

Just as we are writing the introduction to this special issue on AIDS, COVID-19 is designated a pandemic. Should we comment on COVID-19? What are the dangers of trying to bring these pandemics into conversation? What can we not yet think or know about COVID-19? In the AIDS intro we discuss the ongoing need to rethink AIDS — we wrote: "Have we begun to ask good questions about AIDS?" — and then everywhere we see coronavirus testing and quarantining graphed with infection and death rates; countries and demographics becoming axes. Many of our contributors start experiencing the effects of COVID-19: some test positive for the coronavirus; friends and family become sick; everyone is in lockdown, and in the deteriorating mental and physical health of quarantine, deadlines become impossible. Crisis provokes a response: asking better questions is replaced with offering quick solutions — what Elaine Scarry, invoking Hannah Arendt, refers to as "emergency thinking" (2012: 19). And yet, having just put together this special issue on AIDS, we cannot help but notice the echoes. COVID-19 exposes and renews the entrenchment of racism and antiblackness in health care, social services, and the US national response. Media outlets report that people with preexisting health conditions and limited access to health care are especially vulnerable, with demographics showing an unequal impact of COVID-19 on Black and brown communities. Antiblackness is carceral; not surprisingly prisons are the most concentrated sites of COVID-19. Perhaps what AIDS and COVID-19 share is antiblackness and racism. Might COVID-19 be a reiteration of these US legacies? COVID-19 has occurred amidst ritualized state sanctioned murder and warfare against Black people by police, from Breonna Taylor to the shooting of Jacob Blake. The moment of COVID-19 has also been one of waves of sustained activism — daily marches and actions against antitrans

TSQ: Transgender Studies Quarterly * Volume 7, Number 4 * November 2020   **527**
DOI 10.1215/23289252-8665171   © 2020 Duke University Press

and antiblack violence—from the Black trans march in New York City where an estimated twelve to fifteen thousand marched, to the actions and marches and protests for defunding and abolishing the police.

It is uncertain what will happen in the coming months and years of the pandemic, and yet what is already loud and clear is the rhetoric of contagion. Contagion discourse outpaces the virus (about which very little is known, and yet how quickly virology organizes care for the self [Foucault 1988]). "Friends" and "followers" on Instagram, Facebook, and Twitter post photos, memes, and videos about the urgency of social distancing and sanitizing. Face masks, latex gloves, hand sanitizer, and Zoom virtual gatherings (from dinners to classrooms) are civic virtues, demonstrating how safety is the responsibility of the individual (as if neoliberalism needed anymore devotion). Through the moralizing of quarantine and social distancing, modes of intimacy, friendship, and "care" disclose an underside of interpersonal surveillance and paranoid positioning. Contagion shapes and reshapes the personal sphere through posting videos that show "how sexy my boyfriend is in cleaning himself and our apartment," or screen captures of online classrooms that hide student and faculty labor, anxiety, and isolation through responsible and productive connectivity. Our wellness will be determined by personal restraint, abstinence, and abeyance. By this script, the socially distant subject of neoliberal health care is under an injunction to enact proper conduct and protocols figured through personal responsibility alone. Not only does social distancing aim to obscure the state's culpability through personal responsibility, but it also operationalizes autopoiesis. Given the United States government's abysmal response to COVID-19, a neoliberal response is necessitated through a lack of a state response. With self-care comes the enforcement of it, which is the crisis of the neoliberal response: there are no "good" personal responses; or better, there are no "personal" responses. Personal options have already been carved out by the state and are designed to reinforce its social engineering through obfuscation and reification. This is demonstrated in how immediately we recognize our social responsibility (as if pandemic thinking was already at work before COVID-19). As such, the morality of self-care is designed to empower the subject so as to conceal the state's commitment to control.

Self-care is represented as not only well-being, but well-adjustment: a "good" state subject with healthy boundaries. The "bad" state subjects—poor Black and brown communities whose sociality is already criminalized—are further surveilled and targeted by police, who are now also tasked with the enforcement of public health regulations during the COVID-19 pandemic. The police continue what Walter Benjamin (2019: 301–2) diagnosed as their "law making" and "law preserving" violence in the time of the pandemic. In New York City, police are using social distancing as an alibi to continue the policing of Black life on the one hand and to protect whiteness as proper citizenship on the other. Given the rapidity of moralizing self-care, it appears that the logic of distance — in what ways is whiteness an account of social distancing? — was already at work such that COVID-19 was simply an affirmation. These distancing strategies eerily echo racist and homophobic state efforts to close down social spaces used and loved by the unwanted. For instance, some COVID-19 responses appear to respond to the AIDS crisis, confirming social logics that ensured the ongoing pandemic of AIDS. Social and intimate behavior is foregrounded as causal and "risky" so as to hide the state's capitalist and antiblack exploits through globalization, health disparities, economic inequality, environmental injustice, and lack of social services. Another call-and-response to AIDS, there are now instances of the enmeshment of "public health" and criminalization — a woman charged with "bioterrorism" for coughing on food at a grocery store, echoes of HIV criminalization law in which a Black man was charged with bioterrorism in 2010, a charge made possible within the context of HIV/AIDS lawfare and criminalization, which is the backdrop for criminalization of public health — including the criminalization of HIV-positive sex workers.

And yet, how do we complexify these collapsing resonances of one pandemic into another? Perhaps it starts with asking: what does it mean that the ongoing sociopolitical traumas of AIDS are responded to through COVID-19? Already we see popularized science reports that HIV antiretroviral medications are being tested for efficacy in treating COVID-19. Miami gay festivals have already been reported as "spreading coronavirus." "COVID-19 parties" suggest antisociality and abject decadence — the affective logic that subtends HIV/AIDS "risk prevention" rhetoric. This is the technology of analogy. Analogy is a rhetorical device that aims to make meaning through the collapse of difference. A false historicity is one way this collapse occurs: the analogy is itself a retroactive response, a redress or "afterwardness." That we compare these pandemics is a desire to redo (but mostly in the form of repetition) our response. This analogy works to cast AIDS into the past of the novel coronavirus. And yet, for us *TSQ* editors and our contributors — some of whom are living with AIDS, who are Black and trans — we are differently vulnerable to COVID-19. AIDS remains! The expansion of the security state operates in this moment of pandemic as Black and brown trans HIV-positive people are further impacted by joblessness, houselessness, lack of health care. How are those who are disabled facing the state violence of, on the one hand, the robust carceral state apparatus with policing and prisons and, on the other hand, the "organized abandonment" (Gilmore 2015) of the collapse of the welfare state and neoliberal privatization of health so that "remote work" is largely foreclosed? In this "economy of abandonment" (Povinelli 2011), what is inscribed in the self (distance) is the prescriptive discourse of risk and moral hygiene through an epidemiological grid predicated on antiblackness. In the meanwhile, trans women of color are dying removed from friends and loved ones, in hospitals, by themselves, forced to say impossible goodbyes via phone — a social distancing in and of itself (and a cruel reminder of isolationist logic of racism and transphobia).

In contrast to the repulsion for people dying from HIV/AIDS-related illness — the four *H*'s of AIDS: homosexuals, heroin users, hemophiliacs, and Haitians — with coronavirus the initial media response was to prop up a shared sense of the nation as a unified and unifying body that will persevere and overcome illness, recovering as a whole national body. Eric Stanley reminds us that while COVID-19 had nurses and doctors flying to NYC, during AIDS they were trying to escape. But these differences between pandemics are continually under revision. With COVID-19, scientism is mobilized in the name of a self-possessed national immunity; the bodily self is recast as property so as to reactivate the racial schema that made a coherent and contained subject of the state erectable. The idea of national immunity and coronavirus as universally infecting and the fortification of the nation as a shared body is predicated on xenophobia and anti-Asian violence, shored-up border securitization, and the racial and ableist capitalist flow of vulnerability, the racism of what Ruth Wilson Gilmore (2007: 28) has termed "the state-sanctioned or extralegal production and exploitation of group-differentiated vulnerability to premature death." COVID-19 responses are folding people into new biomedical and epidemiological stratagems. What political kinds of organizing will COVID-19 require — echoing the radical health activism of the Black Panthers (Nelson 2011) — to answer Dean Spade's (2020) question: "What would a public health system not rooted in military imperialism and backed by criminalization mechanisms look like? What would a public health system look like in a society grounded in collective care and co-stewardship rather than coercion?"

As we write this response to COVID-19, the rate of coronavirus infection at Rikers Island prison now hugely exceeds New York City to become one of most concentrated and fast-moving sites of COVID-19 in the entire world. Just as AIDS did, COVID-19 is showing the lethality of antiblackness and capitalism as not simply effects of pandemics but the logic on which pandemic deaths are calculated. In the epilogue to *AIDS and the Distribution of Crises*, C. Riley Snorton brings Stuart Hall's work *Policing the Crisis* to bear on HIV/AIDS in an analysis of Hall's reflections on crisis as a pretext for increased policing, as well as AIDS and analogy. The infection discourse of pandemics capitalizes on the very conditions that made infection not only possible but inevitable. If we follow Snorton and Hall, policing COVID-19 looks like police enforcing social distancing through continued criminalization of Black sociality and upholding racial capitalism while incarcerated people at Rikers are left to die. The Federal Bureau of Prisons recently purchased $60,000 of hydroxychloroquine, the drug made infamous by President Trump's hackneyed claim of its effectiveness, to "treat" coronavirus in federal prisons where several have died and nearly two hundred have tested positive. These compounding acts of violence in the name of security echo, as Snorton is proposing, HIV rates for incarcerated people that are five to seven times higher than non incarcerated, and still higher for Black incarcerated people. COVID-19 is reactivating antiblackness through the cultural pathologization and a rhetoric of racial responsibility that has been part of the programmatics of AIDS.

As a way of returning to what we intended to do with our introduction, and in an effort to complicate any simplified analogy between COVID-19 and AIDS, while also foregrounding antiblackness as the structuration of both pandemics, we want to end this brief statement with two reflections by trans women who are navigating this current moment and have also been involved in AIDS activism and prison abolitionist organizing. Both remember the death of Lorena Borjas from COVID-19. Lorena Borjas was a trans Latina activist and a mothering figure for many trans Latinas in Queens. Borjas passed away on March 30 after she was hospitalized due to coronavirus. Memorialized by Cecilia Gentili (2020) in the *New York Times*, Borjas's legacy of resistance included bailing out countless trans people of color and organizing trans sex workers of color "to become" — as Gentili writes — "an unstoppable insubordination." In the article, Gentili contextualizes Borjas's legacy in this time of coronavirus and the landscape of racism and transphobia. Gentili writes,

> Jackson Heights is among the areas in New York City that have been hit especially hard by the coronavirus. As a result we've had to rethink what outreach looks like in the age of a pandemic, and what the specific needs of the community are at this critical moment. Trans sex workers and the undocumented folks in our community are not eligible for unemployment, and they most certainly will not be receiving stimulus checks. They need to know what their housing rights are, as well as food, medications and money to pay their phone bills. . . . Some rare magic has left us. But Ms. Borjas leaves a network of activists who she nurtured, and who have mobilized in her wake.

Tourmaline reflects on how the struggle for housing, food, medication, and access to health care for all and against criminalization was the struggle of Lorena Borjas, and that struggle continues in this moment. In a moving reflection on the life and legacy of Lorena Borjas on Instagram, Tourmaline (2020) writes, "We honor her when we look at the root causes of the pandemic, when we support each other thru mutual aid. When we dream & demand much more than we were trained to and when we come together in the service of that dream."

Introduction: Trans in the Time of HIV/AIDS

As opposed to a crisis of the present, AIDS in the United States is imagined as over, a past that has been overcome. AIDS is a disease of another time, and those with AIDS are either dead or are somehow now well. Even the acronym AIDS calls to mind newsprint, grainy photographs, wavering of VHS tapes, weathered ACT UP posters, and impossibly sick bodies in hospitals. These representations of AIDS define the pandemic as past tense. Even the media of these representations — video, photographic, paper, and other materials — archive AIDS as history, as historically contained. Most are populated by white gay men, ensuing the homophobia of AIDS so as to never remember the racism and sexism of the pandemic. We struggle to use the acronymn *AIDS*. At best it sounds antiquated; at worst, a slur. Language itself aims to relegate AIDS to something unbearable that the present might be free of. This overness of AIDS is a refusal to know through the act of remembering. What is remembered serves to memorialize what we think AIDS "was," ensuring that we never know what AIDS "is." This is the brutality of the AIDS pandemic in the United States: a cruel afterimage — we grieve so as to misunderstand, which makes possible the updating of history to make unthinkable the continued violence of AIDS.

In contemporary representations, Acquired Immunodeficiency Syndrome (AIDS) has been replaced with Human Immunodeficiency Virus (HIV). The biological virus of HIV works as "bare life" (Agamben 1998), as a material reality that symbolically misrecognizes the failure of governments, the forsakenness of the social order that AIDS marks. HIV is the bright, shiny tool of the present; it is another nail in the coffin of thinking AIDS, of grappling with the catastrophe that the AIDS pandemic remains. HIV drug advertisements are full of smiling, healthy, and sexually and racially diverse faces. HIV prevention campaigns emphasize safety over "risk," while continuing to promote Black trans women as a "high risk" and "target" population. This virus — the problem with virology and the immunological — becomes a new representation of AIDS, but strategically designed without attention to the structuration of AIDS: the racism of AIDS, the trans/homophobia and sexism of AIDS. The biologization of AIDS through HIV pivots around good/bad behavior, personal responsibility, and proper care of the self. The focus shifts to prevention — and a discourse of "resilience" — its own form of "post-AIDS" existence wherein there is no unhappy or failed subject living with the devastation of AIDS, only the reformed subject of prevention and pre-exposure prophylaxis (PrEP). In the social imaginary, HIV is no longer a sign of the abjection and negation of AIDS, but a symbol of pharmacological success and inclusion, a reformed subject able to participate in seemingly "post" AIDS epidemic sociality. This is the contemporary (in)visibility of AIDS. The time of AIDS — these new representations seem to propose — is either an obliterated past tense or an HIV+ pharmacological futurity.

Yet, AIDS remains. AIDS continues.

It is the persistence of AIDS that prompted this special issue of *TSQ*. The question that guided this was "How do we think trans with AIDS?" Surely, AIDS is central to trans life and trans death: among the 3 million HIV testing events reported to the Centers for Disease Control (CDC) in 2017, the percentage of transgender people who received a new HIV diagnosis was three times the national average, and nearly half of all new HIV diagnoses are Black trans women. But then again, this is the CDC's story about HIV infection. What about AIDS? Which is to ask about the overlapping with questions about citizenship, belonging, exile, the carceral, the border, antiblackness, disability, queerness, feminism, racialization, biopower, and necropolitics, and much more. It was not until the writing of this issue that the CDC made a trans-specific register public (Johnson 2020). In 2016 the distribution of HIV infection was such that 84 percent of trans women tested positive, 15 percent were trans men, and less than 1 percent had another gender identity. These numbers suggest that thinking AIDS with trans must also theorize difference — to think AIDS, trans theory cannot misrecognize trans as without race. The racial difference of trans and AIDS is significant, so much so that even the shorthand "trans and AIDS" threatens to hide the centrality of blackness in the AIDS pandemic. Moreover, trans theory cannot be sexless and genderless (even if our political ambitions are to abolish sex/gender systems recognizing sex/gender as racial logics). In other words, if we want to start thinking about AIDS and trans, we must break apart a general trans theory. Not just in terms of racial difference, but in terms of the radical differences between, say, trans men/masculine theorical investments, trans gender-nonconforming analytics, and trans femme/woman heuristics. Equally, we must question that which obfuscates the sexualizing and racializing violence of trans and AIDS, such as the cis/trans binary, non/binary gender, and others. The difficult truth of transgender studies—one that this special issue tries to elaborate— is how transphobia has structured its own interrogatives and analytics. Simply, it is time to recognize an implicit racial, sexual, and transphobic violence in the generalizability of trans and to start thinking trans in terms of differences, bodily and otherwise. To think AIDS and trans, then, means we must think racial and sex/gender differences together, even as those investigations destabilize the familiar logics, investments, and protocols of trans theory. But how? In what way? There are so many questions—so much that requires attention—and yet outside public health and the social sciences (both of which rely on the general field of transgender studies to refine their languages, questions, and conclusions), there is little to no theoretical engagement with how AIDS "defines" trans people's experience and—even more startlingly, perhaps—the very field of transgender studies itself.

Special journal issues aim to fill gaps in thinking—ideally—in what has not yet been thought. Mostly, the aim is additive: how to add an issue to another issue, or to divide one theme by some problematic. Transgender studies—and *TSQ*—is no exception to this mathematical logic. Ever proliferating, transgender studies finds attachment to an endless array of questions: trans + aesthetics, trans + decolonialism, trans + feminism, trans + blackness, trans + futures, and onward. Sometimes new knowledge is forged out of these special issue equations. New analytics. New insights. Other times these efforts show the aporetic impossibility of the intersection; that is, how the social organization of one domain actively refuses to think another. Antidisciplinarity. For example, in foregrounding blackness, Treva Ellison, C. Riley Snorton, Kai Green, and Matt Richardson in their special *TSQ* issue "The Issue of Blackness" (2017) question the order of analysis. This is to say, transgender studies and trans theory must confront the racialized logics of sex/gender that have organized its central analytic. To study trans + blackness cannot be simply additive; instead, this line of inquiry demands attention to how trans/cis and sex/gender are effects of (and are made meaningful through) blackness. In other words, sex and gender—what transgender studies often isolates, and centralizes—are what blackness does, what it animates and activates.

Our special issue tries to refuse the certainties and closures of transgender studies and, for that matter, AIDS studies. We have curated this issue to complicate the relationship between trans and AIDS, to stay with uncertainty and a conceptual openness that might incite new and different questions. Our contributors are artists and performers, cultural and media theorists, social scientists, and archivists who think about the relationships between race, immigration, transgender, representation, and HIV/AIDS. Kiyan Williams—who generously allowed us to use their art for the cover of this issue—discusses how their work remembers AIDS through re-imag(in)ing. Art, for Williams, is the AIDS archive, and, through desire, actuality is illuminated into political refusal. Cecilia Gentili refuses the injunctions of visibility as respectability through the brilliant and cutting comedy performances of *The Knife Cuts Both Ways*. Gentili discusses sex worker activism, trans struggles against policing and detention, and working in HIV/AIDS services to expand trans access and programming. Monica Jones discusses her work as a Black trans woman for sex worker decriminalization, how decriminalization is an HIV/AIDS activist struggle (and vice versa), her relationship with and to Sharmus Outlaw, and the pathbreaking report on HIV/AIDS policy on sex worker organizing: *Nothing about Us, without Us: HIV/AIDS-Related Community and Policy Organizing for US Sex Workers*. Through self-retrospection of their work, P. Staff suggests how art can be an effort to feel what has not yet been made sensible or shareable. Art, in this way, is experimental desire intervening in the resistance of the real to symbolization. Christopher Lee and Laura Stamm investigate and question the representation of trans women of color and AIDS in visual and popular culture. In different fields and interpretive frameworks, Adam Geary and Bahar Azadi et al. examine the problem—the impossibility—of trying to study AIDS and trans without attention to antiblackness and xenophobia. Geary provocatively argues that theorizing transgender with AIDS risks obscuring the antiblackness of the US epidemic and reifies the "queer paradigm" that has shaped the pandemic. Through a public health analysis, Azadi et al. shows how high HIV rates for trans women cannot be understood without thinking about anti-immigrant and xenophobic sentiments in France. Ellis Martin and Zach Ozma reflect on Lou Sullivan's diaries and how AIDS mediated sexual and gender identity for Sullivan. Matilda Sycamore reflects on her involvement in political movements, her fiction and nonfiction writing, a long history of AIDS organizing with ACT UP and in radical queer/trans collectives, and on San Francisco as a psychic and material landscape across multiple times of AIDS.

Given the lack of scholarship in transgender studies on AIDS—and conversely, the lack of attention to trans in AIDS scholarship—we do not aim to fill this chasm, but instead to foreground this absence as a provocation. How might lack of attention to AIDS in transgender studies be an opportunity to refocus the field, to redefine its investments, to challenge its assumptions? This special issue works to 1) deconstruct analytic frameworks to better understand how foreclosure (a refusal to think) has been installed (for instance, why has transgender studies not produced much scholarship on AIDS?); 2) help build an account that will aid in unraveling the work that this unthinking has done in forming interpretive logics; and 3) gesture to work, mostly creative and political, outside transgender studies (as an academic field, given that the field, especially in the United States, has remained so silent on AIDS) that has taken seriously the problem of trans people living/dying with AIDS. Given that our special issue sits with these absences, these voids in thinking, we stay with these questions: What is it about transgender studies that refuses to think AIDS; and what is it about AIDS scholarship that refuses to think trans? How might we think about trans and HIV/ AIDS in the present tense? How might the present conjuncture of trans and HIV/ AIDS differ from earlier moments? How can we understand the relationship between HIV/AIDS and "trans visibility" and representation (Tourmaline and Stanley 2017)? Thinking alongside Tourmaline, Eric A. Stanley, and Johanna Burton (2017: xxiv), who argue in the introduction to *Trap Door* that trans visibility is predicated on whiteness, on white trans visibility, how then might the inability to think trans and AIDS be a symptom of the field's own allegiance to whiteness. Even more boldly, what is it about transgender theory and studies that must be abolished to think about AIDS and difference? These are some of the questions that guide this introduction, but also our effort to bring together scholarship, art, and activism that considers "Trans in a Time of HIV/AIDS."

Transgender Studies *Is* AIDS
Given that *TSQ* is an academic journal and an outgrowth of transgender studies, it is important to puzzle over the omission of AIDS in the formation of the field (even as transgender studies has become many things in many different disciplines). Theory—that poetry of thinking—originates from embodied subjects, but never directly, never without contingency, never without the representational field of language. Because theory does not escape representation it never escapes politics. Theory is political—at its most base level—because it is made through representation through symbolization; what Stuart Hall (1997) described as "articulation." Importantly, every effort to represent embodied experience is marked by repression, marked by that which constitutes the subject. Given that AIDS is recognized in the same few years that transgender studies originates itself in the United States, we cannot but wonder how repression is at work. By the 1990s, transgender studies was institutionalizing its specific interventions into the cultural meaning of sex, gender, and sexuality. In that same time nearly 5 million people were reported to be HIV+, and the homophobic and racist stigmas of pandemic were entrenched. So, by repression, we do not mean simply a disregard, but a defense built into the field formation: its figurations and representations, its methodological and interpretive devices.

In *Second Skins: The Body Narratives of Transsexuality*, Jay Prosser (1990) proposed that some of the early architects of queer theory, specifically Eve Sedgwick and Judith Butler, needed a "transgender position" to unify gay and lesbian studies (to find a shared political orientation to sexism and homophobia), particularly in response to the AIDS crisis: "It is transgender that makes possible the lesbian and gay overlap, the identification between gay men and lesbians, which forms the ground for this new theory of homosexuality discrete from feminism." Prosser continues, "And it is surely this cross-gendered identification between gay men and lesbians—an identification made critically necessary by the AIDS crisis—that ushers in the queer moment" (22). Sedgwick (1990: 22) in particular argued for an "irreducibility" of sexuality to gender, which intermeshes desire and identification, transgender and homosexual respectively. Significantly, in this gendering of sexuality, processes of egoic identification are thought to supersede—and then analytically define—the unconsciousness of sexuality. Queer theory, in this form seems to operationalize "transgender" so as to bind the anarchic dimensions of libidinal life. To further illustrate his point, Prosser cites Sedgwick's (1993: 23) confession of her "identification? Dare I, after this half-decade, call it with all a fat woman's defiance, my identity?—as a gay man." Prosser goes on to track the transgender position in the work of Kobena Mercer, Gloria Anzaldúa, and Marjorie Garber to demonstrate how the foundations of this queer theory are organized by a conceptual "transgendering."

While Prosser's genealogy deserves more attention—indeed, it is worth tracking in detail how transgendering emerges and shapes (often whitening—gender is a racial technology; transgendering, then, is made meaningful through race—and normalizing analytics—egoic sexuality—in) both queer theory and transgender studies—what stands out to us is his passing reference to "an identification made critically necessary by the AIDS crisis." What was it about the AIDS pandemic that necessitated transgendering? Was the crossing of genders—as an analytic—a reaction to the particular trauma and silence of AIDS in the 1990s? Prosser's assertion, while insightful, that the AIDS crisis necessitated a transgender position so as to build a shared sense of suffering, solidarity, and personal investment between gay men and lesbians seems an insufficient account of the racism, sexism, and homophobia that is AIDS. Instead, rather than the transgender position functioning as a joint—a point of contact and care—it may also serve as a conversion and translation (repression) of these social violences *into* and *as* theory. More simply put, this queer theory acted out rather than worked through AIDS phobia in its turn to transgendering. Given that queer theory emerges out of a direct critique of homophobia and heteronormativity, why were thinkers like Sedgwick so keen in the late 1980s and early 1990s to displace sexuality with gender *as its* sexuality? This is to ask, what is it about AIDS that activated the displacement of sexuality through cross-gendering as an egoic queer eros? To answer this question exceeds what an introduction to a journal issue can do, but we want to deepen it as a way to invite more scholarship, art making, and activism. So, let us follow a few lines of inquiry.

Cindy Patton argued in *Inventing AIDS* (1991) against the "queer paradigm" of the AIDS epidemic in the United States. This paradigm relied on homophobic and racial abjection to structure a response to AIDS, giving rise to the idea that risky behavior and sexual deviation (particularly among Blacks and gays) were the cause of the epidemic. The paradigm enabled the representation of AIDS as a gay disease, which helped obscure the impact the disease has on Black and Latino men and women. In consolidating homosexuality with illness, the queer paradigm was (and remains) successful in collapsing homophobia with (libidinal) sexuality. The crisis of AIDS, then, was also the danger that unbound sexuality always already poses to the subject itself, making racial and sexual identities the representatives of this threat. It is this collapsing of threats—what we have called, early in this introduction, "compounding"—that may help elucidate Prosser's claim that a transgender analytic emerges as an effect of AIDS. Might the transgender position—gender as sexuality; identification as "the" sexual investment—in queer theory be a disciplining of sexuality (drive sexuality or libido) that was already at work in the US response to AIDS? Contrary to the liberatory power of the transgender position that queer theory promised, it served as a binding of the imagined threat that sexuality posed. It comes as no surprise then that identity (the sexuality as gender) would be asserted (and championed) over the problem of sexuality. Transgendering, for queer theory, was a triumph of processes of identification (at most, the binding of libido into an object of self-hood; mastering the self) over sexuality that had been designated—through the racism and homophobia of AIDS—as a threat in need of administration. Even in the endless permutations of transgendering, the subtending logic is the maintenance of sexual drive through, and as, identity—leaving only the processes of binding (specifically, identification) as acceptable expressions and conceptualizations of sexuality.

That transgender studies has struggled to distinguish itself from queer theory is evidence through the fact that the transgender position has been taken up by both, with only a narrowing investment (though, Jack Halberstam called it a "border war" in 1998) in identity as a distinguishing feature (Chu and Drager 2019; Stryker 2004). The territorialization of gender, for much of the 1990s transgender scholarship, would be a central stake for understanding what transing did that queering did not nor could not. Because of this propped-up relationship between queer theory and transgender studies, to propose a uniquely transgender analytic required ever-expanding or, conversely, ever-narrowing understandings of sexuality, gender, and sex so as to perform a coherent argument. While transgender studies is many things in contemporary academia, it is worth considering how queer theory's 1990s version of transgendering took hold and shaped, and indeed named, transgender studies (the object of study, and site of divestment in the more current trans/trans* studies). David Valentine, Viviane Namaste, and Talia Mae Bettcher have all provided superb accounts of the theoretical and political divides between transgender and queer, but none have foregrounded AIDS as structuring this schism. Transgender studies emerged with—and perhaps, as Prosser suggests, of—AIDS, and it took up the cross-gendered position as its central heuristic, spending over four decades to distinguish itself from queer theory. It would be impossible to not think transgender with AIDS, and yet, curiously, the refusal to think AIDS in transgender studies is pervasive.

To be clear, our inquiry into the inability of the academic field of transgender studies to think AIDS should not be generalized to trans/gender/sexual subjectivity or lived experience. On the contrary, given the alarmingly high rates of HIV infection among transgender people, especially Black and of color trans women, this inability to think about AIDS is specific to the production of cultural and critical theory. We might simply call this absence symptomatic, and leave it at that, but let us consider that transgender studies maintained the enmeshment that Prosser charged Sedgwick and other queer theorists with—the collapsing of identity and sexuality so as to master sexuality through gender. Sandy Stone's germinal "The *Empire* Strikes Back: A Posttranssexual Manifesto" (1991) and Susan Stryker's field-defining essay, "Transgender Studies: Queer Theory's Evil Twin" (2004) offer some guidance for thinking through this question. While the essays do different things—Stone proffers a queerer ontology for transsexuals, and Stryker works to demarcate and constitute the field of transgender studies—both theorists are central to transgender studies, and both essays are constitutive of the ongoing US AIDS epidemic. Indeed, provocatively, transsexualism—a figuration that both Stone and Stryker importantly attend to in their theorization—was not accorded the status of an official "disorder" in the *Diagnostic and Statistical Manual* until 1980, which was a year earlier than the first AIDS cases (classified as such) in the US were reported. While neither essay reflects on AIDS—and this is not a critique, as these essays were significant in institutionalizing transgender studies that allowed and welcomed questions posed by and for trans/gender/sexual people—we are interested in how these essays help illustrate—in ways not necessarily intended by either author, but by the epistemology itself—but also complicate Prosser's claim regarding the transgender position in theory as an effect of AIDS.

Stone (1991: 2) calls on transsexuals—whom she describes as subjects that "commonly blur the distinction" between the "performative character of gender with the physical 'fact' of sex"—to forgo "passing" and to be "read," and to "multiplicatively divide the old binary discourses of gender and sex." There are a number of considerations: firstly, Stone relies on the overcoming of the dualed dynamics of sex and gender through blurring and crossing—that the relationship between these domains unsettle the facticity of both. Secondly, "multiplicatively" serves as unresting of "fact" through the "performative"; that is to say, gender and sex are not simply undone, but sex itself is understood as a domain of gender through the workings of blurring, reading, and passing. Said differently, the posttranssexual *is* the transgender position, and the problem of sex/ism is resolved through the dynamism of gender. In the conclusion of the essay, Stone writes, "Transgender theory would appear to be successfully engaging the nascent discourses of Queer Theory in a number of graceful and mutually productive respects, and this is reason for guarded celebration" (15). Stone brings queer theory's transgender analytic to trans subjects (to be "mixed genres") and to the field of transgender studies. Stone gives trans people another account of themselves—and the importance of this should not be dismissed—and she also authenticates queer theory's own innovation. The self-determination and autonomy that Stone's theory performs on the body may also be symptomatic of the logic of whitening that forms much contemporary trans thought on gender. The posttranssexual is the transgender position in transgender studies—indeed the term *transsexual* is abandoned in the field for the progressive *transgender* and now *trans*. Within transgender studies (and, interestingly, queer theory) the transsexual is rendered as essentializing—as an investment in sex—but with Prosser's reading, one cannot help but wonder if the problematic "sex" of transsexual is the lost sexuality—and whiteness—of queer theory's own transgendering. Which is to ask: How might disinterest in sex and sexuation—what the transsexual complexifies—be part of the erasure of AIDS in transgender studies?

In an effort to differentiate queer theory from transgender studies—and to insist that queer theorists not simply transform trans/gender/sex people's bodies and experiences into heuristics—Stryker (2004) playfully stages a sibling rivalry between sexuality and gender. She writes, "While queer studies remains the most hospitable place to undertake transgender work, all too often *queer* remains a code word for 'gay' or 'lesbian'" (214). Transgender studies, here, is proposed as a gendered study, distinct (to a recognizable degree) from queer theory's privileged object of sexuality. And while this effort at differentiation is important, Stryker also maintains the enmeshment that Prosser charges Sedgwick with—the collapsing of identity and desire. The gendered identities of gay and lesbian, here, subsume the sexuality of queerness itself. In other words, the transgender position in queer theory is claimed by transgender studies, and the claim act becomes differentiation. Stryker continues, "all too often transgender phenomena are misapprehended through a lens that privileges sexual orientation and sexual identity as the primary means of differing from heteronormativity" (214). While this critique remains pivotal in thinking about the inclusions and exclusions of "transgender phenomena" in queer theory, it helps to confirm Prosser's suspicions. It leaves us wondering about Prosser's suggestion that the AIDS crisis produced queer theory and its transgender position that would be claimed and reinvested through the institutionalization of transgender studies. This brief rehearsal of a conceptual theme within transgender studies is meant to refocus the absence of AIDS scholarship in transgender studies (and equally, trans scholarship in AIDS studies—because the confusion of sexuality/identity has not been isolated). Stryker and Stone are not the progenitors of transgendering—they inherited the analytic—nor are they alone in how the analytic of transgendering (and its whitening and desexualizing logic) has defined the field of transgender studies. In many ways, transgender studies only reifies a problem that originates in queer theory.

To answer what about AIDS inaugurated transgender requires many more questions. For the purposes of this introduction, we can propose some directions and routes of inquiry. The contributors to this special issue offer their own insights into this question, sometimes departing from those we offer here. One direction that emerges—what we follow here—is informed by trans of color and Black trans critiques that complicate the ontology of gender. Snorton's *Black on Both Sides: A Racial History of Trans Identity* (2017) and Jules Gill-Peterson's *Histories of the Transgender Child* (2018), to name only two monographs, have challenged the field's understanding of gender by demonstrating that trans studies' investment in gender as ontological obscures the ways race—and blackness in particular—makes meaningful (makes ontological) sex/gender. In other words, the question of race cannot be additive to the problem of gender, but instead schematizes the logic on which "gender trouble" rests. Queer theory's and transgender studies's transgendering—in its nominative claim to cross gender and sex—is already an account of racialization. How, then, might we complexify Prosser's account of transgendering—as an analytic predicated on race—as an effect of AIDS?

In his book *Antiblack Racism and the AIDS Epidemic: State Intimacies*, Adam Geary (2014: 1) writes, "The color of AIDS in America is black." Working against the "queer paradigm" of the US AIDS epidemic that relied on "risk behavior" discourse, he asks, "How does the racial blackness of the US [AIDS] epidemic challenge what we think we know about it?" (2). Geary carefully outlines how AIDS is an effect not of deviancy—the homophobic and racist script of the epidemic—but of "the unequal and violent conditions in which they [people] are forced to live and that are embodied as ill-health and vulnerability to disease" (2). Cathy Cohen (1999) also demonstrated that racist and sexist representations of the AIDS epidemic worked to displace attention from how Black communities were made vulnerable through state formations that resulted in disproportionately high HIV rates. Cohen describes how antiblackness structured disparities in the response to AIDS, and those disparities, particularly among Black women, further differentiated health and life expectancy. Even as womanhood (gender) is forged out of colonial and antiblack violence, gender/sex regimes continue to differentiate vulnerability and livability of Black women—the AIDS epidemic is one such instance. As Zakiyyah Iman Jackson (2020: 9) proposes, "antiblackness itself is sexuating, whereby so-called biological sex is modulated by 'culture.' In other words, at the register of both sign and matter, antiblackness produces differential biocultural effects of both sex and gender." AIDS is an effect of antiblackness, and this effect further materializes differentiations in terms of race, sex, and sexuality. In *Nobody Is Supposed to Know*, Snorton (2014: 5, 42) foregrounds the metaphor of the "glass closet" to show how Black sexuality and genders are dramatized as devious, duplicitous, and errant—figured in a time of HIV/AIDS through the "down low," "marked by hypervisibility and confinement, spectacle and speculation," and surveilled in an extension of racial slavery's "vertical sovereignty" and "biopolitical and necropolitical" regulatory ends. In describing how deviancy AIDS discourse served to displace attention from state-sponsored antiblack racism, Geary (2014:19) offers the trope of "screen discourse" that names the social structuration of displacement and disavowal. He writes, "Telling the story of queers and deviants in AIDS discourse, then, has always been a way of *not* telling the story of how vulnerability to disease is structured" (19). If, then, the AIDS epidemic was administrated through a homophobic "screen discourse" that concealed the structuration of antiblack racism, then how too were major threads of queer theory and transgender studies susceptible to the homophobia and racism of AIDS, building the affective force of both into the foundations of their analytics? Did transgendering not only background sexuality but also foreground gender so as to misread (or fail to read altogether) race?

The question is not to propose a canceling of these critical projects—in both, Black queer and trans critiques have intervened in the contemporary debates. Instead, we ask this question to imagine what a transgender studies would look like that did not disavow the centrality of AIDS in its formation. What might transgender studies have been without a specific liberatory and hyper investment in gender that aimed at subsuming sexuality (and sex), such that questions of race or nation could be theorized—problematically—as simply additive? It might start by not knowing how to think trans and AIDS together, to start from a place of uncertainty and unknowing. It might have to consider how AIDS for trans people is first a question of race and sex, not of gender or sexual identity, which is to complicate how the field often thinks about intersectionality and ontology.

A transgender studies aware of its origin would need to start with this: AIDS is a story of race and of Black death, and Black AIDS activism is part of the duration of Black freedom struggle against the violence of premature death. Che Gossett (2014: 31) precisely describes the inextricable "vectoring" of criminalization, transphobia (especially transmisogyny), antiblack racism, and AIDS phobia when they write, "We are living in a time of 'chains and corpses,' death, loss and mourning, of outrage and activism in response to mass incarceration, mass detention and deportation, HIV criminalization, AIDS phobia and the ongoing AIDS epidemic, anti-queer and anti-trans police violence." Abolition, then, is also the end of AIDS. A transgender studies attentive to AIDS would want to be, could only be, a study of racialization, sexuation, and libidinal sexuality.

Trans Art *Is* the Trans AIDS Archive

Given that the field of transgender studies has not adequately thought the question of AIDS, we look beyond the academy for direction. Specifically, how have art and activism engaged the ongoing relationship between blackness, trans, and AIDS? Art and activism are not here as metaphors for thinking, but as figuring poetics, arguments, and theory. Working through AIDS contemporary Black and trans artists offer an account of the pandemic that refuses the homophobic, transsexist, racist representations that have structured AIDS. These artists make living records of AIDS—loving, lusting, and fighting archives. Artists like Tourmaline and Kiyan Williams further challenge, edit, and alter the representation of AIDS through particular archival modalities? In this, their work asks, how do we archive social violence, and when is the archive itself a violence? This question highlights the problem of representation: the AIDS archive is one of visibility and representation, and yet how have race and trans been the story of hypervisibility, of overrepresentation, of not just visibility but the brute force of the visual, the optical, the perceived real. In turning to art and activism, we are not suggesting these are solutions to the racist and antisexual foreclosures that have structured transgender studies' inattention to AIDS, nor are we proposing that the path forward is only about art making or voice raising. We turn to art for guidance in better understanding how transgender studies and AIDS studies might change or reimagine their own possessive investments.

In attending to the archive of slavery and antiblack violence, Saidiya Hartman (2008) invites us to question the meaning of the archive itself and its institutionalization, to question its authority and expertise. She asks, "Is it possible to exceed or negotiate the constitutive limits of the archive?" (11). Given that AIDS *is* antiblackness—AIDS is part of what Hartman terms the afterlife of slavery—Hartman's interrogative extends to questions of archiving and representing this pandemic. The archive—the problematic representation of AIDS that we described earlier in our introduction—is offered as a complete record; it is built to desire a real account while disavowing the desire that built it. The archive is a promise to the real and, more generally, a contract with what is real, what real-*ly* happened. But, how does the real-ism of the social order—and here, Hartman's proposal is most urgent—reinvest in this orientation to historicizing, collecting, and cataloguing? Michel Foucault (1976: 144) elucidates this question: the archive encompasses the "domain of statements" that are articulable. What creates the archive is "the density of discursive practices, systems that establish statements as events (with their own conditions and domain of appearance) and things (with their own possibility and field of use. They are all these systems of statements (whether events or things) that I propose to call archive" (145). He continues, "The archive is first the law of what can be said, the system that governs the appearance of statements as unique events" (145). For Foucault, it is the work that can be done that incites thought—it is what drives (desire) the making of archives. And here, perhaps, we see what "exceeds" the archive: its incitement, its "fever" (Derrida 1998). How does desire summon archives and then occult them? Might the drive to systemize also, paradoxically, be the unbinding of the archives'—to return to Hartman—"constitutive limits"? And with Foucault's attention to the governing role of "the appearance": What of the aesthetic investments *of* and *in* the archive as the record of archival incitement?

It is this question of aesthetics as a record of the wanting to remember, of artfulness that guides us as editors to try and work through Hartman's call to "exceed" and "renegotiate" the archive, particularly the archive of AIDS. Just as AIDS discourse relied on the "queer paradigm" to "screen" structural forms of antiblack racism, the archive of AIDS has also worked to remember so as to forget. This problem is as much an effect of the unbearableness of AIDS—how do institutions remember death?—as it is a result of failing to ask better questions regarding the pandemic. That is to ask: do we yet know what AIDS was and is? Rather than answer this question, we instead pose it as a provocation. We wonder how aesthetics and art—and the incitement that shapes and reshapes both—offer different insights into the problem of remembering AIDS. Our issue includes artist statements and artwork as a different kind of record or archive, perhaps one that does not want to forget because the problem of desire is foregrounded.

Turning to art as archival is to ask: in what ways is the archive bound up with its own destruction (anarchival)? As much as organization structures the archive, there is also a disorganizing principle that is prior to organizing, to gathering, to collecting. Okwui Enwezor (2007: 16) argues, "The archive achieves its authority and quality of veracity, its evidentiary function, and interpretive power—in short, its reality—through a series of designs that unite structure and function." The archive is an effect of design and artfulness, of aesthetic practice. Enwezor proposes that "archival legacies become transformed into aesthetic principles, and artistic models become historicizing constructs" (22). This aesthetic—rather than a philosophical orientation, we suggest aesthetics as sites of sublimation (Freud 1957, 1990)—*in* and *as* design is a form of delimiting, delimit of the disorderly, of the disorganized that preexists organization. Aesthetic thought, then, exists both before and against the archival thought: ante- and anti- organization.

The organization Visual AIDS foregrounds the constitutive forces of aesthetics and archives. As Esther McGowan recounts: "At the height of the AIDS crisis, many people were ostracized from their families and neighbors, and their art would be thrown out. Frank and David Hirsh came up with the idea of creating an archive of images. People now are living long-term with HIV, so it's not just the legacy of people who passed away, but also of those living with HIV who continue to make work" (Ansari, Reisman, and Bolster 2019). In projecting the images of Kay Rosen's *AIDS On Going Going On* onto the facade of St. Vincent's Hospital and the Guggenheim, Visual AIDS (n.d., 2016) and collaborating artists showed how AIDS haunts the institution of the museum and its archive. Even more than an institutional critique of the "museumological" construction of the memorialization and archiving of AIDS, the projection forces the museum to reckon with the imagined absence and "screen discourse" (screen, here, takes on a literal dimension) of the AIDS crisis.

To illustrate how art serves as anarchival archive, we turn to the artists Kiyan Williams and Tourmaline, who respond to Hartman's stirring interrogation of the archive. They make work that desires through the historical record while also exploring how the historical record is constituted through effacement. Both artists confront the historical erasure of Black trans femmes and women and seek to imagine the un-archivable through an anarchival engagement. Tourmaline's films—*Happy Birthday, Marsha!* (2018), *Atlantic Is a Sea of Bones* (2017), and *Salacia* (2019) have all been works of speculative Black trans cinematic imagination. *Atlantic Is a Sea of Bones* was commissioned by Visual AIDS for the program "Alternate Endings, Radical Beginnings," curated by Erin Christovale and Vivian Crockett.

Thinking about Black queer/trans art in a time of antiblack and antitrans state of emergency that *is* the ongoing AIDS epidemic, Christovale and Crockett commissioned work by Mykki Blanco, Cheryl Dunye and Ellen Spiro, Tourmaline, Thomas Allen Harris, Kia LaBeija, Tiona Nekkia McClodden, and Brontez Purnell. Christovale and Crockett brought Black queer and trans visual theorizing to AIDS. "ALTERNATE ENDINGS, RADICAL BEGINNINGS as a title came from a conversation we had around the idea of radicality and its roots in a black art tradition" (Christovale and Crockett 2017). In their statement, Christovale and Crockett articulate how their work was shaped by and in conversation with Angela Davis's definition of radicality as seizing problems at the root and with Robin Kelley's work on the imaginary that lies at the core of the Black radical tradition. Christovale and Crockett emphasized the radical imperative of Black queer and trans art about AIDS at a time when the AIDS epidemic is being historicized and institutionalized within the space of the museum, even as the epidemic is continuing to disproportionately impact Black communities:

> We've been thinking about what it means to practice radical imagination and what that does for those who are usually marginalized. That notion really speaks to all the filmmakers and visual artists that we commissioned for this program. The artists are radically thinking about the HIV/AIDS epidemic as Black people in this country, asserting themselves and their creative narratives amidst an ongoing discourse around who is invited into institutions." (Christovale and Crockett 2017)

Christovale and Crockett's work in and as "Alternate Endings, Radical Beginnings" is a Black queer and trans radicalization of the museumology and political genealogy of AIDS art and activism. Their bringing together Black queer and trans artists to reckon with AIDS at a moment of the museum archiving of AIDS activism on the one hand and antiblackness as a mechanism of AIDS crisis on the other brings Black queer/trans art to bear not only on collective memory but also its ongoing urgency.

Atlantic Is a Sea of Bones, whose title invokes Lucille Clifton's (2020) poem of the same name, speaks to Black trans life and ongoing violence of displacement. The film centers around Egyptt LaBejia, Black trans performer and witness to the AIDS epidemic, coinciding with the loss of cruising spaces of the piers and meatpacking district in NYC. The film opens from inside the Whitney Museum of American Art, where Eygptt looks out at the piers and says, "I literally lived on that pier that's no longer there." Egyptt says to Hope Dector, pointing to the remnant of one of the piers, "I've never seen it from this angle before." Egyptt says, looking down from inside the museum at the horizon of the piers, "The times of the village, from Christopher Street to 14th Street. People should never forget where they came from." The lens zooms out to the outline of the cityscape over the Hudson River, which drains into the Atlantic Ocean.

Tourmaline's film centers Black trans life, experience, and theory and is a work of cinematic theorizing about AIDS, Black trans dispossession, and memory. Egyptt and Fatima Jamal's casting is an important and powerful directorial imperative because it situates Black trans women and femme and nonbinary artists as the protagonists—critiquing visibility but doing so within the radical imaginary of Black trans art. Lying outside the orbit of the film, Fatima Jamal's own directorial and aesthetic interventions into queer/trans discourse with the film *No Fats, No Femmes* and Egyptt's legacy of the House of LaBeija. The film refuses to be a spectacle for nontrans and/or non-Black consumption, which is so often how Black trans women and femmes both figure and are taken up in academia as in film: as always already dead. Hartman's study of "fungibility" as an effect of enslavement is also illustrated by the hyper-consumption of Black trans women to produce scholarship, and institutionalization, and the operations of transgender studies itself (Hayward 2017). Tourmaline layers in archival documentary video of Egyptt's performances, creating a temporal vibration from the historical to the present. There is hardly any dialogue in the film, except Egyptt's opening invocation to remember, and this Black trans remembrance is facilitated through sound and music by Geo Wyeth. The audience is awash in sounded-light—synthetic effect—compelled by and saturated with what Tourmaline terms "movie magic" (Tourmaline and Wortzel 2018).

Atlantic Is a Sea of Bones bends the binary between "reality" and fantasy until it reaches its breaking point. Even more, the film goes further than blurring and trans-figuring the reality/fantasy binary—the film reveals how fantasy and libidinal sexuality are central to the production of "reality" itself. The film begins and ends with Eygptt at the Whitney Museum of American Art—a loop, traveling full circle—a Black trans radical beginning and ending. The film serves as a critique of the antiblack and antitrans violence of effacement—historical and lived—and also shows Black trans intimacy and "aesthetic sociality" that is forged through and beyond the purview of the archive (Harris 2018). As Tavia Nyong'o (2018) writes of the film: "*Atlantic Is a Sea of Bones* thus posits history through the angular entanglements of transgender subjects who are caught up in non-linear temporalities and non-sovereign subjectivities. Stolen and disposable life finds new dispositions for itself and others. Abandoned to liberty, extimate grounds forge creative kinship."

Saidiya Hartman (2017) contends that "care is the antidote to violence." The affective and aesthetic practices of care are present in the work of Kiyan Williams and Tourmaline, who reimagine the ends of the archive. The archive functions as a technology of veridiction and apparatus for the adjudication of historical truth claims. Troubling the ontology of the archive and the event, Hartman (2008: 11) writes, "I have attempted to jeopardize the status of the event, to displace the received or authorized account, and to imagine what might have happened or might have been said or might have been done." This speculative imagining of life otherwise is central to the work of Tourmaline and Williams. Williams's work explored the film archive of Marlon Riggs, to excavate and bring to the fore a political genealogy of Black trans experiences of the (ongoing) AIDS crisis by exploring the archive of Jesse Harris, interior to Riggs's archive.

"The afterlife of slavery," as Hartman says, "is not only a social and political problem but an aesthetic one as well" (Hartman 2018). Tourmaline's and Williams's work of Black trans un-archiving, speculation, and film show how Black trans art is a critical site and register for confronting the ongoing afterlife of slavery as an aesthetic problem, against the violence of representation and visibility as a "grammar of capture" (Spillers 2003: 14). Trans is reimagined in their work as artistry, as an erotics that takes seriously the libidinal dimensions of subjectivity. Gender is not abandoned—the violence that Black trans women and femmes experience is particular and not generalizable to all transgender positions—but pushed through on a wave of desire marked by aesthetics. Tourmaline's and Williams's work confront the afterlife of slavery as an aesthetic problem through a Black trans abolitionist frame. Williams and Tourmaline show how the violence of antiblackness, antiqueerness and antitransness function through the regulation of the aesthetic that aims to render Black trans captive. Against antiblack metaphysical violence (Wilderson and Douglass 2013; Warren 2018) and antiblack violence of the carceral, Williams and Tourmaline's work theorizes fugitivity (Mary Jones), deconstruction (unmaking of America) and forces viewers to consider Black trans as abolitionist struggle that is ongoing and "interminable" (Sexton 2014: 593).

Tourmaline's recent film *Salacia* reimagines the insurgency of Black trans sex worker Mary Jones in the 1800s, placing her in Seneca Village, on the run—a fugitive from and in defiance of antiblack, antitrans law and order and the protocols of proper citizenship. Tourmaline enacts a cinematic and speculative imaginary akin to what Hartman (2008: 11) terms "critical fabulation." Tourmaline anarchives Mary Jones and, through a historical imaginary of Jones, incorporates and absorbs the historical record—from the 1836 court transcript of Jones's defiance of gender's jurisdiction to dramatizing abolitionist tensions about racial respectability and sex work—to not only refract it but also to extend the imaginary of the historical beyond the coordinates of the archive, turning toward other affective modes of not forgetting presence (as opposed to remembering). In Tourmaline's film time is folded, and Jones swerves between the temporal zones of present and past using magic as a transport. The character of Jones ends the film by exclaiming "we can be anything we want to be"—a Black trans desire—and it is art as imaginary that facilitates this as both a call to history as well as the present.

In Kiyan Williams's *Meditation on the Making of America* (2019)—dirt/earth from a "Vessel/Womb/Abyss" is hurled onto a blank white canvas and launched as a projectile at Williams as well. The onlooking audience is witness to the violent materializing of America. To think with Spillers: America is a grammar of Black trans capture. What is the archive—moreover—the event of America? In this performance America is both made—physically and cognitively mapped out as ground—and radically unmade—its sovereign pretense and ontological authority undone. The Foucauldian archive that is the nation-state America is confronted with its own "anarchive," its own disorder and disordering.

In *Happy Birthday, Marsha!* (2018) Tourmaline and codirector Sasha Wortzel show the interplay between different versions of Marsha P. Johnson, subverting the aesthetic injunction of visibility, the historical record, and the linear conventions of trans narrative form. As Tourmaline and Wortzel (2018) said in an interview: "An impulse we're both following is finding these absences and gaps in the historical record. We're not so much interested in correcting and filling them, as we are in creating entirely new historical documents that are looking to the past in order to imagine what other possibilities could be." Instead they propose and offer a kaleidoscopic and dynamic take on Johnson: "There's a kind of inconsistency in having two different Marshas. We are offering that as a form of disabled beauty, an aesthetic of movie magic that pushes back against an idea that you have to keep it all together. Because we know that Marsha didn't have it all together a lot of the time, and actually that was a part of her beauty" (Tourmaline and Wortzel 2018).

Marsha P. Johnson's memory syncs up with Anohni's art and music, as one of its conditions of possibility and an ancestral presence under whose sign Anohni's work travels. "And the Johnsons" resonates, echoes, responds to, and reverberates with Marsha's memory. In Anohni's 2019 exhibit at The Kitchen, titled *Love*, Anohni thinks through the form of crisis as a "vanishing," as Simon Wu (2019) contends in his review of exhibit in *Brooklyn Rail*, "a sense of time where past, present, and future collapse." The past is enlivened (even lived) through an erotic of posterity (posterior time) enmeshed (hidden in plain sight, subliminated) in aesthetic work, in art making. This time is one that Anonhi wants to acknowledge, and, in acknowledging it, Anohni's exhibit entreats us to be in touch with—to sense through—a past-present as aesthetic. "I think about holding space for vanishing, of people, of communities, of biodiversity, in a way that opens into spectral time, leaking all points at once," says Anohni (2019). In this spatial and temporal topology, time is figured not as a solid—moving along a fixed and isomorphic axis—but as liquid flow, "leaking all points at once." Time overspills with the saturation of the historical present. The "spectral time" of AIDS is not past but past as sedimented presence. Says Anohni (2019), "So much of this work is animist and dealing with ghosts, the living and the dead, with different presences ricocheting among the moments and objects, offering an opportunity to make more intuitive connections between histories, gestures, colors, cataclysms, and ideas."

For this special issue on trans and AIDS, we propose that the artwork by Tourmaline and Williams differently historicize the erasure of Black trans women through the contemporization of AIDS as an effect of antiblackness, sexism, and homophobia. While AIDS was not at the center of transgender studies, it has been theorized, imagined, and problematized by artists for decades, and this provides an entry point into rethinking trans and AIDS. Moving with art and activism means inhabiting a different archive of AIDS and trans theory, aesthetics, and politics. Each of the artists, thinkers, and activists who contributed to this special issue challenge us to imagine and reimagine how we might think together—from representation to archive, from art making to public health practice, from theory to activism—trans and AIDS. For instance—pointing toward a theorization and entanglement of trans, AIDS, and disability—Ellis Martin and Zach Ozma work to publish and conceptualize Lou Sullivan's moving diaries. Sullivan's diaries are, in their words, "auto-archival"—written over the course of decades, and excerpts of them became *We Both Laughed in Pleasure*. The diaries are erotico-political, a record of encounters within a trans- and AIDS-activated network desire that is auto theoretical as well as auto archival. This archive of early trans AIDS activism and desire helps rethink the narration and historicity of AIDS and trans. What Sullivan's diaries demonstrates—and also Williams's and Tourmaline's artwork, as well as our other contributors work—is that to begin to understand why AIDS has been so difficult to think—historically, representationally, politically, and theoretically—requires an irreverence to the discourse of pandemics so that we might ask better questions, become freshly curious about what we do not yet know. This special issue curates a collection of work that confronts the erasure of AIDS in transgender studies—surprisingly, no such curation has happened before this—but it does not resolve the erasure, nor offer "the final word" on AIDS and trans. Instead, we offer this special issue as an invitation for deepening and challenging the questions we offer here.

Che Gossett is a PhD candidate in women's and gender studies and a graduate fellow at the Center for Cultural Analysis at Rutgers University–New Brunswick.

Eva Hayward is an associate professor in gender and women's studies at the University of Arizona.

References

Agamben, Giorgio. 1998. *Homo Sacer: Sovereign Power and Bare Life.* Translated by Daniel Heller-Roazen. Stanford, CA: Stanford University Press.

Anohni. 2019. "ANHONI: *Love.* The Kitchen, April 3–May 11. thekitchen.org/event/anohni-love.

Ansari, Rehan, Sara Reisman, and George Bolster. 2019. "Beyond the Red Ribbon: The Ongoing Legacy of Visual AIDS." *POZ,* February 26. www.poz.com/article/beyond-red-ribbon -ongoing-legacy-visual-aids.

Benjamin, Walter. 2019. "Critique of Violence." In *Reflections: Essays, Aphorisms, Autobiographical Writings,* edited by Peter Demetz and E. F. N. Jephcott, 291–316. Boston: Mariner Books, Houghton Mifflin Harcourt.

Christovale, Erin, and Vivan Crockett. 2017. "Alternate Endings, Radical Beginnings Curatorial Statement." As told to Alex Fialho. *Visual Aids Blog,* November 29. visualaids.org/blog /curatorial-statement.

Chu, Andrea Long, and Emmett Harsin Drager. 2019. "After Trans Studies." *TSQ* 6, no. 1: 103–16.

Clifton, Lucille. 2020. *How to Carry Water: Selected Poems of Lucille Clifton.* Edited by Aracelis Girmay. New York: BOA Editions.

Cohen, Cathy. 1999. *The Boundaries of Blackness: AIDS and the Breakdownof Black Politics.* Chicago: University of Chicago Press.

Derrida, Jacques. 1998. *Archive Fever: A Freudian Impression.* Translated by Eric Prenowitz. Chicago: University of Chicago Press.

Enwezor, Okwui. 2007. *Archive Fever: Photography between History and the Monument.* New York: International Center for Photography.

Foucault, Michel. 1976. *The Archaeology of Knowledge.* Translated by Alan Sheridan. New York: Harper and Row.

Foucault, Michel. 1988. *The Care of the Self.* Vol. 3 of *The History of Sexuality.* Translated by Robert Hurley. New York: Vintage.

Freud, Sigmund. 1957. "Creative Writers and Day-Dreaming." In *Collected Papers,* vol. 4, translated by Joan Riviere, 415–28. London: Hogarth.

Freud, Sigmund. 1990. *Leonardo da Vinci and a Memory of His Childhood.* Translated by Alan Tyson. Edited by James Strachey. New York: Norton.

Geary, Adam. 2014. *Antiblack Racism and the AIDS Epidemic: State Intimacies.* New York: Palgrave.

Gentili, Cecilia. 2020. "What Lorena Borjas Did for the Trans Girls of Queens." *New York Times,* April 11.

Gill-Peterson, Jules. 2018. *Histories of the Transgender Child.* Minneapolis: University of Minnesota Press.

Gilmore, Ruth Wilson. 2007. *Golden Gulag: Prisons, Surplus, Crisis, and Opposition in Globalizing California.* Berkeley: University of California Press.

Gilmore, Ruth Wilson. 2015. "Organized Abandonment and Organized Violence: Devolution and the Police." Vimeo video. The Humanities Institute at the University of California, Santa Cruz, November 9. vimeo.com/146450686.

Gossett, Che. 2014. "We Will Not Rest in Peace: AIDS Activism, Black Radicalism, Queer, and/or Trans Resistance." In *Queer Necropolitics,* edited by Jin Haritaworn, Adi Kunstman, and Silvia Posocco, 31–50. New York: Routledge.

Halberstam, Jack. 1998. "Transgender Butch: Butch/FTM Border Wars and the Masculine Continuum." *GLQ* 4, no. 2: 287–310.

Hall, Stuart. 1978. *Policing the Crisis.* London: Palgrave.

Hall, Stuart. 1997. *Representation: Cultural Representations and Signifying Practices*. London: Sage.

Harris, Laura. 2018. *Experiments in Exile: C. L. R. James, Hélio Oiticica, and the Aesthetic Sociality of Blackness*. New York: Fordham University Press.

Hartman, Saidiya. 2008. "Venus in Two Acts." *Small Axe*, no. 26: 1–14.

Hartman, Saidiya. 2017. "In the Wake: A Salon in Honor of Christina Sharpe." Panel at the Barnard Center for Research on Women, New York, November 28. Vimeo video, 01:34:41. bcrw.barnard.edu/videos/in-the-wake-a-salon-in-honor-of-christina-sharpe/.

Hartman, Saidiya. 2018. "Saidiya Hartman on Working with Archives." Interview with Thora Siemsen. *Creative Independent*, April 18. thecreativeindependent.com/people/saidiya -hartman-on-working-with-archives/.

Hayward, Eva. 2017. "Don't Exist." *TSQ* 4, no. 2: 191–94.

Jackson, Zakiyyah Iman. 2018. "Theorizing in a Void: Sublimity, Matter, and Physics in Black Feminist Poetics." *South Atlantic Quarterly* 117, no. 1: 617–48.

Jackson, Zakiyyah Iman. 2020. *Becoming Human: Matter and Meaning in an Antiblack World*. Sexual Cultures 53. New York: New York University Press.

Johnson, Chris. 2020. "CDC Now Has Data on HIV Infections for Trans People—and They're Going Up." *Washington Blade: Gay News, Politics, LGBT Rights*, May 9. www.washington blade.com/2020/05/08/cdc-now-has-data-on-hiv-infections-for-trans-people-and-theyre -going-up/.

Nelson, Alondra. 2011. *Body and Soul: The Black Panther Party and the Fight against Medical Discrimination*. Minneapolis: University of Minnesota Press.

Nyong'o, Tavia. 2018. "Atlantic Is a Sea of Bones." *ASAP Journal*, January 4. asapjournal.com/b-0-s -6-2-atlantic-is-a-sea-of-bones-tavia-nyongo/.

Patton, Cindy. 1991. *Inventing AIDS*. New York: Routledge.

Povinelli, Elizabeth A. 2011. *Economies of Abandonment: Social Belonging and Endurance in Late Liberalism*. Durham, NC: Duke University Press.

Prosser, Jay. 1998. *Second Skins: The Body Narratives of Transsexuality*. New York: Columbia University Press, 1998.

Scarry, Elaine. 2012. *Thinking in an Emergency*. Norton Global Ethics Series. New York: Norton.

Sedgwick, Eve Kosofsky. 1990. *Epistemology of the Closet*. Berkeley: University of California Press.

Sedgwick, Eve Kosofsky. 1993. *Tendencies*. Durham, NC: Duke University Press.

Snorton, C. Riley. 2014. *Nobody Is Supposed to Know: Black Sexuality on the Down Low*. Minneapolis: University of Minnesota Press.

Snorton, C. Riley. 2017. *Black on Both Sides: A Racial History of Trans Identity*. Minneapolis: University of Minnesota Press.

Snorton, C. Riley. 2020. "Afterword: On Crisis and Abolition." In *AIDS and the Distribution of Crises*, edited by Jih-Fei Cheng, Alexandra Juhasz, and Nishant Shahani, 313–18. Durham, NC: Duke University Press.

Spade, Dean. 2020. "This article also makes me wonder what would a public health system not rooted in military imperialism and backed by criminalization mechanisms look like?" Twitter, April 27, 8:58 p.m. twitter.com/deanspade/status/1254938008643465216.

Spillers, Hortense J. 2003. *Black, White, and in Color: Essays on American Literature and Culture*. Chicago: University of Chicago Press.

Stone, Sandy. 1991. "The *Empire* Strikes Back: A Posttranssexual Manifesto." uberty.org/wp -content/uploads/2015/06/trans-manifesto.pdf.

Stryker, Susan. 2004. "Transgender Studies: Queer Theory's Evil Twin." *GLQ* 10, no. 2: 212–15.

Tourmaline. 2020. "So heartbroken to hear about Lorena Borjas dying today." Instagram, March 30. www.instagram.com/p/B-YADIlBNve/.

Tourmaline, Eric A. Stanley, and Johanna Burton. 2017. Introduction to *Trap Door: Trans Cultural Production and the Politics of Visibility*, edited by Tourmaline, Eric A. Stanley, and Johanna Burton, xv–xxvi. Cambridge, MA: MIT Press.

Tourmaline and Sasha Wortzel. 2018. "Tourmaline and Sasha Wortzel Talk about Their Film *Happy Birthday, Marsha!*" Interview by Alex Fialho. *Artforum International*, March 20. www.artforum.com/interviews/tourmaline-and-sasha-wortzel-talk-about-their-film-happy -birthday-marsha-74735.

Wu, Simon. 2019. "ANOHNI: *LOVE*." *Brooklyn Rail*, May. brooklynrail.org/2019/05/artseen/ ANOHNI-LOVE.

Visual AIDS. n.d. "Kay Rosen Tote." visualaids.org/projects/kay-rosen-tote (accessed April 26, 2020).

Visual AIDS. 2016. "Radiant Presence Projections in New York City." *POZ*, February 13. www.poz .com/blog/radiant-presence-pro.

P. Staff

An Interview

CHE GOSSETT and EVA HAYWARD

Abstract The following is an interview with visual performance artist P. Staff conducted by Che Gossett and Eva Hayward. In the interview Staff thinks about kinship and AIDS, "desire and dispossession," AIDS and art, justice and ACT UP, and a trans aesthetics of refusal. How might art and art-making refuse to represent AIDS and trans? How is the imperative to represent trans and AIDS part of the violence of trans/AIDSphobia? Staff questions the progressive projects of social uplift, of well-being, and the endlessly reparative subject. Working through a "trans negativity," Staff's work tracks the corrosive and unbinding force of sexuality that is hidden by contemporary trans and AIDS discourses.

Keywords refusal, kinship, HIV/AIDS, nonrepresentation

CG and EH: *In an interview with* Crosscuts *magazine of the Walker Arts Center, you describe a political tension and antagonism. On the one side there is the investment in a critique of family by queer studies as a political project and on the other a consolidation around the figure of the family within the mainstream LGBT movement. You saw the latter as one response to the question: "How do you reclaim a notion of 'family' in the wake of AIDS?" What are the ways that you see trans kinship in the wake and in the ongoing AIDS crisis?*

PS: What is compelling to me about notions of kinship, and trans kinship in particular, and feels rarely acknowledged, is its resistance to order. Does kinship really behave that well? I suppose I'm tired of the recuperative demands of working as a queer artist. Works of mine such as *Weed Killer* (2017) or *On Venus* (2019) aim to undo, or trouble, some of the more reparative ideas that can become embedded in work around identity, the body, toxicity, and transness. They also actively seek out difficult—or sticky—forms of kinship, such as pharmaceutical practices related to chemotherapy and hormone therapies in *Weed Killer*. What often troubles the conversation around kinship, or troubles its very conception, in my experience, is the way that people invariably trample over its conceits, in all

TSQ: Transgender Studies Quarterly ∗ Volume 7, Number 4 ∗ November 2020
DOI 10.1215/23289252-8665186   © 2020 Duke University Press

directions. This can be really painful! It can also be gleeful. To fraternize with the enemy, to fuck outside the assigned orientation, to be chemically or sensorially bonded against the grain, and I list these examples with as much conservative potential as there is transgressive. It goes in all directions, cutting across and through sensible bonds.

So it's hard not to perceive the question as a request to synthesize something inherently decomposed, and as Andrea Long Chu so succinctly put it, nothing good comes of forcing desire to conform to political principle. This is not necessarily a revolutionary statement, but it does feel like a concern that has become muddled. My work *The Prince of Homburg* (2019), an anarchic reinterpretation of the play of the same name, tries to work through this, I think—how the inherently troubling nature of desire might be the necessary friction in our politics, but also a catalyst for trouble, in many senses. My 16-mm film work *depollute* (2017) uses a set of instructions for performing a self-orchiectomy and posits them as a sort of liberatory manifesto toward ridding the body of a toxic agent, something potentially cleansing or restorative. Likewise, my collaborative practice with Candice Lin is based around combining our research and interests in herbalism and hormonal therapy to make smoke machines that release vapors laced with hormonal effects, such as antiandrogenic properties (fig. 1). I am aware when showing these works of the contradiction in terms, of the complicating positing of the toxic and the natural, or of harm and becoming. But the aim, again, I think, is to fuck with the predetermined apparatuses of desire and dispossession. I don't know where that leaves us, but it feels more productive to name these things, and to be diligent about what is driving the work we do. I once had a therapist ask if I thought my work made the world a better place. I was horrified at the idea. The only metaphor that I could think for its productive potential was a twisting of the knife.

The ways that I actually see trans kinship in the wake of and amidst the ongoing crisis is deeply unruly. But I think this is necessary; the wrong wrong community, made up of the wrong wrong bodies; the dread of, and the pleasure of, desire's ungovernability. Again, I think this has been a fundamental part of queer organizing historically, and is something to hold onto amidst what feels like a gentrification of our politics and desire in recent times. So as an artist, I am resistant to the project of sense making even when we believe the work we do to "make sense" to be in good faith. There has to be something else to offer.

CG and EH: *How has your art been thinking through HIV/AIDS? Can you talk about your work* Clean Needles Now & Now *and AIDS activism around needle exchange and how you folded that into your performance? Also, how that particular work explores virality, networks, contagion, toxicity, intoxication as queer/trans registers? How you might see that in relationship to trans AIDS activism and drug criminalization and "war on drugs" as an intensifier of HIV/AIDS?*

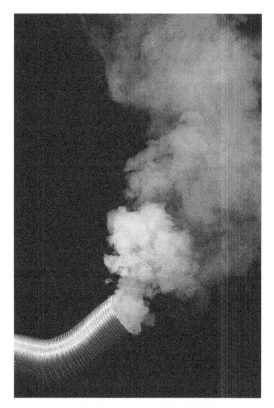

Figure 1. P. Staff and Candice Lin, *Hormonal Fog (Study #5)* (2018). Hacked fog machine and timer, testosterone-inhibiting herbal fog tincture, wooden crate, bungee cords, C-clamp, jars, and miscellaneous household goods, 22 × 12 × 48 in. (56 × 30 × 122 cm). Courtesy of the artists.

PS: The epidemic suffuses my practice, and I think that's inevitable and inextricable. I was born in 1987. That February, the first panel of the AIDS quilt was sewn; ACT UP was founded that March. The U.S. Public Health Service added HIV as a "dangerous contagious disease" to its immigration exclusion list with mandated testing for all visa applicants, and this HIV ban wasn't lifted until 2010. It's durational. I grew up in the United Kingdom under section 28, which was in place until 2003—the majority of my years in school. [Section 28 was enacted in 1988, stating that local authorities "shall not intentionally promote homosexuality or publish material with the intention of promoting homosexuality" or "promote the teaching in any maintained school of the acceptability of homosexuality as a pretended family relationship."] Social relations in my lifetime have been completely redefined. To return to the previous question, HIV/AIDS and the current pandemic turn fundamental ideas of the home and kinship and the family inside out. It only serves to reveal the constitutionally unsafe nature of private property, privatized relations. So, for me, there isn't art that does or does not deal with HIV/AIDS in its wake, it's just a case of how and where.

For a long time I was interested in live work, working as a choreographer, with bodies, with live encounter. I think that I am always working for the place of that encounter in the work, to be thinking primarily in terms of a somatic experience, rather than, say, a predominantly visual one. This is, I think, where the place of HIV/AIDs is also potentially felt most keenly in the work, perhaps it seems obvious to say, but in this space of bodily awareness. However, a number of my works, including the one you mention, use strategies that come from thinking through HIV/AIDS contemporarily, through virality, contagion, toxicity, and intoxication as queer/trans registers, as formal strategies, as interior logics. I think of these as methodologies that come from a lineage of queer and feminist art-works and artists, but also as strategies that are born of and completely inter-twined with HIV/AIDS. I see the effect of the Imagevirus everywhere.

Since 2015 I have been organizing these performative screening nights to engage archival material in a sort of louche, convivial space, with music and readings. People lie on the ground, can wander in and out between films. I usually try to encourage a bit of intoxication, "bad" behavior for the context of a screening in a gallery. The first was *Dreams of Travel* (2013), where I tried to use other artist film to talk about time travel, displacement, and illness; *Uniform Smoke* (2015), which explored material from kink and leather archives alongside the imper-manence of smoke and ghosts; and *Missives* (2016), which was a collaboration with curator Robin Simpson, looking at Canadian trans video art, in particular *Man from Venus* by James Diamond, *Gender Troublemakers* by Mirha-Soleil Ross and Xanthra Mackay, and *Rupert Remembers* by Xanthra Mackay. *Clean Needles Now & Now* (2018) was another one of these evenings and looked more specifi-cally at HIV/AIDS and was riffing, in a way, on the relationship between art in Los Angeles and the Clean Needles Now exchange program in the city. This wasn't only done through looking at or discussing archival materials, but also through questioning the sociality of a gathering of that sort in the city, now. I tried to use the format to resist a reductive narrativization of the history of needle exchanges or harm reduction. I wanted to talk about the permeability of boundaries; trans-mission and carriers; cleanliness and immunity; the sharing, use, and reuse of images and practices; occupied territories of the body; the toxic and the intoxicated. There is a tension I think, in how to work outwardly while still holding a room together in these performance/screening/events I'm describing. They are using a particular form of conviviality as a communal space of encounter, to go somewhere together with a specific set of materials. That sounds kind of spiritual, which maybe it is, but I think it comes from a lot of studying and thinking about choreography. Abstraction or extrapolation can seem like a difficult thing to consider as a group. Therein lies the challenge, to make it communal, or social, while resisting trying to force that encounter into a place of consensus about what the past might mean, or what is happening now.

CG and EH: *What are the challenges you have encountered in artistically representing AIDS and trans? What representations do we need, and do you see other artists taking up this challenge as you have done?*

PS: I think the challenges arise from the presupposition that we need represen-tation, that representation is always good, that art and artists are primarily a representation-producing mechanism. So much of our interpretation of con-temporary art is based on the decoding of analogies in order to arrive at the moral position that we guess the artist—and by extension the institution—is advocating for. And this expectation is of course disproportionately put on, and unevenly distributed between, artists who occupy a marginal position of some kind. I think the challenge then of representing HIV/AIDS and transness is to resist producing a representation that is definitive, because my question is: for whom? As a queer and trans artist, it often feels like the expectation and desire of the institution is that I make myself more and more visible, over and over again. For whom, I really don't know. I'm not interested in that, and I'm not convinced that it benefits my community. I feel much more compelled to speak about the many intersecting structures that foreclose community, identity, the body, agency. Visibility and representation can be deeply affirming, but I do think we have to be vigilant. If nothing else, perhaps art's use is to challenge the latent assumptions embedded within the visible, the representational, or the semantic.

My most recent large-scale work was an exhibition called *On Venus*, which was presented at the Serpentine Galleries in London. It was perhaps my most ambitious work to date in terms of attempting to address and challenge the ways in which discipline—whether economic, biopolitical, industrial, or architectural—becomes manifest, how its models arouse dogma, and, crucially, how its structure contends with dissent, debility, virality, and trans identity. Its central work is a video, also entitled *On Venus*, which comprises two sections: the first consisting of warped archival footage of industrial farming for the production of meat, fur, and hormones; the second featuring a poem about life on the uninhabitable planet Venus, conjuring a state of near-death that has parallels with trying to survive as a queer person in a heteronormative world. The idea of being on Venus became a useful sort of leitmotif for the exhibition, in the poem, in the work, in which I try to use the idea of being on Venus as a way to describe a slow but perpetual or consistent state of being, a sort of pushing through this liquid, a sort of shorthand to or for describing parallel forms of life, dispossessed living, or ulterior states of near-death, nonlife, nondeath. This could also be a description of intense anxiety, of intense pressure or perhaps, most acutely for me, an intense and disorienting form of dysphoria.

Pipes suspended from the ceiling leak a blend of natural and synthetic acids into steel barrels, causing chemical corrosion. I wanted to create a feeling of collapsing infrastructure, the sharing of bodily fluids, and the uncontrollable, networked spread and collection of viruses and data. Producing work through corrosive qualities became another guiding methodology. A series of intaglio etchings—steel plates, washed with acid—documents a British tabloid fixation from 2017, which wrongly claimed that Ian Huntley, a notorious convicted child murderer, planned to undergo gender reassignment in order to be moved to a women's prison. I became interested in the story around the time that the retractions and clarifications began to circulate. In 2017 and 2018, the *Daily Star*

Figure 2. P. Staff, *On Living* (2019), detail. MDF boxes and steel etchings, dimensions variable. Courtesy of the artist and Commonwealth and Council, Los Angeles. Photograph by Hugo Glenndinning.

began to run tabloid articles stating that Ian Huntley was planning to transition (fig. 2). This got picked up by a number of other tabloid newspapers, and repeated. The reports claim he was buying wigs and stockings, asking to be referred to as Lian or Nicola, and so forth.

    What you see in the etchings is that these stories were denied by Huntley and the prison services. They were retracted, incredibly small and meager clarifications were posted, and online, stories were just deleted entirely. These stories were pushed as part of a vicious, media-generated backlash against trans rights amidst debate over the Gender Recognition Act in the United Kingdom, and the rise of ethno-nationalist government policies globally. Through the stories we see clearly how the discrete categories of *man* or *woman* do not serve people, but rather whiteness, borders, the denial of care. It mirrors the gay panic stories of my childhood, situating queer identity in proximity to threat toward the child, good health, safety. There is a provocation in these etchings that goes beyond just redressing harmful tabloid articles. On what grounds are subjects given the permission to agency? And how does that sit with the social appetite for punishment, incarceration, death? And where is that contained: in our museums, in our newspapers, in our prisons, in our medicines and poisons. In part, the works organize a set of potentially simplifying analogies—the institution as a body, the animal body as an incarcerated body, the trans body as an incarcerated body, the trans body as an animal body. But they fissure, they splinter. They can't contain the analogy; that is intentional. I want for the work to break under the structures we build, the conceits that we put on language, a virus, a body; to collapse under the weight of our expectation, to ultimately betray us.

Che Gossett is a PhD candidate in women's and gender studies and a graduate fellow at the Center for Cultural Analysis at Rutgers University–New Brunswick.

Eva Hayward is an associate professor in gender and women's studies at the University of Arizona.

Undetectability in a Time
of Trans Visibility

CHRISTOPHER JOSEPH LEE

Abstract The advancement of medical treatments of HIV has given rise to the term *undetectability*, which has become synonymous with HIV survival and the promise of an otherwise normal life. This article explores the concept of undetectability as it relates to a theory of trans visibility as protection, epitomized by *Time Magazine*'s 2014 declaration of a "trans tipping point." Following critiques that trans visibility offers little guarantee of safety, the author traces the emergence of the term *undetectability* alongside calls for and against trans recognition. The author grounds arguments about undetectability's possibilities through a critique of the documentary *Death and Life of Marsha P. Johnson* (2017), examining its framing as a detective story that seeks answers around Johnson's mysterious death. More specifically, the author analyzes how the murder-mystery form reinforces a carceral fantasy of individual culpability running adjacent to the privatization of HIV as a matter of personal management. The article concludes by turning to Tourmaline and Sasha Wortzel's *Happy Birthday, Marsha!*, not just to pose a divergent narrative frame for Johnson's life but to also understand how undetectability might offer a resource in navigating the violence of exposure itself, toward a space of trans opacity.
Keywords highly active antiretroviral therapy (HAART), Marsha P. Johnson, medical treatments of HIV

I n 1996, the advent of highly active antiretroviral therapy (HAART) as an effective treatment for HIV marked a watershed moment in which a commonly fatal infection could be seen as a manageable chronic condition. In the wake of this medical breakthrough, researchers investigating the effectiveness of antiretroviral medication found that early and prolonged use of HAART could also serve as a deterrent to spread of HIV, suggesting that treating the virus contributed to its prevention. Put simply, by suppressing viral load to a level undetectable by conventional testing, HAART also suppressed transmission of the virus. More recently, this concept of treatment as prevention (TasP) has gained traction in public health campaigns, designating "undetectability" as an essential tool and term in the fight against HIV.[1]

TSQ: Transgender Studies Quarterly ★ Volume 7, Number 4 ★ November 2020 **561**
DOI 10.1215/23289252-8665201 © 2020 Duke University Press

While undetectability guides the promise of a once unimaginable normal life, critics, curators, and activists have also pointed to the limits of undetectability discourses, asking how overemphasizing treatment as prevention might leave out broader discussions of access, class, education, race, and community care. In his essay exploring HIV, incarceration, and art, Ted Kerr (2019) suggests that public health campaigns' embrace of undetectability simultaneously promotes the effectiveness of HIV treatment as prevention and the "individual work of ending the crisis by choosing to become undetectable." Jan Huebenthal (2017: 2) argues, likewise, that undetectability signals fitness for good citizenship, promising "a post-AIDS world inhabited by gay men who, having suffered though the horrors of AIDS, have returned to their healthy, authentic selves." In reflecting on the relative privilege necessary to access treatment, Nathan Lee (2013) posits that undetectability might "displace the positive/negative binary with the more urgent categories of the insured/uninsured." Registered collectively, these critics suggest that, far from acting as a guarantee of HIV destigmatization, undetectability might overdetermine questions of individual responsibility and health at the cost of forgoing discussions of the structures barring access to widespread testing and treatment.

Beyond its medical and public health definitions, the term *undetectable* carries different resonances in a time of heightened trans visibility predicated on a theory that more or better trans representation might better protect trans people.[2] This discourse of trans visibility has crept into public HIV/AIDS campaigns that name trans people of color as an underrecognized risk group, and, according to the *US News and World Report*, warn of a growing trans population of the "infected and invisible" (Marcus 2018). But while nonprofit organizations like the Human Rights Campaign continually call for greater trans "visibility and inclusiveness" within HIV/AIDS campaigns, scholars like Eric Stanley and Toby Beauchamp have highlighted the imbrication of trans visibility with targeted surveillance practices (Human Rights Campaign n.d.). In *Going Stealth* (2019), Beauchamp examines how overemphasizing trans recognition can expand the reach of surveillance programs like identification documents and airport body screening that monitor gender conformity. Beauchamp's interrogation of visibility dovetails with Stanley's (2017: 617) movement from trans "optics" to "opacity," putting forward a call to interrogate a "visual regime hostile to black trans life." In short-circuiting the seeming promise of trans recognition, Stanley asks: "How can we be seen without being known and how can we be known without being hunted?" (618).

Such critiques of trans visibility offer another inroad to unpacking undetectability, not just as a shorthand for the management of viral risk but also as a space for navigating the violence of surveillance and exposure in a "discourse of concealment" germane to trans life (Beauchamp 2019: 32). To invoke undetectability in a time of trans visibility might mean exploring how demands for trans recognition parallel an enduring and equally fraught demand to recognize those living with and lost to HIV/AIDS, in a time before undetectability could even be imagined. Bound up with the problem of trans representation and visibility, moreover, is the struggle to represent HIV/AIDS altogether, given what Paula A. Treichler (1987: 31) has called, in her early analysis of the AIDS crisis, an "epidemic of signification." Treichler's call to reckon with the multitude of interpretations seeking to signify the virus is a reminder that the battle against HIV/AIDS has always comprised medical and scientific breakthroughs as well as a crisis of meaning. When confronted with undetectability, as with the social construction of the virus itself, we are wrestling with the many contradictions this term might hold for those living with HIV/AIDS and for those living in an intensified moment of trans visibility and precarity. Can undetectability serve as an adjacent term to trans opacity or trans invisibility? And what lessons might follow from thinking about undetectability alongside metaphors of vocalization from silence, visibility from opacity, and clarity in the absence of clear or certain narratives?

Undetectability and the Detective Story

In the midst of these discussions, I want to turn to David France's *Death and Life of Marsha P. Johnson* (2017) as an attempt to constellate questions of undetectability, trans visibility, exposure, and remembrance. In recent years, a resurgent attention has been devoted to the revolutionary figure, Marsha "Pay It No Mind" Johnson, owing largely to the work of community historians in shining a light on her roles as freedom fighter, activist, and cofounder, alongside Sylvia Rivera, of the Street Transvestite Action Revolutionaries (STAR). Simultaneously, such an attention has also revived intrigue around the mysterious circumstances of Johnson's death, which, to this day, remains unsolved. In 2017, France, director of the Oscar-nominated film *How to Survive a Plague*, released *The Death and Life of Marsha P. Johnson*, which centers Johnson's unexplained death as well as the efforts of Victoria Cruz, a close friend of Johnson's, to find answers. That France's latest film features the death of Marsha P. Johnson—a black, trans woman noted for her revolutionary movement work—appears to serve as a corrective to critiques that *How to Survive* privileged the perspectives of white men over queer people of color, life over death, and medical advancements over direct action and activism.[3] The narrative emphasis that *Death and Life* places in Johnson's mysterious demise poses another frame of detection and undetectability connected to trans life and antitrans violence: the detective story. France's film folds in archival footage, Cruz's investigation, and the present-day trial of Islan Nettles, a trans woman beaten to death in 2013, as a means to explore how detection can potentially mediate and deter, or potentially fail to resolve antiqueer violence.

By weighing *Death and Life*'s emphasis on detective work—namely, the film's tracking of Cruz's investigation as a means of closing a chapter on transphobic violence—I reflect on both detection and undetectability as tools for confronting acts of transphobic violence, as well as the multiple causes, spectacular and otherwise, of trans precarity. While the film's privileging of forensic detection, investigation, and state-sponsored resolution strikes an odd contrast to Johnson's movement work on behalf of people living the HIV/AIDS, prisoners, sex workers, and other survivors of state violence, I argue that the film points both to the affective thrill of pursuing detection *and* its inevitable disappointments. Revisiting undetectability within these efforts to memorialize Johnson—who herself had been living with HIV prior to her mysterious death—reminds us how practices of looking, investigation, and the fantasy of "knowing" operate in the interlocking discourses of trans and HIV/AIDS visibility, both of which demand forms of secrecy and disclosure.

In one of the first scenes of *Death and Life*, we are introduced to Victoria Cruz, a counselor at the Anti-Violence Project who serves as the narrator of much of France's film. Cruz remarks that Johnson's case, in particular, has been "cold" for twenty-five years, and that she seeks justice for slain trans women of color, beginning with Johnson. As Cruz asks, "If we can't bring justice to Marsha, how can we bring justice for all these other unsolved cases?" Cruz's nondiegetic narration plays out in this early scene, where she assembles a rough time line in the days leading up to Johnson's death (fig. 1). Writing on various Post-it notes, Cruz pins one note after another to a largely bare wall of corkboard. A close-up of one note reads, "July 6 1992, found at 5:23 PM," the time at which Johnson's body was first discovered. This scene launches the long investigatory arc of France's film, in which Cruz's attempt to bring justice to Johnson's unsolved death dovetails with a broader effort to confront and resolve the violence facing trans women of color. As Cruz conducts interviews and chases leads, the once empty space of the corkboard fills up with printed articles, interviews, and diagrams relating to Johnson's death, all annotated with Cruz's hand-written comments. This wall becomes a recurring visual motif for the investigatory motor of France's film, in which Cruz assembles clues and details that will point to answers in Johnson's cold case.

This quest for justice is at the heart of France's film as well as Cruz's investigation, but the question of justice—whose justice, what type of justice is served, and whom it serves—is far murkier. Cruz's method of detection, whereby she pores over eyewitness accounts and forensic reports, places her firmly in the frame of the hard-boiled crime story, which, according to Bill Pronzini and Jack Adrian (1997: 3), generally centers "a social misfit" in the role of the amateur or professional sleuth and deals principally with "disorder, disaffection, and

Figure 1. Victoria Cruz assembles evidence relating to Marsha P. Johnson's death, including a hand-written timeline of events. From *The Death and Life of Marsha P. Johnson* (2017).

dissatisfaction" with the prevailing social order. The detective story, especially of the hard-boiled variety, serves as a well-worn genre through which to channel frustration with the failures of the police to adequately address Johnson's mysterious death. By beginning with death, the film suggests that detection, foremost, can clear the fog of mystery hanging over Johnson. In Jeffry J. Iovannone's (2017) account, France's film deemphasizes Johnson's remarkable contributions to queer liberation in favor of "focusing disproportionately on the more spectacular and suspenseful details of her death." *Death and Life*'s meditation on Johnson's mysterious demise follows a broader trend to draw political and symbolic meaning from trans death. Though memorials might serve as a crucial outlet to publicly mourn the loss of trans lives, scholars like Jin Haritaworn and C. Riley Snorton have also critiqued the ritualized remembrance of transphobic attacks and murders. As they discuss, public memorials for trans women of color increasingly feed the institutionalization of a trans politics that converges with rather than against state power. Haritaworn and Snorton (2013: 74) describe how trans-of-color death is invoked to "accrue value to a newly professionalizing . . . class of experts whose lives could not be further removed from those they are professing to help." In this way, it is only through death that "poor and sex working trans people of color are invited back in" to policy, legal, and nonprofit discussions of trans protections and rights.

As Victoria Cruz and many of those in Johnson's close community seek answers for the loss of a friend and sister, their quest for personal justice is frustrated by the ineffectiveness of state-sponsored inquiries. Their anger at do-nothing cops is channeled at an effort to carry out their own investigation. But even this provisional opposition to the state is another feature of the hard-boiled crime story, as the detective will often have "a jaundiced view of government, power, and the law" (Pronzini and Adrian 1997: 3). And despite capturing a palpable anger at the police, France's film remains enmeshed in a model of detection that privileges forensic investigation and state-sponsored inquiries into transphobic violence. In a secondary arc of the film, Cruz and other activists seek justice for Islan Nettles, a trans woman of color beaten to death in an act of brutal transphobia. One of the last sequences of France's film takes place in a New York courtroom, where Nettles's killer is sentenced to ten and a half years in prison. Xena Grandichelli, a volunteer with the Anti-Violence Project and an attendee of the court proceedings, is shown to be outraged at the judge's decision, indicating that the relatively light sentencing amounts to a failure of the system in deterring and accounting for transphobic violence.

Nettles's death in 2013 marks a significant but contested moment in which trans=of=color death drove public and media narratives around antiqueer violence, including efforts to propose and advance carceral expansion.[4] As Lena Carla Palacios (2016: 43) writes, Nettles's case "has been used as a poster child by journalists, legislators, and even members of their own kin to expand police surveillance in racially marginalized communities and to bolster the passage of criminal punishment—enhancing laws that purportedly address transphobic violence." In her broader study, Palacios suggests that reductive accounts of Nettles's death discount the circumstances contributing to transphobic harm, like gentrification and increased police surveillance of Harlem. *Death and Life* plays a part in this flattening of context, and its narrative centering of a courtroom sentencing scene suggests that carceral resolutions of transphobic violence mark, in its framing, a horizon of trans justice. To be clear, though, the trans activists depicted in France's film are not merely mouthpieces for the documentary's carceral model of justice. Any critique of *Death and Life*'s framing of justice must also weigh the extent to which trans women themselves—Cruz, Grandichelli, and others—push for longer sentencings and punitive responses to transphobic violence. Palacios's analysis of the media outcry following Nettles's death cautions that trans women of color's responses vary in their responses to the institutionalization of trans remembrance, and they can both "reproduce and challenge dominant logics of social value" (45). While capturing a passionate outcry for state intervention into trans violence, the film overlooks what Palacios calls an "outlaw vernacular" that works against a straightforward politics of recognition and visibility (39).

How might we rethink detecting the origins of transphobic harm and, in doing so, reconceptualize its supposed resolution? And what relationship might the fantasy of criminal guilt have to a term like *undetectability*? *Death and Life* investigates the untimely deaths of Johnson and Nettles in search of an individual perpetrator to account for the enormity of transphobic violence. Likewise, discourses of undetectability that emphasize personal management follow what Trevor Hoppe (2017: 118) has called a "responsibility politics" that emerged in the late 1990s and early 2000s, just as the advancement of antiretroviral treatments "transform[ed] HIV-positive people from passive victims into active managers." In analyzing the Centers for Disease Control and Prevention's (CDC) shift from promotion of condom use and "safer sex" to campaigns like "HIV Stops With Me," Hoppe describes how efforts to endow HIV-positive people with a sense of individual responsibility "resonate[d] with efforts to assign blame, punish, and, ultimately, criminalize individuals viewed as failing to live up [to] those [expectations]" (119). These notions of individual responsibility, well-meaning or otherwise, drive, in Hoppe's terms, an "epidemic of criminalization" that expands HIV-specific laws to punish the spread of disease (294).[5] As with carceral solutions to transphobic harm, it is within this punitive framework of detection, exposure, shame, and guilt that an individual wrongdoer must surface.[6]

The quest to find a missing perpetrator to account for Johnson's death defines the investigatory arc of France's documentary. By the end of the film, though, Cruz appears to hit a limit in her own investigation. Methodically removing her notes and clues, she files her evidence into a hefty dossier, stripping the corkboard wall as bare as it had begun. She hand addresses the file folder, and the camera follows her as she delivers the binder to the Federal Bureau of Investigation's (FBI) New York office. France's film thus ends with the transfer of Johnson's case to a bureau that notoriously utilized state power throughout 1960s to infiltrate, surveil, and quell the activities of the Black Panthers, suspected communist organizations, and civil rights groups.[7] Framed as a search for Johnson's presumable killer(s), *Death and Life* ends in this melancholic space, with Cruz looking off mournfully into the New York skyline. Cruz's search for justice is forestalled, perhaps indefinitely. My argument suggests that *Death and Life*'s framing as a hard-boiled detective story, complete with forensic detail and intrigue, offers a poor juxtaposition to Johnson's lifelong struggle with the police and state power (by her own count, having been arrested over a hundred times). However, I also argue that in offering up an ultimately failed detective story, the film lays bare the limits of forensic investigation.

In searching for a criminal account to clear the mystery around Johnson's death, *Death and Life* takes on the impossible task of mediating transphobic harm writ large, which, as Eric Stanley (2011: 7) reminds us, is more a foundational and "epistemic force" than a state of exception. Without an individual perpetrator to account for Johnson's death, the film suggests that something—a narrative thread or piece of evidence—is missing. In his account of HIV criminalization, Kane Race (2017: 117, 120) argues that "criminal law aims to isolate the human subject in its framing of responsibility for HIV events," and he asks, alternatively, "What capacities exist within juridical discourse to conceive the participation of a wider range of actors . . . in undesirable events such as HIV infection?" The same question might be asked of the death of Marsha P. Johnson: that is, how can the juridical frame account for a death absent an explicit cause or human actor? I am not suggesting that viral exposure, death, and potentially murder are at all commensurate in scale, but rather, that the logic of criminalization demands that a perpetrator emerge in each instance.[8] Without a culpable subject to anchor such a loss, what sense of justice remains?

Undetectability in Trans Remembrance

Shortly after the release of *The Death and Life of Marsha P. Johnson*, a controversy erupted around France's film, ignited by claims that his ideas were heavily borrowed, if not outright lifted, from the historical and archival research of filmmaker Tourmaline, who herself had been working on a documentary about Johnson.[9] The revelation that France's well-funded *Netflix* film might derive from the intellectual labor of an underfunded trans woman raises serious questions about the institutionalized remembrance of trans life (and death), particularly in its reproduction of violent power asymmetries that Johnson herself negotiated. Tourmaline, alongside codirector Sasha Wortzel, released her own short film about Johnson entitled *Happy Birthday, Marsha!* in 2018. Though there is much evidence and significance to weigh in this controversy, I want to, instead, close by taking note of the striking formal contrast between France's handling of Johnson's legacy and her depiction in *Happy Birthday, Marsha!*

If *Death and Life* is premised on exposure and detection—a documentary-cum-detective story that drives toward state-sponsored and forensic resolution of Johnson's mysterious demise—*Happy Birthday, Marsha!* is premised on exploring Johnson's legacy through a lens of opacity. With Mya Taylor cast in the role of Marsha P. Johnson, Tourmaline and Wortzel's film combines elements of archival research and fantastic reimagining, depicting the hours in Johnson's life leading up to the famous Stonewall Uprising of 1969, the police riot widely considered to be the modern birthplace of the gay liberation movement. As Jeannine Tang (2017: 382) remarks, *Happy Birthday, Marsha!* is steeped in a soft-focused aesthetics of glamour that works against a visual logic that features "trans bodies as . . . mangled and murdered." Rather than linger on Johnson's mysterious death, Tourmaline and Wortzel craft a small, intimate portrait of Johnson that culminates in a stand off with the police at the Stonewall Inn. Notably, the film stops meaningfully short of the uprising itself, though Johnson (as played by Taylor) is shown to throw the shot glass that, legend has it, launched the multiday demonstrations (fig. 2). The historical and temporal space that Tourmaline and Wortzel work in is relatively contained but rich with affection, style, and intrigue. Cutting

Figure 2. Marsha P. Johnson (as played by Mya Taylor), shot glass in hand, faces off with police at the Stonewall Inn. From *Happy Birthday, Marsha!* (2018).

between recorded footage and a fictional reimagining of Johnson, the film intermingles what is apprehensible in the archive with what remains (or must remain) unseen. Thinking alongside *Happy Birthday, Marsha!* and France's documentary is one space in which to reflect on undetectability, trans visibility, and the promise of opacity.[10]

What would it mean to sit with the historical and archival registers and gaps in Marsha P. Johnson's legacy and leave what is unexposed, unruly, and undetectable? What would it mean to refuse criminal investigation—beginning first with the FBI and forensic investigation altogether—and decline declaring any singular cause of transphobic harm?

There is little doubt that the state-sponsored justice system failed Johnson in overlooking the circumstances of her death. There is little doubt, however, that this system was built on that failure, punishing and criminalizing people like Johnson: poor people of color, sex workers, houseless people, and those living with HIV/AIDS. In her time, Johnson saw many of her own community, "transvestites," as she called them, locked up "for no reason at all" (Jay 1992: 113). She observed how the justice system trapped her trans sisters by demanding bail and legal fees from those who had no money to give. She marched on Wall Street with ACT UP to decry the overpricing of AIDS medications and called on people to "stand as close to [people living with AIDS] as much you can . . . help them out as much as you can."[11] Honoring Johnson's legacy asks us to reflect on crafting a sense of justice commensurate with those who have lived under and resisted, in oftentimes revolutionary ways, the reach of the carceral state. What is left unknown, I argue, moves beyond the mysterious causes of her death, extending into the remarkable political imaginary that she crafted, a portrait of mutual aid that we have yet to fully realize. This model of collective liberation necessitates rethinking the privatization of viral management and the joint orientation of criminal investigation toward individual choice, responsibility, and guilt.

Christopher Joseph Lee is a zine maker, writer, and PhD candidate at Brown University, where their research explores narratives of antiqueer violence. Their writing has appeared in the *New Inquiry*, *Women and Performance*, and the *Baffler*.

Notes

1. The Undetectable=Untransmittable movement (U=U) launched in 2016 with a consensus statement affirming that "people living with HIV on HAART with an undetectable viral load in their blood have a negligible risk of sexual transmission of HIV." U=U has played an especially significant role in promoting undetectability to normalize and destigmatize HIV as a manageable condition. See Prevention Access Campaign 2016.

2. The edited collection, *Trap Door*, offers a number of reflections on the paradox of trans visibility, questioning, in the editors' words, whether it is "a goal to be worked toward or an outcome to be avoided at all costs" (Burton, Stanley, and Tourmaline 2017: xx).

3. France's earlier work, *How to Survive a Plague*, has been the subject of both mainstream acclaim and intense scrutiny. Despite the film's offering an oftentimes moving account of the early years of the AIDS crisis, scholars like Jih-Fei Cheng (2016: 73) point to the gaps in *How to Survive*'s framing, depicted through a "lens of white male heroes" that largely overlooks queer-of-color contributions to early AIDS activism. Cheng describes how the film trains its attention to the search for a medical breakthrough (like undetectability). White men are positioned as central to the eventual development of HAART, and the survival of some of these men "become[s] the film's evidence that biomedical interventions can and should work for everyone" (74). See also Shahani 2016.

4. Dean Spade's (2015) work on critical trans politics has been particularly instructive in illuminating the failure of hate crime legislation to effectively deter transphobic harm.

5. As of today, according to the CDC, twenty-six states in the United States have laws criminalizing HIV exposure. See CDC n.d.

6. Perhaps the most infamous example of HIV/AIDS discourses' intersecting with individual responsibility resides in the case of Canadian flight attendant Gaëtan Dugal, the man popularly dubbed "Patient Zero." Through a work of investigative journalism by Randy Shilts, *And the Band Played On*, Dugal was sensationally scapegoated as the man who brought the AIDS virus to the Western world. Philip James Tiemeyer (2013: 258) describes the speed with which the "patient zero" mythos ignited a new narrative in which "AIDS was a disease born of gay immorality, a threat to the nation that came from the post-Stonewall gay credo of unchecked sexual excess." Tiemeyer suggests that the popularization of the term *patient zero*, though only tenuously based in truth, served as an effective bogeyman for conservative lawmakers to rapidly advance the criminalization of people with HIV. In the case of Dugas, detecting "patient zero" helped propagate even more emphasis on medical exposure of and criminalization of potentially "dangerous" individuals.

7.   In David Cunningham's (2004: xi–xii) analysis of the FBI's counterintelligence programs, he remarks that COINTELPRO and other actions taken up by the bureau should not be seen as "purely historical artifacts" but rather as "key to comprehending the FBI's fragile orientation to civil liberties generally."

8.   In a time before undetectability was understood and accepted, such comparisons between viral exposure and murder were commonplace. Gay journalist Charles Kaiser was infamously quoted as saying, "A person who is HIV-Positive has no more right to unprotected discourse than he has the right to put a bullet through another person's head" (quoted in Jacobs 2005).

9.   Two articles in *Teen Vogue* (Weiss 2017 and Tourmaline 2017) offer a clear portrait of this controversy. For more on the question of narrative authority and *Death and Life*, see Calafell 2019.

10.   As with visibility, there are limits to the promise of opacity. To be marked illegible, or to mark oneself in such a way, is also to be uncounted, unheard, and potentially discarded; indeed, the tactics of early AIDS organizing demanded visibility and vocalization amidst a deafening silence. In a time of trans exposure and HIV criminalization, though, we must also weigh, in Ted Kerr's (2019) words, how "visibility has become a state-enforced demand."

11.   From an interview in an earlier documentary, *Pay It No Mind: Marsha P. Johnson* (Kasino 2012).

References

Beauchamp, Toby. 2019. *Going Stealth: Transgender Politics and U.S. Surveillance Practices*. Durham, NC: Duke University Press.

Burton, Johanna, Eric Stanley, and Tourmaline. 2017. "Known Unknowns: An Introduction to Trap Door." In *Trap Door: Trans Cultural Production and the Politics of Visibility*, edited by Johanna Burton, Eric Stanley, and Tourmaline, xv–xxvi. Cambridge, MA: MIT Press.

Calafell, Bernadette Marie. 2019. "Narrative Authority, Theory in the Flesh, and the Fight over *The Death and Life of Marsha P. Johnson*." *QED* 6, no. 2: 26–39.

CDC (Centers for Disease Control and Prevention). n.d. "HIV-Specific Criminal Laws." www.cdc.gov/hiv/policies/law/states/exposure.html (accessed June 15, 2020).

Cheng, Jih-Fei. 2016. "How to Survive: AIDS and Its Afterlives in Popular Media." *WSQ* 44, no. 1: 73–92.

Cunningham, David. 2004. *There's Something Happening Here: The New Left, the Klan, and FBI Counterintelligence*. Berkeley: University of California Press.

France, David, dir. 2017. *The Death and Life of Marsha P. Johnson*. Netflix.

Haritaworn, Jin, and C. Riley Snorton. 2013. "Trans Necropolitics: A Transnational Reflection on Violence, Death, and the Trans of Color Afterlife." In *The Transgender Studies Reader 2*, edited by Susan Stryker and Aren Z. Aizura, 66–76. New York: Routledge.

Hoppe, Trevor. 2017. *Punishing Disease: HIV and the Criminalization of Sickness*. Oakland: University of California Press.

Huebenthal, Jan. 2017. "Un/Detectability in Times of 'Equality': HIV, Queer Health, and Homonormativity." *European Journal of American Studies* 11, no. 3. journals.openedition.org/ejas/11729.

Human Rights Campaign. n.d. "Transgender People and HIV: What We Know." www.hrc.org/resources/transgender-people-and-hiv-what-we-know/.

Iovannone, Jeffry J. 2017. "Should Netflix Viewers Boycott *The Death and Life of Marsha P. Johnson*?" *Medium*, October 8. medium.com/queer-history-for-the-people/should-netflix-viewers-boycott-the-death-and-life-of-marsha-p-johnson-cdf0a4057217.

Jacobs, Andrew. 2005. "Gays Debate Radical Steps to Curb Unsafe Sex." *New York Times*, February 15. www.nytimes.com/2005/02/15/health/gays-debate-radical-steps-to-curb-unsafe-sex .html.

Jay, Karla. 1992. *Out of the Closets: Voices of Gay Liberation*. New York: New York University Press.

Kasino, Michael, dir. 2012. *Pay It No Mind: Marsha P. Johnson*. Redux Pictures.

Kerr, Ted. 2019. "From Tactic to Demand: HIV Visibility within a Culture of Criminalization." *ONCURATING*, no. 42. www.on-curating.org/issue-42-reader/from-tactic-to-demand -hiv-visibility-within-a-culture-of-criminalization.html.

Lee, Nathan. 2013. "Becoming-Undetectable." *E-flux, no.* 44. www.e-flux.com/journal/44/60170 /becoming-undetectable/.

Marcus, Noreen. 2018. "Infected and Invisible: Fla. Housing Troubles Hit Transgender Residents." *US News and World Report*, April 11. www.usnews.com/news/healthiest-communities /articles/2018-04-11/hiv-transgender-residents-hit-by-south-florida-housing-crunch.

Palacios, Lena Carla. 2016. "Killing Abstractions: Indigenous Women and Black Trans Girls Challenging Media Necropower in White Settler States." *Critical Ethnic Studies* 2, no. 2: 35–60.

Prevention Access Campaign. 2016. "Consensus Statement." July 21. www.preventionaccess.org /consensus.

Pronzini, Bill, and Jack Adrian, eds. 1997. *Hardboiled: An Anthology of American Crime Stories*. Oxford: Oxford University Press.

Race, Kane. 2017. *The Gay Science: Intimate Experiments with the Problem of HIV*. New York: Taylor and Francis.

Shahani, Nishant. 2016. "How to Survive the Whitewashing of AIDS: Global Pasts, Transnational Futures." *QED* 3, no. 1: 1–33.

Spade, Dean. 2015. *Normal Life: Administrative Violence, Critical Trans Politics, and the Limits of Law*. Durham, NC: Duke University Press.

Stanley, Eric. 2011. "Near Life, Queer Death: Overkill and Ontological Capture." *Social Text*, no. 107: 1–19.

Stanley, Eric. 2017. "Anti-trans Optics: Recognition, Opacity, and the Image of Force." *South Atlantic Quarterly* 116, no. 3: 612–20.

Tang, Jeaninne. 2017. "Contemporary Art and Critical Transgender Infrastructures." In *Trap Door: Trans Cultural Production and the Politics of Visibility*, edited by Johanna Burton, Eric Stanley, and Tourmaline, 363–92. Cambridge, MA: MIT Press.

Tiemeyer, Philip James. 2013. *Plane Queer: Labor, Sexuality, and AIDS in the History of Male Flight Attendants*. Berkeley: University of California Press.

Tourmaline. 2017. "Why Transgender People Should Be the Ones Telling Transgender Stories." *Teen Vogue*, October 11. www.teenvogue.com/story/reina-gossett-marsha-p-johnson-op-ed.

Tourmaline, and Sasha Wortzel, dirs. 2018. *Happy Birthday, Marsha!* San Francisco: Frameline, DVD.

Treichler, Paula A. 1987. "AIDS, Homophobia, and Biomedical Discourse: An Epidemic of Sig-nification." *October*, no. 43: 31–70.

Weiss, Suzannah. 2017. "'The Death and Life of Marsha P. Johnson' Creator Accused of Stealing Work from Filmmaker Tourmaline." *Teen Vogue*, October 8. www.teenvogue.com/story /marsha-p-johnson-documentary-david-france-reina-gossett-stealing-accusations.

Paradigmatic

ADAM M. GEARY

Abstract When we bring together trans and HIV/AIDS, what are we trying to know, and what are we trying to do with that knowledge? In this essay the author argues that antiblack racism is the nexus for critically thinking the epidemiology of trans and HIV/AIDS, not simply black trans people's disparate suffering. Antiblackness has been paradigmatic and fundamental to the structural relations of domination and violence that have organized both group vulnerability to exposure to HIV and the ecologies of human susceptibility to illness and disease through which HIV has dispersed historically. Thus, within the public-health surveillance category "transgender," racial disparities in HIV prevalence and incidence rates point toward the true paradigm for thinking HIV/AIDS as an epidemic and the enfoldment of trans people within it.
Keywords HIV/AIDS, trans, antiblack racism, epidemiology

W hen we bring together trans and HIV/AIDS, what are we trying to know, and what are we trying to do with that knowledge?

Paradigm 1: Identity

Michel Foucault (1980, 1991) taught us that knowledge is a technology of power, and that in modern societies, expert knowledges are at the very least technologies of government. In approaching knowledges about HIV and AIDS, then, we should consider the ways that this knowledge has been generated for the problem of a particular governing, and then we must ask ourselves what we are doing with these knowledges and to what ends. So when invoking HIV rates for trans women, as well as other trans people living with HIV, we must ask ourselves not only what program of governance generates the knowledges we are invoking, but also how any attempt to redeploy those knowledges might be limited by the originating governmentality.

Knowledges about trans people and HIV, like all official knowledges generated regarding people living with HIV, emerge from what Cindy Patton (1985a; 1985b), writing at the beginning of the known epidemic, named "the queer paradigm." Patton discovered that in social discourse, public health knowledges,

TSQ: Transgender Studies Quarterly ∗ Volume 7, Number 4 ∗ November 2020 **573**
DOI 10.1215/23289252-8665215 © 2020 Duke University Press

and policy, people found to be living with HIV are always presumed to be somehow queer, behaviorally or culturally. HIV is the sign of some sort of pathological difference on the part of the person or group living with, or dying from, HIV. From this disposition, the problem of governing HIV became a problem on the one hand of governing the perversity of groups and individuals through behavioral and cultural modification programs (Geary 2011; Patton 1996; Schiller 1992), from safer sex and drug-injection harm reduction to abstinence and criminalization; and on the other hand, of pursuing the techno-pharmaceutical "silver bullet" of a cure or a vaccine for HIV (Brandt 1987).

In retrospect, we might describe Patton's critique as a queer intervention into the neoliberalization of health and medicine in the United States. Indeed, her oeuvre on HIV and AIDS has made a strong case that AIDS governance, rather than simply reflecting neoliberal rationality, has been one of the key problem-spaces for developing and articulating neoliberal rationalities and techniques of governance in the United States especially but not only (esp. Patton 1996; see also Patton 2002). The neoliberal governmentalization of HIV/AIDS "risk" involves a double movement. The HIV/AIDS epidemic was first problematized as a technical problem within a "population" conceived as a "market" and amendable to technocratic rationality: primarily public-health advertising and new or old technologies like condoms, vaccines, and other pharmaceutical therapies. Questions of incentives and disincentives were (and continue to be) debated by national and international policy makers and public health officials to produce new forms of "rational" decision making (market logic) around risk both within and between populations. This effort to instill market logics, in turn, revitalized and produced new forms of subjectification. Groups and individuals were targeted by national and international public health institutions for elaborate (but also shallow) therapeutics to produce subjects oriented around the moralities of health, responsibility, and security (Geary 2007). Increasingly, this moralized subjectification is articulated with techno-pharmaceuticals under the rubrics of "treatment as prevention" and "pre-exposure prophylaxis" (PrEP), aligning neoliberal subjectification and consumer technology markets. This governing logic also justified and revitalized older biopolitical state repressions, including the criminalization of (potential) HIV exposure and immigration exclusions (Farmer 2005; Hoppe 2015). The division between moral subjectification and state repression often falls directly on the fault line of race.

Descriptions of a governmental program always sound rather ideal. Of course, the program is marked by widespread failure and both organized and unorganized resistance, and people employ the pharma-technologies and techniques of subjectification in unauthorized and novel ways. For the governmental apparatuses, however, failure registers as impetus to improve the knowledge, techniques, and strategies of the program; resistance and underground novelties are signs of failed or willfully perverse subjectivity. We need not, and should not, allow neoliberalism to define us, but it seems wise to remember that discursively and technically, it is prepared to absorb and manage nearly any ideological resistance that falls short of mass revolt.

A critique of the queer paradigm, as a name for AIDS neoliberalism, provides context for my hesitations about the use of knowledge about trans and HIV. AIDS neoliberalism governs through identity; it treats identity as the proper site of governance, which proceeds through public health behavioralism as moral subjectification. Intervening in the problem of HIV risk is staged as a problem of knowing and reforming kinds of people and their communities or cultures (Fassin 2002; Geary 2011; Patton 1996). Indeed, it would be difficult to find a more perfect example of the deployment of power and subjectivity outlined by Foucault in volume 1 of his *History of Sexuality* (1990). Thus for trans women and other trans people at risk of HIV, the problem of risk and vulnerability is addressed within epidemiology and public health by knowing who they are, just as it has been for the other "risk groups" in the history of this pandemic. Which is to say that within neoliberal public health reasoning and practice, trans women are treated as a problem to be solved, and in solving the problem of trans women, public health will solve the problem of their HIV risk and its governance. In this entanglement, it is nearly impossible to distinguish "trans" from risk and governance.

Paradigm 2: Antiblackness

Neoliberalism is first and foremost an ideological defense against left critique and governance. AIDS neoliberalism is no exception to this rule. One of the key lessons that I have drawn from Patton's thinking on the queer paradigm is that the phobic attention to perversity in HIV/AIDS discourses and risk sciences has blocked, or attempted to block, investigations into the structuring of social and embodied vulnerability to HIV, or how the relations of inequality and violence that we call transphobia, homophobia, racism, sexism, class domination, and imperialism have structured both vulnerability to exposure to HIV *and* embodied susceptibility to infection if exposed, as well as the living and dying of people living with HIV. Again and again, critical AIDS scholars are forced to prove the inadequacy of sexual deviance, including the perverse pleasures of drug use, for thinking the HIV/AIDS pandemic: sexuality and sexual differences in behavior simply cannot explain the scale or distribution of HIV in the world (Katz 2002; Stillwaggon 2006). The persistence of the story of perversity, however, suggests that it must be seen as a story rehearsed and repeated in part to ward off telling other stories. The representational politics of perverse identities functions as what we might call a screen discourse, masking and drawing attention away from social inequality and structured vulnerability to HIV. Although the division in risk discourses between "queers" and "innocent victims" has engaged and recirculated racist, homophobic, and misogynist stereotypes as a rule, the primary discursive effect of this division has been to draw narrative energy to those so-called risky behaviors and cultural pathologies in discussions of disease vulnerability, away from questions of social structure and social violence. The inflated, phobic attention to gay men, drug users, "down low" black men, sex workers, and other queers in AIDS discourses has always been a way of not telling a story of how vulnerability to disease is structured through social inequality and structural violence.

The long tradition of left, materialist health science and epidemiology, however, demonstrates that epidemic disease burden is organized socially and structurally, because disease incidence (like HIV infection rates) is more than a simple representation of exposure to an infectious agent (see Krieger 2011). Rather, infection patterns depend on the general health of populations of people prior to exposure. Epidemics are structured "social facts" (Stark 1977) rather than the simple unfolding of a biological given. While individuals and groups of people are exposed to disease agents relatively randomly and relatively often, those agents only generally emerge as diseases, let alone epidemics, in welcoming sociobiological ecologies, especially the welcoming ecologies of human bodies made vulnerable through malnutrition, environmental poisoning, parasitosis, and other indices of impoverishment and social violence. Any given individual's susceptibility to an infectious agent will depend in part on the mode of exposure and the qualities of that agent, but also and more importantly on their general health and ability to ward off infection prior to exposure, as well as the general health of others around them. While specific forms of immune compromise may increase susceptibility for an individual, epidemics require kinds of population-level vulnerability that come from political, economic, and environmental immiseration.

This is as true of the global HIV/AIDS pandemic as it has been for other disease epidemics (Katz 2002; McBride 1991; Poku 2001; Singer 1994; Stillwaggon 2006). Compromised health has been shown to increase the likelihood that exposure to HIV will result in infection and to increase an individual's infectiousness to others. Over the long term, compromised health within given populations has led to greater disease burden in those populations, even if they engage in the same distribution of potential transmission behaviors as healthier populations.

Against prevailing wisdom, I propose that within "transgender" as an identity category within public health surveillance, racial disparities in HIV prevalence and incidence point toward the true paradigm for thinking HIV/AIDS as an epidemic and the enfoldment of trans people within that epidemic.

Conservative estimates suggest that, while overall HIV prevalence rates for trans women are approximately 14 percent—an already alarming number—nearly 45 percent of black trans women are living with HIV, as are roughly 25 percent of trans Latinas (Becasen et al. 2019: e3).[1] Prevalence rates for black trans women are more than six times greater than white trans women's, and prevalence rates for trans Latinas are more than three times greater. Additionally, from 2009 to 2014, more than half of all new HIV diagnoses for trans women were made in black trans women, and approximately 30 percent were in trans Latinas (Clark et al. 2017: 2779), suggesting that future prevalence disparities will continue to look about the same, if not greater.

A little over 3 percent of trans men are believed to be living with HIV. From 2009 to 2014, however, nearly 60 percent of all new HIV diagnoses for trans men were made in black trans men, with white and Latino trans men each at around 15 percent of the total (Clark et al. 2017: 2779).

These racial disparities are mirrored in every demographic breakdown. Of the approximately 1 million people in the United States currently living with HIV, more than 40 percent are black, as are more than 40 percent of all people newly infected with HIV each year, even though black people account for only 12 percent of the total US population (CDC 2018). Sixty percent of all women living with HIV in the United States are black women, as are nearly two-thirds of all women globally. Also mirroring the global pandemic, there are more black people living with HIV in the United States than whites or any other racial/ethnic group, with the prevalence rate for black people being nearly eight times greater than for whites and three times greater than for Latinos. At current rates of infection, epidemiologists project that one in sixteen black men and one in thirty-two black women in the United States are likely to be diagnosed with HIV infection in their lifetimes.

In my *Antiblack Racism and the AIDS Epidemic: State Intimacies* (2014), I demonstrated that deep investigation of the color of the US epidemic—its racial blackness—reveals antiblack racial formation as structuring the social, institutional, and physiological conditions that allowed HIV to establish itself and emerge as an epidemic per se. Antiblack racism is the political economy of HIV/AIDS, its paradigm. Two state institutions of antiblack racism have been foundational to the US HIV/AIDS epidemic overall, and especially to the epidemic among black people: the production of ecologies of intensified social and physiological immiseration within the apartheid structure of the black urban ghettos, and the post–Civil Rights era redeployment of the prison as a technology of antiblack racial domination—what has since become known as "mass" or "hyper" incarceration. Health geographers have demonstrated that the US epidemic emerged historically from the synergistic context of highly marginalized and concentrated gay communities and the immiseration of the racialized urban ghettos of the major US cities, traveling along the urban hierarchy and then to surrounding communities (Gould 1993; Wallace 2007; Wallace and Wallace 1995; Wallace et al. 1999). In this way, the socially produced conditions of urban despair fulfilled their historical function in being the incubators of epidemic, with the HIV epidemic being only a more recent example rather than something exceptional (McBride 1991). The formation of the US urban ghetto within the history of antiblack racism (Massey and Denton 1993) is therefore structurally essential to a nonreductionist account of the US HIV/AIDS epidemic, not as emerging from the sexual excesses of gay men but as emerging and dispersing through the compromised human ecologies of the mid-century urban ghettos.

The urban ghetto as an ecology of immiseration has been determined not only by segregation and planned destruction; it has also been determined by direct relations of state violence in the form of the policing-prison apparatus authorized by the race war in its various guises: the wars on poverty, on crime, on drugs, on terror, against communism, and so forth (Sexton and Lee 2006; Wacquant 2002). The extraordinary expansion of the prison beginning in the 1970s under the war on crime, and accelerating dramatically under the war on drugs, has reached a sociological threshold in which incarceration and its effects, both individual and aggregate, have become a part of the everyday lived experience of black Americans, especially those concentrated in the urban ghettos. Recent research, in turn, has demonstrated that these effects include increased vulnerability to HIV, not only for those incarcerated but also for the communities from which they come and to which they return (Johnson and Raphael 2009). Indeed, statistical modeling suggests that between 70 and 100 percent of black-white AIDS diagnosis disparities in the United States for both men and women can be explained by the extremely disproportionate incarceration of black men starting in the 1970s. This is due not solely, or even firstly, to risk practices and HIV transmission in prisons. Rather, what sociologist Loïc Wacquant (2001) has called the "deadly symbiosis" of mass incarceration and the black ghetto degrades the overall health of those captured within its continuum by structuring and deepening racial and classed inequality, damaging the health of the incarcerated over their lifetimes (even if not always while incarcerated), increasing and concentrating the possibilities of exposure to HIV and other transmissible diseases, and decreasing the overall health of those communities from which the incarcerated are captured and to which they are released. In each of these modes, and especially in their interarticulation, mass incarceration functions as an active technology for producing ill health and vulnerability to disease, including HIV, in communities of black urban poverty, the communities most thoroughly articulated into the apparatuses of mass incarceration. As mass incarceration has intensified and expanded over the last four decades, so has this social and physiological vulnerability of the ghetto, indexing almost exactly the organization of the US HIV/AIDS epidemic as an affliction visited on the black poor.

My argument in *State Intimacies* was not only that antiblack racism has structured health and disease disparities—including HIV/AIDS disparities—for black people in the United States, but that as a fundamental antagonism not only in US state formation but in global Atlantic modernity (Sexton 2008; Wilderson 2010), antiblackness has structured the emergence and history of the HIV/AIDS epidemic overall. Antiblackness has been paradigmatic and fundamental to the structural (as opposed to purely interpersonal) relations of domination and violence that have organized both group vulnerability to exposure to HIV and the ecologies of human susceptibility to illness and disease through which HIV has dispersed historically. In addition to their other functions for racial domination, the ghetto and the prison and their synergism have produced, and continue to produce, population-wide, embodied vulnerability to diseases, including HIV. What I have called "state intimacy"—organized, antiblack, racial domination as relayed through state apparatuses—has structured vulnerability to HIV exposure and susceptibility to infection in the United States far beyond the capacity of any individual or community to mitigate or control. This structuring of ecologies and relations, of course, is not confined to black people; it is, rather, the matrix through which multiple life worlds have been organized and brought into relation.

The formation of antiblack racism, additionally, is internally differentiated through relations of class, gender, sexuality, and other axes of difference and inequality. For instance, in *State Intimacies*, I argued that understanding the link between incarceration and HIV makes sense of gendered difference in HIV rates for black people in the United States. Black men suffer HIV prevalence and infection rates dramatically higher than all other men, but also at least twice that of black women. Recognizing the role of incarceration helps us understand HIV rate differentials between black men and women as being related to a gendered insertion into relations of domination. As many critical scholars have argued, poor, urban African Americans are dominated and exploited in a fundamentally gender-differentiated apparatus of workfare and incarceration (e.g., Wacquant, Eick, and Winkler 2011). Through the so-called welfare reform legislation of 1996, black women have been reorganized as a pool of highly exploitable labor, while black men have been rendered surplus and inassimilable to the labor market. To control this surplus population, black men have been incarcerated. Black men's higher rates of HIV, then, index this gendered distribution of violence and exploitation directed at black people—the concrete relations of domination and violence. What is essential, however, is the organization of violence and exploitation, which is antiblack racial formation.

I suggest that antiblackness is the nexus for critically thinking the epidemiology of trans and HIV/AIDS, not simply black trans people's disparate suffering. Even seemingly progressive common sense in public health tends to treat HIV as a given, or brute fact, in relation to which subjects are made more or less vulnerable in the arithmetic of identity and inequality. It attends only to the individual subject's social vulnerability, which it treats as a personal or situated deficit that can be overcome through personal empowerment strategies. Thus trans women's HIV rates emerge as the sum of inequalities—gender + trans + poverty + race—which are conceived fundamentally as deficits in power and resources. Racial disparities among trans women therefore mark the addition of racial inequality to other deficits in power and resources structured by gender and class (see Crenshaw 1989, for the critique of this additive logic). This deficit model approaches the problem, but its individualizing focus tends to occult the ordered relations of domination and violence that produce these deficits and are them-selves the true engine of epidemic disease (Krieger 1994; Stark 1977), as I have argued is the case for antiblack racism in structuring the emergence, dispersion, and replication of HIV.

Pursuing an account of violence and domination as structuring, however, would differently inflect accounts of HIV infection that rely on deficit arithme-tic or depend too heavily, or even solely, on structured, gendered inequality in interpersonal sexual relations, including sex work (Katz 2002; Patton 1994). The latter, in particular, is too late in the story. Those unequal and even violent relations absolutely exist, but they are finally but the last link in much larger, organized sets of relations that exceed them. Not only is the larger structuring of antiblack racism fundamental to living or dying with HIV, it is also fundamental to the texture of those gendered, interpersonal relations, as well as the presence or absence of HIV in them. Approaching that larger structuring, however, would involve investigating the ways that trans women and men exist within and in relation to institutional arrangements in such a way that these institutional arrangements structure not only their vulnerability to exposure but also their susceptibility to infection with HIV. How are trans women and men multiply articulated into ecologies of racialized poverty and the wholesale destruction of life worlds, into the racially organized withholding or denial of health care and medicine, into networks traversing the carceral and the military-imperial appara-tuses, into the production of human surplus, and into the ever-increasing pre-caritization of wage labor? Which is to say, how has antiblack racial formation structured the concrete relations of exposure to HIV for trans women and men as well as the ecologies of immiseration and susceptibility in which exposure so easily leads to infection? This might yield something other than a general theory of trans identity, life, or oppression. (Although it might yield a general theory, too.) As I discussed above in relation to gendered differences in HIV rates between black men and women, some kinds of domination and violence make one more susceptible to particular diseases than others. But answering any of these socio-logical and epidemiological questions would be anything but straightforward or easy, even for the most sophisticated statistical researchers. The data available to us was generated for other ends, stripped of contexts that might make sense of patternings that exceed the most immediate, personal contexts or qualities. What we can know has been actively constrained.

Paradigmatic Politics

In concluding, I want to return to my opening question: When we bring together trans and HIV/AIDS, what are we trying to know, and what are we trying to do with that knowledge? Is the goal to end the HIV/AIDS epidemic, to govern it, or to survive it? Is it a general theory of trans identity or oppression? These questions may be related. It depends. But they are not the same question.

In general, of course, my argument reaffirms the foundational critical movement of black feminism and its extensions, including the emerging trans-of-color critique: that the experience of oppression and possibility is constituted in a matrix of domination (Collins 2000) whose proper name is "The Master's House" (Lorde 1984). The structuring of the structural continues to follow/flow from the political and libidinal economies of the plantation (Hartman 1997; King 2013; Sexton 2016; Wilderson 2010). I have argued that this structuring of the matrix of domination is reaffirmed in the history and epidemiology of the HIV/AIDS epidemic: a critical account of the epidemiology of HIV demonstrates that social vulnerability to exposure to HIV and embodied susceptibility to infection from exposure have been structured within a matrix of dominations organized by antiblackness. Furthermore, I am arguing here that trans vulnerabilities to HIV—even vulnerabilities that might be unique to transing—must also be emplotted within that matrix. Trans would therefore be analytically decentered, which—to be clear—is not the same as marginal or incidental.

Within this analytical matrix, then, what sorts of trans pragmatics or politics of HIV/AIDS are possible, or desirable? I don't want to be glib. On the one hand, I have warned against the impulse toward governance through identity in HIV risk and treatment research. But in a context like the United States, where individualized risk reduction and treatment protocols are the only game in town, what I am calling deficit arithmetic research on risk environments—the imme-diate environments in which subjects, including trans subjects, negotiate risk and vulnerability—may yield real survival knowledges.

And yet, this survival knowledge will never be enough. If my reading of the epidemiology of HIV/AIDS is correct, the matrix of domination and violence through which the epidemic replicates itself—antiblack racism—will necessarily overwhelm individual or even community efforts to mitigate it. That's what structural domination means. All of which is to say that there is a difference between research generated in the service of risk or harm reduction, which may be organized through identity categories (or not), and knowledge oriented toward the paradigmatic structure and replication of HIV/AIDS as an epidemic. And then there is the problem of a politics of the paradigm, which may or may not have any specific relation to the pragmatics of immediate, defensive risk/harm reduction. My point, however, is that these are different levels of conceptualization, and failing to recognize this difference only contributes to the repetitive collapse in thinking HIV/AIDS: from political outrage over the structured violence and domination of antiblack racism into pragmatic problems for the neoliberal governance of health and disease. For those of us actively committed to a paradigmatic politics of HIV/AIDS, in a context committed to depoliticization and confusion, we must learn, relearn, and remind ourselves how to think and act at both levels and in their entwining.

Adam M. Geary is the author of *Antiblack Racism and the AIDS Epidemic: State Intimacies* (2014).

Note

1. In the studies reviewed by Becasen et al. (2019), 84 percent of respondents identified as transgender women, 15 percent as transgender men, and 1 percent as otherwise transgendered.

References

Becasen, Jeffrey S., Christa L. Denard, Mary M. Mullins, Darrel H. Higa, and Theresa Ann Sipe. 2019. "Estimating the Prevalence of HIV and Sexual Behaviors among the US Transgender Population: A Systematic Review and Meta-Analysis, 2006–2017." *American Journal of Public Health* 109, no. 1: e1–8. doi.org/10.2105/AJPH.2018.304727.

Brandt, Allan M. 1987. *No Magic Bullet: A Social History of Venereal Disease in the United States since 1880.* Expanded ed. New York: Oxford University Press.

CDC (Centers for Disease Control and Prevention). 2018. *HIV Surveillance Report, 2017.* Vol. 29. www.cdc.gov/hiv/library/reports/hiv-surveillance.html.

Clark, Hollie, Aruna Surendera Babu, Ellen Weiss Wiewel, Jenevieve Opoku, and Nicole Crepaz. 2017. "Diagnosed HIV Infection in Transgender Adults and Adolescents: Results from the National HIV Surveillance System, 2009–2014." *AIDS and Behavior* 21, no. 9: 2774–83. doi.org/10.1007/s10461-016-1656-7.

Collins, Patricia Hill. 2000. *Black Feminist Thought: Knowledge, Consciousness, and the Politics of Empowerment.* 2nd ed. New York: Routledge.

Crenshaw, Kimberlé Williams. 1989. "Demarginalizing the Intersections of Race and Sex: A Black Feminist Critique of Antidiscrimination Doctrine, Feminist Theory, and Antiracist Politics." *University of Chicago Legal Forum* 1989: 139–67.

Farmer, Paul. 2005. "Pestilence and Restraint: Guantanamo, AIDS, and the Logic of Quarantine." In *Pathologies of Power: Health, Human Rights, and the New War on the Poor*, 51–90. Berkeley: University of California Press.

Fassin, Didier. 2002. "Embodied History: Uniqueness and Exemplarity of South African AIDS." *African Journal of AIDS Research* 1, no. 1: 63–68.

Foucault, Michel. 1980. "Truth and Power." In *Power/Knowledge: Selected Interviews and Other Writings 1972–1977*, edited by Colin Gordon, 109–33. New York: Pantheon.

Foucault, Michel. 1990. *An Introduction*. Vol. 1 of *The History of Sexuality*. New York: Vintage.

Foucault, Michel. 1991. "Governmentality." In *The Foucault Effect: Studies in Governmentality*, edited by Graham Burchell, Colin Gordon, and Peter Miller, 87–104. Chicago: University of Chicago Press.

Geary, Adam M. 2007. "Culture as an Object of Ethical Governance in AIDS Prevention." *Cultural Studies* 21, nos. 4–5: 672–94.

Geary, Adam M. 2011. "Inessential Theory: Culture and AIDS Risk Governance." *Eä: Journal of Medical Humanities and Social Studies of Science and Technology* 2, no. 3. www.ea-journal .com/en/numeros-anteriores/63-vol-2-no-3-abril-2011/580-inessential-theory-culture -and-aids-risk-governance-2.

Geary, Adam M. 2014. *Antiblack Racism and the AIDS Epidemic: State Intimacies*. New York: Palgrave Macmillan.

Gould, Peter. 1993. *The Slow Plague: A Geography of the AIDS Pandemic*. Oxford: Blackwell.

Hartman, Saidiya V. 1997. *Scenes of Subjection: Terror, Slavery, and Self-Making in Nineteenth-Century America*. New York: Oxford University Press.

Hoppe, Trevor Alexander. 2015. "Disparate Risks of Conviction under Michigan's Felony HIV Disclosure Law: An Observational Analysis of Convictions and HIV Diagnoses, 1992–2010." *Punishment and Society* 17, no. 1: 73–93.

Johnson, Rucker C., and Steven Raphael. 2009. "The Effects of Male Incarceration Dynamics on Acquired Immune Deficiency Syndrome Infection Rates among African American Women and Men." *Journal of Law and Economics* 52, no. 2: 251–93.

Katz, Alison. 2002. "AIDS, Individual Behaviour, and the Unexplained Remaining Variation." *African Journal of AIDS Research* 1, no. 2: 125–42.

King, Tiffany Jeannette. 2013. "In the Clearing: Black Female Bodies, Space, and Settler Colonial Landscapes." PhD diss., University of Maryland, College Park. search.proquest.com /docview/1461804097.

Krieger, Nancy. 1994. "Epidemiology and the Web of Causation: Has Anyone Seen the Spider?" *Social Science and Medicine* 39, no. 7: 887–903.

Krieger, Nancy. 2011. *Epidemiology and the People's Health: Theory and Context*. New York: Oxford University Press.

Lorde, Audre. 1984. "The Master's Tools Will Never Dismantle the Master's House." In *Sister Outsider: Essays and Speeches*, 100–113. Berkeley, CA: Crossing.

Massey, Douglas S., and Nancy A. Denton. 1993. *American Apartheid: Segregation and the Making of the Underclass*. Cambridge, MA: Harvard University Press.

McBride, David. 1991. *From TB to AIDS: Epidemics among Urban Blacks since 1900*. Albany: State University of New York Press.

Patton, Cindy. 1985a. "Heterosexual AIDS Panic: A Queer Paradigm." *Gay Community News* (Boston), February 9.

Patton, Cindy. 1985b. *Sex and Germs: The Politics of AIDS*. Boston: South End.

Patton, Cindy. 1994. *Last Served? Gendering the HIV Pandemic*. Bristol, PA: Taylor and Francis.

Patton, Cindy. 1996. *Fatal Advice: How Safe-Sex Education Went Wrong*. Durham, NC: Duke University Press.

Patton, Cindy. 2002. *Globalizing AIDS*. Minneapolis: University of Minnesota Press.

Poku, Nana K. 2001. "Africa's AIDS Crisis in Context: 'How the Poor Are Dying.'" *Third World Quarterly* 22, no. 2: 191–204.

Schiller, Nina Glick. 1992. "What's Wrong with This Picture? The Hegemonic Construction of Culture in AIDS Research in the United States." *Medical Anthropology Quarterly* 6, no. 3: 237–54.

Sexton, Jared. 2008. *Amalgamation Schemes: Antiblackness and the Critique of Multiculturalism*. Minneapolis: University of Minnesota Press.

Sexton, Jared. 2016. "The *Vel* of Slavery: Tracking the Figure of the Unsovereign." *Critical Sociology* 42, nos. 4–5: 583–97.

Sexton, Jared, and Elizabeth Lee. 2006. "Figuring the Prison: Prerequisites of Torture at Abu Ghraib." *Antipode* 38, no. 5: 1005–22.

Singer, Merrill. 1994. "AIDS and the Health Crisis of the U.S. Urban Poor: The Perspective of Critical Medical Anthropology." *Social Science and Medicine* 39, no. 7: 931–48.

Stark, Evan. 1977. "The Epidemic as a Social Event." *International Journal of Health Services* 7, no. 4: 681–705.

Stillwaggon, Eileen. 2006. *AIDS and the Ecology of Poverty*. New York: Oxford University Press.

Wacquant, Loïc. 2001. "Deadly Symbiosis: When Ghetto and Prison Meet and Mesh." *Punishment and Society* 3, no. 1: 95–134.

Wacquant, Loïc. 2002. "From Slavery to Mass Incarceration: Rethinking the 'Race Question' in the U.S." *New Left Review*, no. 13: 41–60.

Wacquant, Loïc, Volker Eick, and Karen J. Winkler. 2011. "The Wedding of Workfare and Prisonfare Revisited." *Social Justice* 38, nos. 1–2: 1–16.

Wallace, Roderick. 2007. "Plague and Power Relations." *Geografiska Annaler, Series B: Human Geography* 89, no. 4: 319–39.

Wallace, Roderick, and Deborah Wallace. 1995. "U.S. Apartheid and the Spread of AIDS to the Suburbs: A Multi-city Analysis of the Political Economy of Spatial Epidemic Threshold." *Social Science and Medicine* 41, no. 3: 333–45.

Wallace, Roderick, Deborah Wallace, J. E. Ullmann, and H. Andrews. 1999. "Deindustrialization, Inner-City Decay, and the Hierarchical Diffusion of AIDS in the USA: How Neoliberal and Cold War Policies Magnified the Ecological Niche for Emerging Infections and Created a National Security Crisis." *Environment and Planning A* 31, no. 1: 113–39.

Wilderson, Frank B. 2010. *Red, White, and Black: Cinema and the Structure of U.S. Antagonisms*. Durham, NC: Duke University Press.

HIV Prevention and Care of Transgender Women in an HIV and STI Clinic in the Paris Metropolitan Area

A Qualitative Assessment from Medical Care to Social Integration

BAHAR AZADI, JULIA ZÉLIE,
FLORENCE MICHARD, and YAZDAN YAZDANPANAH

Abstract HIV infection burden is globally high among transgender women (TGW) and particularly in TGW migrant sex workers and TGW subpopulations with structural inequalities like racism and classism. In addition to stigma related to transphobia, migrant TGW face multiple forms of discrimination because of intersection with other experiences of stigma related to migration and working as sex workers in the host society. This study explores the experiences of TGW seeking care in an HIV and STI clinic in Paris, to evaluate medical adherence, namely, the degree to which a patient is regularly followed up in care and adequately takes the treatment, and trans individuals' social inclusion in this health institution. We examined the different forms of HIV-associated stigma among TGW. A qualitative study was conducted using semistructural in-depth interviews with TGW receiving HIV care and HIV preventive measures. A description is given of how a community-based participation policy and practice in this clinic integrate an intersectional approach among TGW. This results in a high rate of medical adherence in TGW migrants and could lead to social integration.

Keywords TGW, HIV care, community-based participation (CBP), intersectionality, medical adherence

Previous research has shown that health care is a setting in which transgender individuals experience discrimination in various forms, including fear of discrimination (anticipated stigma) and previous experiences of discrimination (enacted stigma) (Reisner et al. 2015). Marginalization and the experience of stigma related to cis-normativity, gender-nonconformity, classism, racism, and previous pathologization of trans identities are the primary reasons transgender

TSQ: Transgender Studies Quarterly ∗ Volume 7, Number 4 ∗ November 2020   **585**
DOI 10.1215/23289252-8665229   © 2020 Duke University Press

women (TGW) avoid seeking medical treatment or prevention. Moreover, the lack of trans identity recognition and noninclusion in national census data, in many countries, as a form of trans identity erasure, exclude transgender individuals from proper health-care services and appropriate information accessibility. Transgender women and in particular TGW sex workers of Latin America, TGW of color in the United States, and ethnic minorities in Europe have been identified as being highly vulnerable to human immunodeficiency virus (HIV) (Baral et al. 2007; Baral et al. 2013; Habarta et al. 2015; Poteat et al. 2016). The risk of acquiring HIV is forty-nine times higher in TGW than in adults of reproductive age globally, although the distribution of HIV prevalence varies across TGW subpopulations and geographic regions across the globe (Baral et al. 2013).

The question of high burden of HIV and sexually transmitted infections (STIs) among TGW despite many recent trans-inclusive research and prevention programs could be analyzed by focusing on the permanent and global situation of vulnerability in this group. In Western Europe in particular, in addition to stigma related to transphobia, a high proportion of TGW face multiple forms of marginalization because of intersection with other experiences of stigma related to immigration, sex working, and race/ethnicity. This could be illustrated by HIV prevalence differences based on the rate of vulnerabilities in the analyzed population; for example, a recent French study targeting immigrant TGW sex workers and another surveying trans individuals by the internet showed important HIV prevalence disparities (Freire Maresca et al. 2007; Almeida Wilson et al. 2008). Other studies report comparable results (Pommier et al. 2011; Baguso, Gay, and Lee 2016). Faced with these results, we initiated a qualitative study in TGW seeking care in our clinic to assess their experience, to evaluate medical adherence from their perspective, and to clarify their needs. Medical adherence was defined as the degree to which a patient is regularly followed up in care and adequately takes the treatment. Social factors affect medical adherence to HIV care and preventions beyond TGW. Through this study, we attempted to understand whether these types of HIV and STI care and prevention clinics could be a counterexample of perceived transgender stigmatization in health care services and, if so, how. The intersectional precarious condition of migrant TGW impacts not only the process of medical care and prevention but also the process of social integration in the host society (WHO 2018). We therefore also discuss the impact of medical care on social integration in this population.

Participants and Procedures

We conducted a semi-structured in-depth interview with TGW who attended the Bichat-Claude Bernard Hospital HIV and STI clinic from November 1, 2018, to January 31, 2019. Convenience sampling was used for interviewing the participants who were available for interview after medical consultations. The size of the sample was based on thematic and code saturation. We enrolled a random sample of 30 out of 306 HIV-positive TGW followed up regularly at the HIV clinic for more than one year, and 15 (out of 52) HIV-negative TGW followed up for HIV and STI prevention. The HIV-positive and HIV-negative trans median age was forty. Respectively, 90 percent and 93 percent were from Latin America, mainly Peru and Brazil. In HIV-positive TGW, median time of follow-up was seventy-nine months. Of HIV-positive and HIV-negative trans individuals, 63 percent and 93 percent, respectively, were sex workers. Interviewees were informed about the interview by their doctor, and interviews were held in French, English, Spanish, and Portuguese in a private room at the hospital. The length of the interviews varied from fifteen to ninety minutes. Interviews were recorded, transcribed, coded, and analyzed. The protocol is registered and has received approval from the Ethics Evaluation Committee of the Institutional Review Board of the French Institute of Medical Research and Health (CEEI-Inserm).

From Social Exclusion to Social Inclusion in Health

Previous studies have shown the impact of marginalization on the health of trans people (Bockting, Robinson, and Rosser 1998; Sugano, Nemoto, and Operario 2006). Concentrated epidemics in most countries show the impact of social exclusion (erasure) on health in which the low prevalence of HIV in the overall population is generally in the presence of the much higher prevalence in certain groups (WHO 2013). Transgender women face not only multifactorial barriers to access to HIV care but also frequent complications (e.g., silicon injections, surgical complications, and hormonal intake). However, despite low medical adherence to care, many transgender individuals need and follow gender-affirmative therapy to accomplish the desirable gender identity transformation (Namaste 2000). According to some studies, negative psychosocial factors increase vulnerability to preventable diseases (Singer and Clair 2003). Other risk factors like multiple sexual partners, condomless receptive and insertive anal intercourse, previous sexually transmitted infections, sharing syringes for injecting drugs and hormones, and physical and sexual abuse and assault are the social and behavioral factors that increase the risk of infection in this population (Neumann et al. 2017).

Measuring social exclusion depends on the elements we use to analyze this concept beyond a particular group and in a particular institution (O'Donnell, O'Donovan, and Elmusharaf 2018). In this article, social exclusion covers people who have been stigmatized and marginalized and also migrants and refugees as a group at risk of social exclusion (Shaw, Dorling, and Smith 2005). In recent years, despite a growing amount of research showing the difficulties experienced by transgender individuals in accessing reliable health care, few studies have analyzed the relationship between the feeling and experiencing of discrimination and stigma and delaying health care or noninclusive health care in this population (Grant et al. 2011; Seelman et al. 2017). All of the participants in this study experienced violence and discrimination in their country of origin, and they have also been experiencing different forms of violence ranging from insult to the worst physical aggression as sex workers in France. Moreover, 90 percent of the participants after experiencing physical aggressions as sex workers did not submit any complaint to the police, while most of them individually first presented to a hospital (Le Bail, Giametta, and Rassouw 2018). This shows that in France undocumented migrant TGW have more trust and feel more secure in hospitals and health services than a judicial institution. Although, for undocumented HIV-positive sex workers, the obligation to leave French territory is becoming more frequent when HIV treatments are available in their country of origin. In response to this, some health-care workers and activists state that existence of treatment does not guarantee access to care and adequate follow-up. Transgender erasure in health-care services, practices, and research takes two forms: passive and active. Active erasure involves clear and radical refusal of trans individuals by health services (e.g., dentist's rejection of transgender individuals living with HIV [Bourrelly and Mora 2018], or refusal of health services in countries where trans identity is illegal), which heightens the risk of death related to HIV and the risk of other infections. Passive erasure of transgender individuals includes a lack of global and appropriate knowledge about trans issues, (e.g., erasure in information production and in institutional protocols and policies; Bauer et al. 2009). This may also happen in health research and policies without trans community-based participation. Bearing this in mind, we tried to find the difficulties in and obstacles to medical follow-up. To measure medical adherence of TGW to HIV care, we asked participants to describe their positive and negative experiences during follow-up.

Results: From Satisfaction to Stigma

1. Technical and Interpersonal Satisfaction

When we asked the participants if they were satisfied with the Bichat-Claude Bernard Hospital HIV and STI clinical care services, 95 percent of participants responded that they were satisfied, although 30 percent stated that they also experienced stigma during their follow-up. This could be in line with the results of an epidemiologic quantitative study on transgender follow-up in this clinic conducted at the same time as this study, which showed that adherence in TGW living with HIV and followed up in our clinic between 2008 and 2018 was comparable to that of cisgender men, cisgender women, and men who have sex with men followed up during the same period (Maisonobe 2019). In this study, the proportion of TGW living with HIV who were lost to follow-up (i.e., who did not attend clinical visits for twenty-four months) during the study period was estimated at 20.5 percent. In another epidemiological quantitative study of 4,796 HIV patients living with HIV followed up in our clinic between January 2010 and October 2014, the risk of medical care interruption was not found to be higher in patients born in sub-Saharan or other countries, including TGW from Latin America, than those born in France (Fournier et al. 2019). Overall these data show that TGW, despite a high rate of social exclusion, are satisfied with and adherent to health services offered by our medical institution.

We defined two forms of satisfaction/dissatisfaction: technical and interpersonal. The main expectation of the majority of participants is focused largely on the technical aspect of treatment as the most important reason for satisfaction. One of the participants explained, "I am satisfied when my doctor tells me everything is fine, congratulations! That's all I want from the hospital."

A high rate of technical satisfaction could be a result of noninclusion in health services in the country of origin or other European countries before arriving in France. In a second phase of satisfaction, the interpersonal aspect of treatment was highlighted. This phase is particularly related to interaction with physicians, nurses, and staff, for example, when the staff member displays a caring attitude, shows understanding, speaks in the patient's mother tongue, and calls patients by their desired gender identity. A TGW stated, "I didn't speak French at all, and Dr. X made things easier because I could speak Spanish with her. When I discovered my illness, the hospital for me was the end, goodbyes, and death. But I followed my treatments and the hospital saved me. My doctor isn't just my doctor, she is also my friend."

Interpersonal aspects may seem to be less important than technical aspects in measuring satisfaction among TGW. Moreover, unfulfilled expectations linked to interpersonal aspects may not necessarily lead to less satisfaction or medical care interruption. However, they may have an important impact on the process of social integration. The health-care worker, when we consider the interpersonal aspect, is not a technician but a member of society: "The doctor isn't just my doctor; she is also my friend." Interestingly, those TGW who were more sensitive and maybe aware of the stigma related to transphobia were those who are mostly members of nongovernmental organizations (NGOs) and are informed about their rights, not only as transgender individuals but also as migrants and sex workers. Satisfaction may decrease when awareness increases.

Participants who stated that they experienced stigma primarily mentioned gender-inappropriate terms of address by the clinical personnel or the administrative staff of the hospital. One of the participants told us about this experience: "There is respect and sometimes no respect; there are people who like to piss off people, for example, a nurse in front of you who looks at you and sees a woman but still calls you sir."

Experience of gender-inappropriate terms of address can even, in some cases, lead to medical interruption, as voiced by another participant: "It has happened to me that the doctor calls me sir and I ask him to call me madam. I told him, 'Look at me, I'm a woman,' but he repeated, sir. I left the consultation and never wanted to continue my treatment with him."

Although many participants reported that mistakes regarding their gender can happen, they stated that repeated use of gender-inappropriate terms of address generates the experience of stigma. They stated that they mostly prefer that their doctor and staff use the pronoun they identify with. Another experience of stigma related to a mismatch between the gender status indicated on identity cards or insurance cards and the lived gender of the TGW. This could be avoided without huge policy and administrative changes, as one of the participants explained: "My doctor noted in my medical records my real name, which I identify with. Since then, my real name and gender are mentioned in my medical records, and so other doctors and nurses call me with my true name."

2. Intergroup Stigma

We asked participants why TGW generally abandon HIV care. The answers were mostly as follows: "lack of motivation," "not to be responsible for her illness," "not to be aware of the severity of her illness," "lack of mental maturity," and "irresponsibility." It seems that among TGW, we can observe a form of intergroup valorization regarding HIV disease: on the one hand, between TGW who live with HIV and TGW who are HIV-negative, and, on the other hand, between TGW who regularly attend follow-up meetings and TGW who attend irregularly. Intergroup stigmatization exists between TGW who are HIV-negative and who seek HIV prevention and pre-exposure prophylaxis (PrEP) in particular, and those who live with HIV. Regarding this, one of the participants explained: "I know some TGW don't follow PrEP because they believe that they will be mistaken for HIV-positive TGW. I don't care and I want to get my PrEP anyway, but for so many it's an important obstacle. I think we should separate the location or the waiting room of HIV treatments and PrEP."

3. Gender-Affirmative Therapy

We assessed whether participants wanted gender-affirmative care (i.e., hormonal therapy, psychological therapy) to be integrated into HIV prevention and care. The idea behind this is to provide medical care in addition to that concerning HIV and/or STI oriented to TGW. This way we may not only improve this population medically but also increase their chance of social integration. When asked whether they need any hormonal therapy in our clinic while following HIV care or prevention, 60 percent of HIV-positive TGW and 75 percent of HIV-negative TGW stated that they think it is a good idea to integrate hormonal therapy management into HIV prevention and care. Compared to trans people living with HIV, HIV-negative TGW use more hormones and practice more self-medication. We discovered different beliefs about hormone therapy among TGW. Some TGW believe that hormone injections create complications while following HIV care; others consider that hormones cause problems in their work as sex workers. When we considered during interviews their willingness to integrate psychological care into HIV prevention and care, most TGW (70 percent) first answered in the negative. However, when we proposed psychological support and care in their mother tongue, they were more open to the idea.

HIV Clinic as a Counterexample of Trans Medicalization

Trans medicalization refers to the pathologizing of trans identity and stigma related to medical and pathological models of trans identity categorizations. It affects the lived experiences of trans people and more specifically their adherence to medical recommendations. HIV prevention research and interventions have generally focused on behavioral risk factors, and little attention has been paid to social complexities and the experiences of stigma and discrimination that directly impact overall health (Fredriksen-Goldsen et al. 2013). Furthermore, a limited number of studies have validated these factors as syndemic (socially produced intertwined epidemics) drivers of HIV among transgender people. The term *syndemic* highlights the multiplicity of determinants that reinforce HIV risk factors in vulnerable populations (Freudenberg et al. 2006).

Syndemic theory highlights the impact of stigma and social disparities that produce these multifaceted collections of epidemics and therefore increase health disparities. However, syndemic research has treated vulnerable groups without paying attention to diversity and diverse degrees of vulnerability related to class, geography, age, and ethnicities within vulnerable subgroups. In addition to pathologization of trans identities as a barrier to access to health services, violence against TGW regularly overlaps with other axes of oppression predominant in a host society, such as racism, sexism, xenophobia, and anti–sex worker sentiment and discrimination. For example, the majority of recently reported trans femicides in Paris are of TGW from Latin America who are sex workers. To this end, intersectionality as a conceptual framework has been proposed in health research (Ferlatte et al. 2014). Intersectionality as a notion is rooted in early criticism of the separation of issues related to race and gender. An intersectional strategy in HIV care addresses syndemic processes and the influence of stigma in TGW experience of HIV care and prevention. A syndemic intersectional approach provides a critical framework for understanding the conditions that create and sustain overall community health (Egan et al. 2011). Transgender women who attend HIV care clinics are at the intersection of precarity related to gender, class, and race (Dhamoon 2011).

Intersectional care and prevention strategies seem to be applied in our HIV care clinic. First, institutional health policies and practices have been largely developed through community-based participatory interventions. Recalling TGW's experience of violence in work, hospitals have been mentioned as the first institution to which they present. In this context, intersectional care takes into account anticipated stigma and discrimination as a barrier to lodging complaints with the police. In this regard, intersectional policies integrate social workers and NGOs so as to extend medical care to include social care. Collaboration with NGOs at Bichat-Claude Bernard Hospital started in 1994, specifically, between one of the infectious disease specialists and Prévention Action Santé Travail pour les Transgenres (PASTT). After that, the links with NGOs grew over time to include Arcat and Acceptess-t, with which close links and a memoranda of understanding (MoU) have been established. Nongovernmental organizations play an important role not only by bringing and accompanying TGW who are new migrants living with HIV to the HIV clinic, but also by raising new arrivals' awareness of prevention and linking them to care. Among HIV-negative individuals we enrolled in our study, 73 percent of TGW seeking HIV prevention (PrEP) were brought to the hospital directly by NGOs, and 20 percent by a friend already following PrEP. Only one person had started PrEP in her country of origin. Of TGW living with HIV, 66 percent were brought to the HIV clinic by another already infected TGW who had settled in France. Friends who bring new migrant TGW to the HIV clinic are generally members of an NGO. Twenty-three percent were directed to HIV care by a member of an NGO and only 10 percent attended the HIV clinic on their own initiative.

Community-based collaboration leads to a trans-inclusive approach and policies that impact barriers to access to health services, like issues related to the lack of appropriate information or previous experience of stigma or problems related to self-esteem, language, and mental health. Community-based participation with TGW who live with HIV and their presence at the HIV clinic help newly arrived TGW to overcome stigma and shyness. Community-based participation has recently extended the practice of prevention by exploring PrEP not only in the hospital via doctors' prescriptions but also at NGO premises. In this way, HIV care and prevention target the TGW group not only as a high-risk HIV population but also as a major stakeholder in prevention and commitment to care.

Bichat-Claude Bernard Hospital is located in the 18th arrondissement (district), one of the poorest areas in Paris (Bayardin et al. 2017). Moreover, this area hosts a high proportion of immigrants. For example, among more than the five thousand persons living with HIV and followed in our clinic, 40 percent are from sub-Saharan Africa, and 20 percent are from other regions and in particular Northern Africa and Latin America, percentages that are much higher than in French national HIV cohorts. Care provision has been organized to take into account the vulnerability of this population, and, in addition to NGOs, social workers, psychologists, and health-care workers are asked when they are hired whether they will be willing to work with this population. Note that the French care system provides universal access to care whatever the person's legal status and also limits discrimination regarding origins, which may help integration. Since 1998 migrants have been able to ask for state medical care (Aide Médicale d'Etat, or AME) and have permanent access to free hospital drop-in clinics (permanences d'accès aux soins de santé [PASS]; twenty-four-hour healthcare clinics.)[1]

We therefore suggest that care provided by this kind of HIV clinic, which could of course be improved as stated above, may be a counterexample to transgender pathologization and the attendant perceived stigma and a possible gateway to social integration in the host society. The trajectory of a TGW with whom we had an in-depth interview may well illustrate how medical adherence can influence social integration.

She is a forty-four-year-old TGW who lives with HIV and is from Ecuador. HIV care in this patient was initiated in 2005. She appears in a 2006 documentary entitled *Les travestis pleurent aussi* (*Transvestites Also Cry*) (D'Ayala Valva 2006). At this time she was working as a sex worker in Paris and dreaming of a home, a husband, and a safe ordinary life. When I met her for the interview, she was wearing a white coat and told me that she had only one hour because she had to return to her training. In the corridors of the clinic, she met the doctors, who were very happy to see her in the hospital this time not as a patient but as a trainer. She communicated warmly with staff and doctors, and with tears in her eyes stated, "My dream is to become a nurse in this hospital. When I arrived here, I was totally pessimistic, I thought that having HIV was the end of life, but I followed my treatments, my doctor encouraged me, I left prostitution, which was like an endless loop, but I wanted to quit. I found this caregiving training and I'm really motivated to finish it perfectly. I want to be a nurse in this hospital and give back what it gave me. Transgenders are strong, we can achieve what we dream for, our social milieu is not just prostitution, we can also be useful in society." She recently started working as a caregiver in the emergency sector of Bichat Hospital.

The example of this TGW as migrant and sex worker who was adherent to care in Bichat Hospital, although not frequent, could be a counterexample of transgender's social exclusion in health service related to perceived stigmatization of trans people in that setting. The high degree of adherence to care and treatment in her case probably will have an impact on her social integration in the host society.

Conclusion

The universal health-care system of France provides health care for every citizen, regardless of wealth, age, or social status. However, the lower use of health-care services among immigrant populations is attributed to their socioeconomic situation in France. Social inclusion beyond HIV prevention in a vulnerable population like TGW migrants needs the implementation of a wide range of strategies that contain an intersectional approach to health policy and practices. This study highlights how integrating gender-affirmative care into HIV-related services can, on the one hand, increase medical adherence and satisfaction and, on the other hand, promote appropriate and accessible information about gender-affirmative practices and services. Moreover, it describes a model of community-based participation in which multilevel challenges related to stigma have been taken into account. The complexity of stigma experienced by TGW is associated with the intersectionality of stigma in different forms: institutional, interpersonal, and intergroup. The community-based participation model in this clinic uses an intersectional approach to decrease the disparity between the real needs of TGW and the health service's policy and practices. This model seeks to propose global health service and care that include gender-affirmative therapy to enhance access to HIV care and prevention. High rates of medical adherence in this clinic may be a consequence of the nonstigmatizing behavior of its health-care providers, which may in return influence social integration, although these nonstigmatizing behaviors are constantly being improved.

Bahar Azadi is a postdoctoral fellow at the University of Paris 1 Sorbonne. She received her doctorate in philosophy from University of Paris Descartes Sorbonne. She is currently a part-time researcher in unit U1037 Inserm at the Faculty of Medicine Bichat, University of Paris 7. Her main area of interest is the subject of trans identity, subjectivation, and resistance. She dedicated her thesis to the subjectivation of trans identity in Iranian society after the Islamic Revolution of 1979. Her postdoctoral research is on female genital mutilation in France.

Julia Zélie is a study coordinator at Bichat-Claude Bernard Hospital. She is currently working on HIV studies in the Infectious and Tropical Diseases Department of the hospital. She also participates in working groups on transgender people and users of psychoactive substances within the framework of COREVIH (Regional Comittee of the Fight against HIV Infection).

Florence Michard is a medical doctor who graduated in 1991 from University of Paris 7, and has been working as a clinician in the Bichat-Claude Bernard Hospital Infectious and Tropical Diseases Department since 1993, especially in the HIV field and in particular TGW living with HIV.

Yazdan Yazdanpanah is head of the Infectious and Tropical Diseases Department at Bichat-Claude Bernard Hospital in Paris, professor of medicine at Paris University, and head of the DeSCID (Decision Science in Infectious Disease Prevention, Control, and Care) team within the French National Institute of Health and Medical Research Infection, Antimicrobials, Modelling, Evolution laboratory at the University of Paris. Graduated in medicine by the Lille University France, he has a master's of science in epidemiology from the Harvard School of Public Health and a PhD in public health from the Bordeaux School of Public Health.

Acknowledgments

The authors gratefully acknowledge the assistance of the clinicians who participated in data collection at the HIV and STI Clinic of the Bichat Hospital. We thank Dr. Jad Ghosn, Dr. Annie Lepretre, Dr. Florence Michard, and Pr. Yazdan Yazdanpanah, whose insight, expertise, and comments greatly assisted the research and improved the manuscript. We are indebted to Sylvie Legac and Julia Zélie for their assistance with data management during the course of this research. We thank Dr. France Lert for her critical review of the article. We are also grateful to Giovanna Rincon, Giovanna Magrini, and members of Acceptess-t for their earlier comments on the study. Any errors are our own and should not tarnish the reputations of these esteemed persons. We would also like to show our special gratitude to TGW who agreed to participate in this research.

Note

1. AME. Direction de l'information légale et administrative. Aide médicale d'état. Art. L. 711-7-1 Public Health Code.

References

Almeida Wilson, K., F. Lert, F. Berdougo, and H. Hazera. 2008. "Transsexuel(le)s: Conditions et style de vie, santé perçue et comportements sexuels. Résultats d'une enquête exploratoire par Internet, 2007" ("Transsexuals: Lifestyle and Conditions, Perceived Health, and Sexual Behavior. Results of an Exploratory Internet Survey"). *Bulletin épidémiologique hebdomadaire* (*Weekly Epidemiological Bulletin*), no. 27: 240–44.

Baguso, Glenda N., Caryl L. Gay, and Kathryn A. Lee. 2016. "Medication Adherence among Transgender Women Living with HIV." *AIDS Care* 28, no. 8: 976–81. doi.org/10.1080 /09540121.2016.1146401.

Baral, Stefan D., Tonia Poteat, Susanne Strömdahl, Andrea L. Wirtz, Thomas E. Guadamuz, and Chris Beyrer. 2013. "Worldwide Burden of HIV in Transgender Women: A Systematic Review and Meta-analysis." *Lancet Infectious Diseases* 13, no. 3: 214–22. doi.org/10.1016 /s1473-3099(12)70315-8.

Baral, Stefan, Frangiscos Sifakis, Farley Cleghorn, and Chris Beyrer. 2007. "Elevated Risk for HIV Infection among Men Who Have Sex with Men in Low- and Middle-Income Countries 2000–2006: A Systematic Review." *PLoS Medicine* 4, no. 12: e339. doi.org/10.1371/journal .pmed.0040339.

Bauer, Greta R., Rebecca Hammond, Robb Travers, Matthias Kaay, Karin M. Hohenadel, and Michelle Boyce. 2009. "'I Don't Think This Is Theoretical; This Is Our Lives': How Erasure Impacts Health Care for Transgender People." *Journal of the Association of Nurses in AIDS Care* 20, no. 5: 348–61. doi.org/10.1016/j.jana.2009.07.004.

Bayardin, Vinciane, Julie Herviant, Danielle Jabot, and Corinne Martinez. 2017. *En Île-de-France, la pauvreté s'est intensifiée dans les territoires déjà les plus exposés* (*In Île-de-France, Poverty Has Intensified in the Territories Already the Most Exposed*). Insee Analyses, no. 76. Île-de-France: INSEE.

Bockting, W. O., B. E. Robinson, and B. R. Rosser. 1998. "Transgender HIV Prevention: A Qualitative Needs Assessment." *AIDS Care* 10, no. 4: 505–25. doi.org/10.1080/09540129850124028.

Bourrelly, Michel, and Marion Mora. 2018. *Trans and VIH*. Paris: ANRS.

D'Ayala Valva, Sebastiano, dir. 2007. *Les travestis pleurent aussi* (*Transvestites Also Cry*). France: Kanari Films.

Dhamoon, Rita Kaur. 2011. "Considerations on Mainstreaming Intersectionality." *Political Research Quarterly* 64, no. 1: 230–43.

Egan, James E., Victoria Frye, Steven P. Kurtz, Carl Latkin, Minxing Chen, Karin Tobin, Cui Yang, and Beryl A. Koblin. 2011. "Migration, Neighborhoods, and Networks: Approaches to Understanding How Urban Environmental Conditions Affect Syndemic Adverse Health Outcomes among Gay, Bisexual, and Other Men Who Have Sex with Men." *AIDS and Behavior* 15, suppl. 1: S35–50. doi.org/10.1007/s10461-011-9902-5.

Ferlatte, Oliver, Travis Salway Hottes, Terry Trussler, and Rick Marchand. 2014. "Evidence of a Syndemic among Young Canadian Gay and Bisexual Men: Uncovering the Associations between Anti-gay Experiences, Psychosocial Issues, and HIV Risk." *AIDS and Behavior* 18, no. 7: 1256–63. doi.org/10.1007/s10461-013-0639-1.

Fournier, Anna Lucie, Yazdan Yazdanpanah, Renaud Verdon, Sylvie Lariven, Claude Mackoumbou-Nkouka, Bao-Chau Phung, Emmanuelle Papot, Jean-Jacques Parienti, Roland Landman, and Karen Champenois. 2019. "Incidence of and Risk Factors for Medical Care Interruption in People Living with HIV in Recent Years." *PLOS ONE* 14, no. 3: e0213526. doi.org/10.1371/journal.pone.0213526.

Fredriksen-Goldsen, Karen I., Hyun-Jun Kim, Susan E. Barkan, Anna Muraco, and Charles P. Hoy-Ellis. 2013. "Health Disparities among Lesbian, Gay, and Bisexual Older Adults: Results from a Population-Based Study." *American Journal of Public Health* 103, no. 10: 1802–09. doi.org/10.2105/AJPH.2012.301110.

Freire Maresca, A., C. Dupont, C. Olivier, J. Leporrier, V. Daneluzzi, R. Quercia, and E. Rouveix. 2007. "Sexually Transmitted Infections (STI) Detected in the Transgender Population Followed at the University Hospital Center (CHU) Ambroise Paré." Conference presentation, 27th Interdisciplinary Meeting of Anti-infectious Chemotherapy, Paris, December 7.

Freudenberg, Nicholas, Marianne Fahs, Sandro Galea, and Andrew Greenberg. 2006. "The Impact of New York City's 1975 Fiscal Crisis on the Tuberculosis, HIV, and Homicide Syndemic." *American Journal of Public Health* 96, no. 3: 424–34.

Grant, Jaime M., Lisa Mottet, Justin Edward Tanis, Jack Harrison, Jody Herman, Mara Keisling. 2011. *Injustice at Every Turn: A Report of the National Transgender Discrimination Survey.* Washington, DC: National Center for Transgender Equality and National Gay and Lesbian Task Force.

Habarta, Nancy, Guoshen Wang, Mesfin S. Mulatu, and Nili Larish. 2015. "HIV Testing by Transgender Status at Centers for Disease Control and Prevention-Funded Sites in the United States, Puerto Rico, and US Virgin Islands, 2009–2011." *American Journal of Public Health* 105, no. 9: 1917–25. doi.org/10.2105/ajph.2015.302659.

Le Bail, Hélène, Calogero Giametta, and Noémie Rassouw. 2018. *Que pensent les travailleur.se.s du sexe de la loi prostitution?* (*What Do Sex Workers Think about the Prostitution Laws?*). France: Médecins du Monde.

Maisonobe, Lucas. 2019. "Étude quantitative 2008–2018. Patientes transgenres masculin vers féminin vivant avec le VIH: Prise en charge des hôpitaux Ambroise Paré et Bichat-Claude Bernard" ("2008–2018 Quantitative Study. Male-to-Female Transgender Patients Living with HIV: Hospital Care of Ambroise Paré and Bichat-Claude Bernard Hospitals"). Master's thesis, INSERM.

Namaste, Vivian K. 2000. *Invisible Lives: The Erasure of Transsexual and Transgendered People.* Chicago: University of Chicago Press.

Neumann, Mary Spink, Teresa J. Finlayson, Nicole L. Pitts, and JoAnne Keatley. 2017. "Comprehensive HIV Prevention for Transgender Persons." *American Journal of Public Health* 107, no. 2: 207–12. doi.org/10.2105/ajph.2016.303509.

O'Donnell, Patrick, Diarmuid O'Donovan, and Khalifa Elmusharaf. 2018. "Measuring Social Exclusion in Healthcare Settings: A Scoping Review." *International Journal for Equity in Health* 17, no. 15. doi.org/10.1186/s12939-018-0732-1.

Pommier, J. D., F. Michard, G. Castanedo, S. Lariven, and P. Yeni. 2011. "Évaluation des caractéristiques médico-sociales des personnes transgenres infectées par le VIH" ("Assessment of the Medico-Social Characteristics of Transgender People Infected with HIV"). *Médecine et maladies infectieuses* 41: 72–75.

Poteat, Tonia, Ayden Scheim, Jessica Xavier, Sari Reisner, and Stefan Baral. 2016. "Global Epidemiology of HIV Infection and Related Syndemics Affecting Transgender People." *Journal of Acquired Immune Deficiency Syndromes* 72, suppl. 3: S210–19. doi.org/10.1097/qai.0000000000001087.

Reisner, Sari L., Jaclyn M. White Hughto, Emilia E. Dunham, Katherine J. Heflin, Jesse Blue Glass Begenyi, Julia Coffey-Esquivel, and Sean Cahill. 2015. "Legal Protections in Public Accommodations Settings: A Critical Public Health Issue for Transgender and Gender-Nonconforming People." *Milbank Quarterly* 93, no. 3: 484–515. doi.org./10.1111/1468-0009.12127.

Seelman, Kristie L., Matthew J. P. Colón-Diaz, Rebecca H. LeCroix, Marik Xavier-Brier, and Leonardo Kattari. 2017. "Transgender Noninclusive Healthcare and Delaying Care Because of Fear: Connections to General Health and Mental Health among Transgender Adults." *Transgender Health* 2, no. 1: 17–28. doi.org/10.1089/trgh.2016.0024.

Shaw, M., D. Dorling, and G. D. Smith. 2005. "Poverty, Social Exclusion, and Minorities." In *Social Determinants of Health,* vol. 2, edited by M. Marmot and R. Wilkinson, 196–223. Oxford: Oxford University Press.

Singer, M., and S. Clair. 2003. "Syndemics and Public Health: Reconceptualizing Disease in Bio-Social Context." *Medical Anthropology Quarterly* 17, no. 4: 423–41.

Sugano, Eiko, Tooru Nemoto, and Don Operario. 2006. "The Impact of Exposure to Transphobia on HIV Risk Behavior in a Sample of Transgendered Women of Color in San Francisco." *AIDS and Behavior* 10, no. 2: 217–25. doi.org/10.1007/s10461-005-9040-z.

WHO. 2013. *Guidelines for Second Generation HIV Surveillance. An Update: Know Your Epidemic.* Geneva: World Health Organization.

WHO. 2018. *HIV/AIDS Surveillance in Europe 2018–2017 Data.* Copenhagen: WHO Regional Office for Europe, European Centre for Disease Prevention and Control.

Lou Sullivan and the Future of Gay Sex

ELLIS MARTIN and ZACH OZMA

Abstract Editors of the recent publication *We Both Laughed in Pleasure: The Selected Diaries of Lou Sullivan* consider Sullivan's writing as an assertion of transmasculine embodiment and pleasure in gay sex culture via his "portal to historical thinking." With intertextual appearances by Ann Cvetkovich, Elizabeth Freeman, John Giorno, Audre Lorde, José Esteban Muñoz, Liam O'Brien, @archivalrival, and a SCRUFF anon.
Keywords Lou Sullivan, gay sex

Question:

The Future of Gay Sex: Is There One?

Figure 1. *Bay Area Reporter* 20, no. 25, June 21, 1990.

Answer:

> When I sleep with poz guys now, I joke to myself that we're going on each other's resumes. A little curiosity.
> —Liam O'Brien, 2019

Several people have told us they've been taking turns with their partners reading out loud from Lou Sullivan's diaries in bed. One friend sent us a screenshot of a SCRUFF profile:

What I'm looking for

Come over and read the horniest bits of We Both Laughed in Pleasure out loud with me.

Figure 2. Excerpt of SCRUFF profile, unknown user, 2019.

TSQ: Transgender Studies Quarterly ★ Volume 7, Number 4 ★ November 2020   **598**
DOI 10.1215/23289252-8665243   © 2020 Duke University Press

In these situations, we see Lou Sullivan (b. 1951, Milwaukee, d. 1991, San Francisco) facilitating an erotic encounter. In "Uses of the Erotic: The Erotic As Power," Audre Lorde[1] (1993: 54) describes the erotic as "a measure between the beginnings of our sense of self and the chaos of our strongest feelings. . . an internal sense of satisfaction to which, once we have experienced it, we know we can aspire." Lou's erotics, transmitted into the present via his own documentary descriptions of his carnal pleasures, now cocreate new erotics, new moments of satisfaction, sense of self, and strong feeling. He teaches us to what we can aspire.

In "Ghosts of Public Sex," José Esteban Muñoz[2] (1996: 36) proposes that John Giorno's[3] similarly lavish records of gay pleasure function as "a disseminator of public sex culture. The idealization his prose enacts is . . . an example of the way in which a rich remembrance of sexual utopia feeds a transformative queer politics." Through his own rich remembrances, Lou also functions as a disseminator of public sex culture, a disseminator whose active presence in the scene broadens the lens of this erotohistoriography[4] to include the "female to gay male."

While there may be an urge to validate Lou's gayness (and perhaps masculinity) in his HIV status, it remains our goal in this diary project to illuminate Lou's gayness in its most primary forms. Lou's erotic desire made him gay, not his diagnosis. He was gay because he chose it. He was gay because of his passion: he consistently sought gay love, gay sex, and gay pleasure. He was gay because he went to the places gay people went. He spoke in the way that gay people have spoken–and, indeed, the way we have begun to speak again as we enmesh ourselves in his language through the diaries.

How do we understand Lou's intersecting subject positions: gay, trans, and poz? The measure between his sense of self and the chaos of his strongest feelings. Lou's diaries offer one way to fold a transmasculine body into the erotic utopic imaginary of gay sexual life. Similarly, his record disavows the view that AIDS ended public sex culture. Lou's body was in many ways ahead of the discourse, enacting in real time and texture the practices of a trans-and-gay-and-poz life beyond the imagination of both experts and the public in his time. Muñoz (1996: 38) continues, "The picture rendered through Giorno's performative writing is one of a good life that both was and never was, that has been lost and is still to come." We understand Muñoz's use of the word *performative* in the sense of a *performative utterance*, a speech act that both describes the current situation and shifts that situation as it is spoken (promises, bets, orders, etc.). When a promise is made, it describes a current arrangement and creates a new situation, a bond of trust. When Lou recounts in his diary a brief tryst in a porno theater, for example, he also creates a new situation in which trans men are among the cruising possibilities of the dirty movies. A promise in its own way to living trans men: you can go to gay places; I have been there before. The picture rendered through Lou's performative erotic writing recounts his real activities and affirms the realness of a "good trans life" for himself and his imagined reader:

> Wow. I'm all spaced out. Finally something FUN happened. Went to the Nob Hill Cinema, gay men's porno. A good one came on with 2 guys fucking in a New York subway car. The movie theatre was deserted, except for me. I figured, well, I'll watch this good one + then leave. So I was playing with myself + suddenly I realize there's someone standing up behind me, so I look back + there's a guy TOTALLY BARE! I thought, wow, talk about BOLD.
>
> He's hanging his dick right on my shoulder + I had to think fast. OK . . . what is safe sex?? I grabbed him with one hand + kept playing with myself with the other. (Sullivan 2019: 375)

Can this passage be thought of as a "portal to historical thinking"? We certainly hope so. Imagine something opening between two lovers or two strangers as they read "the horniest bits of We Both Laughed in Pleasure" out loud. If Lou's writing gets you hot, surely that is some kind of portal, Lou's hand on his own genitals, his other on an anonymous man's genitals, his other on yours. Not to mention the actors in the subway porno, another idealized (aspirational) public sex narrative in the lineage. Not to mention Nob Hill Theatre, closed in 2018, but a little present when we read this scene. An important goal of our project as editors has been to stake a place for Lou in the lineage of gay literature, with Giorno, with John Rechy.

What kind of validation would it require to place Lou in this canon? Validation is top-down, when the nondominant asks the dominant for acceptance, or power. When we consider the reader response from the journals, a swell of trans people who have made their own forms of queerness come to mind. It is not as though Lou only sought the approval of the dominant, cis gays. Rather he became a touchstone in a now highly visible trans+gayness to which cis queers do not have access.

One way to think about this is to consider two different iterations of one of Lou's most famous lines—a highly quotable statement that seems in context to be filled with sincere feeling and his typical tongue-in-cheek wit. In chronological order, the first was a diary entry. The second accompanied a photograph of Lou that was displayed at San Mateo County Hall of Justice along with fifty-nine other portraits taken by photographer Jim Wigler.

> It really hasn't hit me that I am about to die. I see the grief around me, but inside I feel serene + a certain kind of peace. My whole life I've wanted to be a gay man + it's kind of an honor to die from the gay men's disease. (Sullivan 2019: 360)

> I am a female-to-male transsexual living as a gay man. AIDS was the last thing I
> expected—I haven't had that many contacts. They told me at the gender clinic that
> I could not live as a gay man, but it looks like I will die as one. (Sullivan 2019: 371)

Lou as a type of gay man, a type of gay author, is one among the many recognizable flavors of gay specificity—little curiosities, as O'Brien says. Ann Cvetkovich (2012: 75) writes, "The AIDS memoir, which has been crucial in depathologizing the HIV survivor, offers a queer take on personal narratives about illness and disability that can provide alternatives to medical discourse by giving agency to the patient." While a diary, written over decades in real time is not quite a memoir, Lou's diaries position him as an agent in his fully fleshed-out world. Neither his queer writing nor his queer life was created in isolation. Rather, Lou moved fluidly between communities and subcultures, forming a politic and a lifestyle around coalition and community. He recounts getting tired at San Francisco Pride in 1989:

> So I found out where the Handicapped and Special Needs Seating Area was and
> asked the guard what I needed to do to prove I had a "Special Need." "I could show
> you my AZT," I suggested. The guard answered, "I could show you mine." So they
> had no proof requirement, so I just went in and got this front row seat, no people
> standing in front of us, met 2 guys there I knew from our Gay Men's Disability
> Group. It was great! (Sullivan 2019: 396)

Because of Lou's specific, layered identities and his rare auto archival practices, it is possible to view him in isolation as "the only" or "the first." But in this brief interaction with the guard and two friends, we see Lou in his broad queer network at a time when HIV/AIDS devastated communities.

In a previous project, one of us was project archivist on the GLBT Historical Society's *Bay Area Reporter* digitization project. *Bay Area Reporter (BAR)* is a weekly queer news, arts, and culture newspaper that covers the Bay Area and national news. Lou's obituary is one of twenty in the April 4, 1991, issue of *BAR*. Eighteen of the other obituaries either mention AIDS or allude to it. One woman died of an unrelated cancer. In this section, which accounted for an entire page spread, each queer person becomes, temporarily and metonymically, "▼," the symbol used to signal the end of each obituary.

The digitization project, one of GLBT Historical Society's many vital imaging projects, consisted of scanning the issues in reverse chronology—witnessing the past by moving backward, past hopefulness and answers into a time of deep fear and anxiety. Further back to the time before *BAR* had an obituary section.

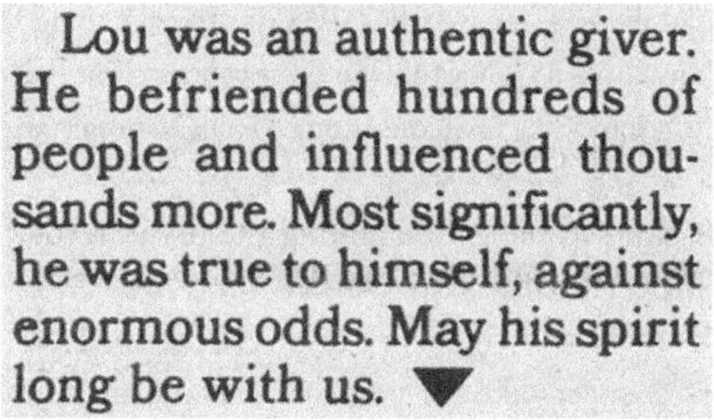

Lou was an authentic giver. He befriended hundreds of people and influenced thousands more. Most significantly, he was true to himself, against enormous odds. May his spirit long be with us. ▼

Figure 3. *Bay Area Reporter* 21, no. 14, April 4, 1991.

In January 1985, the "Deaths" header appeared in print. In terms of imaging, each page of the issue functioned like the others: same size, comparable amounts of text and image, similar color palettes. The effect of scanning in reverse chronology was a disintegration. Often many pages would flash by in a haze of *press foot pedal to cue overhead scanner, pause for scan, flip page, foot pedal, pause, page, repeat.* In the intermediary pause there was a moment to take in the page—a brief flash that created an uneven view of already uneven reporting. The steady quickness of digitization still did not protect from the sharpness of flipping to the weekly page dedicated to obituaries, "DEATHS."

Here again a type of kinship between interconnected but temporally separate queers. Lou articulated his desires like many others: some made it to print, some did not. Readers resume Lou's story in the present, finding resonance and dissimilarity, community, camaraderie, wayfinding, repetition, and, yes, aspiration. Rich remembrances not only of sex but also of death, community suffering, pleasure alongside sickness. The good life Muñoz saw in Giornio's writing, the good story Lou wanted to recount to his implicit audience, threading together people who may not have experienced the 1980s or 1990s but persist in the ongoing AIDS crisis.

What if we return to the idea of validation, but consider the medical-industrial complex as the dominant entity? Lou's experiences with medicine as a poz trans man resonate with his earlier and concurrent experiences trying to access paths to medical transition: encountering doctors who are ignorant. The early AIDS days were rife with moments in which poz people had to educate themselves to counteract failures in the medical system. The exclusionary nature of transphobia in medicine carries to the present day. For example, in 2019 a French PrEP study found that an on-demand dosage of the HIV prevention medication is just as effective as the previously prescribed daily dosage (ANRS 2019). The test centered white, cis men: another instance of the dominant eliding gay, trans experiences.

What if the dominant entity becomes the unknown cis, het viewer of Jim Wigler's portraits at the San Mateo County Courthouse? This is an example of a space that certainly isn't specifically for queer, trans people. The tonal difference between the two entries, written within the space of a few months is vast. The first is about something Lou was perpetually fascinated by: looking at his feelings in comparison to those around him, not as a metering tool but as a reflective moment. The honor is his own. While the buzziest part of both quotes is the punch line, they are not expressly concerned with validation. In the second quote, Lou reminds the viewer that the dominant entity does not actually hold the power to confirm or deny his gayness, and that he has moved beyond a search for validation.

Seeing Lou as someone who was hung up on cis approval presumes that he wasn't accepted, or perhaps that he was exclusively stealth. He had multiple *out* experiences with gay cis men where he was surprised by the lack of questions: "My scarred chest now visible to him. Wondering what he's thinking of me. I offer to make coffee + gathering up all my self-confidence, got out from under the blankets + walked by him naked, my lack of genitals very plain. But he never said a word to me about it" (Sullivan 2019: 245). Here Lou has gay sex that isn't enhanced or affected by a contemporary understanding or awareness. His top surgery scars do not signify a transmasculine body where they may now. Lou continues: "I am so glad not to explain what's the matter with me. I still wonder at this kiss, wonder what he thought I was, and why he didn't care about it. . . . I spend the day feeling his caresses, glad to be what I am" (246).

So what do Lou Sullivan's diaries mean for trans studies, for how we conceptualize HIV/AIDS today, for the future of gay sex? We see a life built on both self-reflection and intentional relationship building. Through correspondence, community newsletters, interviews, support groups held in his home, gay bars, archives, panels, pamphlets, the disabled men's group he frequented before and after his diagnosis, the porno theater, the pride parade, and these diaries Lou Sullivan both reached out and opened himself to receive. He was always oriented toward the erotic. Lou Sullivan's diaries mean connectivity and collectivism are an antidote to queer loneliness.

 lou
@archivalrival

the opposite of loneliness is Lou Sullivan's diaries

8   6:35 AM - Sep 29, 2019

Figure 4. Tweet, @archivalrival, September 29, 2019.

Ellis Martin works in the interstice of art and archive. Martin holds a visual and critical studies BA from Mills College. Martin coedited *We Both Laughed in Pleasure: The Selected Diaries of Lou Sullivan* (2019). He has generated large-scale digitization projects at Oakland Museum of California, Mills College Art Museum, John J. Wilcox, Jr. Archives, and the Gay, Lesbian, Bisexual, Transgender Historical Society.

Zach Ozma is an interdisciplinary artist. Employing mimesis, humor, surprise, and reward, he works in a variety of materials and modes, including ceramics, found objects, performance, writing, and works on paper. He is the author of *Black Dog Drinking from an Outdoor Pool* (2019) and coedited *We Both Laughed in Pleasure: The Selected Diaries of Lou Sullivan* (2019). He holds a BFA in community arts from California College of the Arts.

Notes

1. Lorde (b. 1934, Harlem, d. 1992, Saint Croix, Virgin Islands) was a poet, writer, librarian, activist, and teacher. She continues to be beloved as a visionary who fought against racism, classism, homophobia, and sexism, and identified as black, lesbian, mother, warrior, poet. She authored *Zami: A New Spelling of My Name*, *Sister Outsider*, and *The Cancer Journals*, among other titles.
2. Muñoz (b. 1967, Havana, d. 2013, New York) was a scholar of queer studies, cultural studies, performance studies, and critical theory. He authored *Cruising Utopia*, *Disidentifications*, and *The Sense of Brown*, published posthumously in 2020.
3. Giorno (b. 1936, New York, d. 2019, New York) was a poet, interdisciplinary artist, and AIDS activist. He authored *You Got to Burn to Shine*, among many other titles, and created Dial-A-Poem.
4. Elizabeth Freeman (2010: 59) defines erotohistoriography as "a politics of unpredictable, deeply embodied pleasures that counters the logic of development." Freeman asks, "How might queer practices of pleasure, specifically, the bodily enjoyments that travel under the sign of queer sex, be thought of as temporal practices, even as portals to historical thinking?" (59).

References

ANRS. 2019. "ANRS Prévenir: On Demand and Daily PrEP Both Safe and Effective." Press release, ANRS, July 23.

Cvetkovich, Ann. 2012. *Depression: A Public Feeling*. Durham, NC: Duke University Press.

Freeman, Elizabeth. 2010. *Time Binds: Queer Temporalities, Queer Histories*. Durham, NC: Duke University Press.

Lorde, Audre. 1993. *Zami / Sister Outsider / Undersong*. New York: Quality Paperback Book Club.

Muñoz, José Esteban. 1996. "Ghosts of Public Sex: Utopian Longings, Queer Memories." In *Policing Public Sex: Queer Politics and the Future of AIDS Activism*, edited by Dangerous Bedfellows, 33–48. Boston: South End.

O'Brien, Liam. 2019. "No Funny Business." *A&U*, October 30. aumag.org/2019/10/30/no-funny-business-nonfiction-by-liam-obrien/.

Sullivan, Lou. 2019. *We Both Laughed in Pleasure: The Selected Diaries of Lou Sullivan*. Edited by Ellis Martin and Zach Ozma. New York: Nightboat.

Kiyan Williams

An Interview

CHE GOSSETT and EVA HAYWARD

Abstract The following is an interview conducted by Che Gossett and Eva Hayward with Kiyan Williams, multidisciplinary artist and assistant professor at Virginia Commonwealth University. William's visual art—sculpture and video—on blackness and ecology, dirt and displacement, brings Black trans poetics, aesthetics, and politics to bear on questions of the afterlife of slavery and plantation geographies. Their work also engages Black trans archives and historicity. Here they discuss their work *Reflections* on Marlon Riggs, Jesse Harris, Black trans archives, their works *Meditations on the Making of America* and *Trash and Treasure*, and their engagement with various artistic mediums.

Keywords Kiyan Williams, blackness, HIV/AIDS, ecology

CG and EH: *Your work* Reflections *mines the archive of Black gay filmmaker Marlon Riggs, bringing to the fore Black trans femme experiences of the (ongoing) AIDS crisis by focusing on the figure of Jesse Harris, a Black trans femme whose haunting interview in* Tongues Untied *(1989) discloses a Black trans archive of AIDS. Your work allows for Harris to be heard. Can you speak about what this means to you, aesthetically, affectively/emotionally, and personally to find the interview, and what was the message that you hope to communicate through this stunning piece? Also, can you speak to how this particular piece ties into and interlaces with your broader work on Black queer/trans death, ecology, and sociality?*

KW: In 2010 as an undergraduate I first saw the film *Tongues Untied*, a choreopoem by Marlon Riggs that gave voice to the lives of Black gay men in America and that pushed the conventions of traditional documentary. I was intrigued by a short thirty-second clip from the film in which a figure sitting on a bench smokes a cigarette as Billie Holiday sings the blues about heartbreak and unrequited love. The moment was both unremarkable and remarkable: a short transitional frame between scenes, the subject is transfeminine, it's one of the only scenes in which the subject doesn't speak, and a blue overlay gives it a haunting and

TSQ: Transgender Studies Quarterly * Volume 7, Number 4 * November 2020 **605**
DOI 10.1215/23289252-8665257 © 2020 Duke University Press

melancholic mood. The subject doesn't have a name and doesn't appear in the film credits. I was compelled to find this person, whose five o'clock shadow and high cheekbones, broad shoulders in a strapless blue dress was a reflection of my own gender embodiment. I scoured Marlon Riggs papers and tapes at Stanford University in search of the original footage from *Tongues* and in search of the figure in the blue dress.

I encountered Jesse in box 28 on a Sony Beta Max cassette tape. I found her/his/their name in the production, "Jesse Harris in Park." In the original interview Jesse unravels a white sheet of folded paper and reads poetic accounts of familial abandonment, of spending over a decade displaced in homeless shelters and on streets, and of dreams of performing on stages across the country as a pianist and poet. In fifteen minutes we hear Jesse talk about the quotidian violence he/she/they experience and in the same breath insist on the capacity of art to change his/her/their life. Jesse's reading is interrupted by a passerby who spews homophobic and transphobic slurs. Jesse confronts the assaulter, curses them out: "If you come over here we'll beat your motherfucking ass—." The video cuts to black. We don't get to see the outcome of the confrontation. In another clip, which is my favorite from the video of Jesse, Jesse is walking down a street in New York at night with another unnamed Black gay man. They compare the different vernacularisms of Black LGBT culture between DC and New York. Jesse starts speaking in pig latin, and they both laugh at Jesse's words, which only those who speak pig latin would understand.

I wanted to bear witness, to acknowledge, Jesse's story and exhume Jesse's voice from the archive. In live performances I dress up in clothes and in an affect similar to Jesse's, with the original image projected onto my body. I hold a mirror while sharing a monologue about my search for Jesse. I project the original interview through reflective surfaces, mylar, suspended mirror, such that the viewer is implicated in Jesse's world, and they see themselves when they see Jesse. Simultaneously, the suspended mirrors cast shadows on and obscure the image, reflecting, refracting, and catapulting Jesse's image throughout the room and beyond the frame of the film. The installation is an attempt to render a fugitive image in which the subject and the moving image are not bound by the limitations of the rectilinear frame, but instead Jesse bleeds through and around the space, is projected on to the viewer and into the present. Jesse's image is not static, flat, or relegated to the universe of the interview, but is dynamic, an image in perpetual flight that cannot be easily contained or captured. Complicating systems of viewing and spectatorship. Projecting Jesse's image on to the viewer and into the gallery, while also reflecting the viewer's image into the plane of the interview, connect the past and present, in particular the forms of quotidian anti-Black and transphobic violence Jesse experiences as well as the resistance Jesse experiences when she/he/they confront the person in the park accosting them and calling them a faggot and a man in a dress. Part of my desire to exhume Jesse's voice and show the film was because I had yet to see a gender transgressive person stand up and fight for themselves on-screen. At the time when I was doing the research at Stanford University archives, I had become inundated with images of Black binary and nonbinary trans folks being murdered or relegated to the trope of the tragic trans figure.

In the first iterations of the performance I had hopes that I would encounter someone who would know Jesse, that the project would create a sociality that would connect me to an intergenerational Black LGBT community with connections to Jesse. In early 2016 I shared a still from the video in preparation for my first performance of *Reflections* at the University of Pittsburg studio theater in a presentation organized by the Center for African American Poetry and Poetics. One of my friends from Oakland, a deejay, responded to my post that Jesse was her uncle and had been missing for the past thirty years. I later met cinematographers and collaborators who worked with Marlon on *Tongues* who remember filming Jesse in Tompkins Square Park but who were unable to provide any other context about Jesse's whereabouts. In this way I think of the piece as a tribute that insist on remembering Jesse, and also as a tribute to the quotidian lives of Black people who refuse normative gender. Rooted in testimony and not as spectacle or entertainment. And as a refusal of the disposability of Black queer and trans life.

Marlon Riggs's archive, and Jesse's interview, gesture toward a Black queer fugitivity and fungality. Blackness queerness and transness as fungal, proliferating in subterranean spaces beyond the shadow of white supremacy and building interdependent and intersubjective networks. Sites through which hegemonic and normative gender are decomposed and decayed and from which alternative and otherwise gender embodiments and socialities emerge. In my forthcoming creative and critical work I look toward Marlon's archive alongside my visual art practice to articulate a theory of Black queer and trans fungality.

CG and EH: *Your work is often performative, and in some of it you force the audience to literally confront painful or occluded pasts that operate in the present tense: your work* Trash and Treasure, *for example, which is about the death and disposability of two Black queer women, Britney Cosby and Crystal Jackson in Texas, where you emerge from trash to confront viewers with this violent archive, forcing the spectators to witness, forcing this past into the present so that it cannot be absented. Does witnessing, perhaps in the James Baldwin sense, feel important to your work?*

KW: In my earlier work (including *Trash and Treasure*) I used my body as a material, a site or terrain imbued with social, political, historical meaning and through which state-sanctioned regimes of policing, surveillance, and regulation were enacted. In these early works, performance was a means to challenge hegemonic power and social norms by inserting myself in and disrupting public space. At the same time, performance was a means through which I could name the conditions that attempt to make Black queer and trans life an impossibility. Indeed, at best I am simply bearing witness to the things that haunt me, to the intimacy with which I know violence, tragedy, and loss; in the words of James Baldwin (1989: 225) a "witness to whence I came, where I am. Witness to what I've seen and the possibilities that I think I see."

CG and EH: *In your work* Meditations on the Making of America *which is now part of the permanent collection of the Hirschorn Museum in Washington, DC, you invoke Saidiya Hartman in "Venus in Two Acts" with the "vessel/womb/abyss." This also brings to mind Édouard Glissant, who in* Poetics of Relation *refers to the hold of the ship a womb and an abyss. Your work reflects not only on America but also its relation to the Caribbean and the planetary geography of the plantation. "Evoking the shape of a slave ship and a sarcophagus, the sculpture is made of soil from plantations in the Carribean and the American South" (Williams 2020). You've brilliantly described* Meditations on the Making of America *as exploring "the ecological devastation of racial capitalism that continues to make the planet inhospitable for black people (and many human and non human life forms)," and you emphasize that "still the work insists on life and living and gestures toward possibilities of otherwise ecosystems within (or after) the ruined landscape of America" (Williams 2019b). In your performance we witness the deconstruction of America. There's also the mushrooms that grow in the vessel/womb/abyss. You say "I want to consider the capacity for Blackness (and queerness and transness), like fungi, to emerge in conditions that are inhospitable and hostile toward life" (Williams 2019b). Can you talk about how you use and think about matter, blackness, ecology, and survival?*

KW: *Meditations on the Making of America* was informed by and was an embodied and performative meditation on the notion that chattel slavery and the transatlantic slave trade are the birthing and foundational catastrophes that gave shape to America and the modern world. As so many scholars like Hortense Spillers, Saidiya Haartman, Christina Sharpe, and others have theorized, our contemporary lives are so deeply entangled and informed and haunted by chattel slavery and its afterlives. The land, the soil is imbued with historical memory of violence and trauma. When I began developing the gestures for that performance, and as I engaged in the act of throwing and marking and smearing and whipping soil on canvas, I thought about my great-great grandparents who cultivated crops and worked the land under the systems of slavery and sharecropping. I thought about my great grandmothers who were domestics for white families in New York and New Jersey, whose job it was to do the grueling labor of cleaning up white people's dirt. I thought about my childhood and being called a dirty faggot. The soil embodied the abjection of being Black and queer and poor, the structural violence and conditions that shaped my life. But it too represented the possibility for transformation. Soil is the basis for life, literally holds and incubates and cares for a range of human and nonhuman beings. The possibility for transformation, for growth, for the emergence of otherwise forms and being under hostile conditions is embodied in the sprouting mushrooms. That life can proliferate in conditions it was not meant to. The species of mushrooms that grew in the sculpture, cup fungi, grow in soils that are nutrient deficient. The mushrooms again were a metaphor to me for the capacity of Black and trans and queer and poor folks and people deprived of resources to emerge.

CG and EH: *Reflecting on your work with dirt and how you traveled to St. Croix for your work—thinking here of* Dirt Eater *and* An Intimate Encounter with Dirt— *you offer an excerpt from Rachel Kaadzi Ghansah to help us think about loss and historical materiality and loss that might be unable to be sutured, that is marked by dehiscence and wounds that refuse to close: "This is what happens when names of cattle and crops are recorded alongside those of your foremothers. Mud. That was it. Mud, that was us" (Ghansah 2012: 5).*

You continue:

> And so I dug up the mud, bricks, and coral from the ruins of my great grandmother's house, stuffed them in suitcases, smuggled them back to my studio in Harlem. Reminiscent of Hilton Als' gesture of collecting stones from the terrace of James Baldwin's house in the south of France and exhibiting them in "A Collective Portrait of James Baldwin" last winter. Land holds memory. Sometimes all we have to bring us closer to those who made our lives a possibility are bricks, stones, and mud" (Williams 2019a)

Can you talk about land and place and how your work reflects on these or troubles these categories?

KW: My work is a means for me to grieve and reckon with the persistent displacement of Black life that informs my own existence. In this current moment accessing stable and consistent housing is a challenge I face, as do so many other Black, trans, queer, from the hood. All of the places that were once places of belonging for me as a kid and young adult, Black queer clubs in New York City, queer hoods in the West Village, my old high school building in Newark, have all been closed and demolished by urban development, gentrification, and building luxury housing for the wealthy. The material displacement of Black people in the present is part of the larger Black diasporic experience: the transatlantic slave trade, the many migrations of Black folks from the American South and Caribbean to northern cities. When my high school building was being demolished, alumni went to the site and collected bricks from the facade as mementos. I noticed a similar sentiment in Hilton Als's presentation of rocks from James Baldwin's garden. This inspired me to collect debris, soil, and residue from sites of loss—ruins of slave plantations, the remains of my ancestors' house in St. Croix, low-income residential buildings demolished by corporate developers— and incorporate them into visual art. The materials are imbued with memory, history, trauma, and a sense of belonging.

Che Gossett is a PhD candidate in women's and gender studies and a graduate fellow at the Center for Cultural Analysis at Rutgers University–New Brunswick.

Eva Hayward is an associate professor in gender and women's studies at the University of Arizona.

Reference

Baldwin, James. 1989. *Conversations with James Baldwin.* Jackson: University Press of Mississippi.

Ghansah, Rachel Kaadzi. 2012. "My Mother's House." *Transition: An International Review,* no. 109: 3–19.

Williams, Kiyan. 2019a. "Last December I visited St. Croix, United States Virgin Islands." Instagram, December 23. www.instagram.com/p/B6bI_QaFoM8/.

Williams, Kiyan. 2019b. "The Vessel / Womb / Abyss, 2019, soil, fungi, gnats, nematodes, plant, steel armature." Instagram, July 24. www.instagram.com/p/B0TeOZ9Fy8d/.

Williams, Kiyan. 2020. "Intersectionality in the Studio: Kiyan Williams." Leslie Lohman Museum of Art, June 8. www.leslielohman.org/archive/intersectionality-in-the-studio-kiyan-williams.

Monica Jones

An Interview

CHE GOSSETT and EVA HAYWARD

Abstract The following is an interview with activist Monica Jones conducted by Che Gossett and Eva Hayward. In this interview, Jones talks about her activism against the criminalization of sex work, recounting how the program Project ROSE, which was a revealing collaboration between the university and the police, functioned through carceral logics to detain and then according to a carceral economy of innocence, criminally prosecute or "reeducate" sex workers or those profiled as sex workers. Jones shows how the university is part of the carceral continuum and is a site of Black trans and sex worker and prison abolitionist struggle, which has intensified in the current organizing against police on campuses and entanglement of university and the prison-industrial complex and the policing functions of administration and university governance. Jones also shows how this is an HIV/AIDS activist issue given that the criminalization of sex work is bound up with from gentrification, displacement, and how that is exacerbated with COVID-19.
Keywords Monica Jones, criminalization, sex work, Project ROSE

CG and EH: *Your phenomenal work for sex worker decriminalization has extended over years and has been situated in many different places—from Arizona protesting against Project ROSE, to Melbourne, Australia—and has also taken many different forms, including speaking—such as the incredible keynote speech you gave at the Desiree conference in 2016 in New Orleans—but also being visible in the media and in PJ Starr's documentary about you. How do you navigate media and turn it toward struggles that you are invested in sustaining and growing?*

MJ: When speaking to the media, I always maintain control of the interview, and I always bring the conversation back to my key talking points about why I am giving the speech or interview. This requires preparation and focus. When talking about sex work, I make sure I state that sex work is work, I describe the reasons for ending criminalization, and I always address the conflation of sex work and human trafficking. I am seen as a spokesperson, and I have been public about my activism, but I do not see my voice as one individual because I represent community. As a

Figure 1. Monica Jones holding a red umbrella—a symbol of sex worker rights activism—and smiling. Photograph by PJ Starr.

Black trans woman I always center myself in the struggles of my community and my lived experience as a member of our community. When we are talking about violence against trans women, as a Black trans woman I always highlight that we are more vulnerable to violence due to the social construction of our identity and the historical trauma of our community. Another way this plays out is in the context of conversations about SESTA/FOSTA when activists of greater privilege use street-based sex work as a scare tactic in the media to legitimize their voices as nonstreet-based sex workers. The street is held up as the ultimate danger, and street-based sex workers are seen as lesser than, to be spoken about and for. This approach does not allow us as Black trans women to defend our right to be in public space, and it undermines strategies for economic justice for low-income sex workers of all genders and experiences who are in public space. I am invested in struggles that always raise up the collective voices of Black trans women as leaders in the movement for the rights of all sex workers, that link our struggle to our history as I do via my own organization named for Sharmus Outlaw (the Outlaw Project founded in 2016), and that celebrate our survival, our resilience, and our desire to thrive.

CG and EH: *How do you see the criminalization of sex work as an HIV/AIDS activist issue?*

MJ: In 2014 at the first International AIDS Conference I was able to attend, I learned that with the decriminalization of sex work, HIV transmission rates decrease by 45 percent globally for everyone. This information came from a special issue of the *Lancet*. Here in the United States, sex workers are seen as vectors of disease and are assumed to be the ones who spread infections to "unsuspecting victims." This stigma, that is, of course, not based on any science, feeds into laws that penalize individuals who engage in sex work, specifically, those who are living with HIV. These laws against "transmitting HIV" carry stricter punishment and longer jail sentences. The people who are arrested and charged under these HIV-related laws are almost always Black transgender women and sex workers. Policies allow police to use condoms as evidence to arrest women on suspicion of sex work and contribute to an environment where we cannot keep ourselves safe through best-practice harm reduction. Policing and these policies take the autonomy away from us to have safe sex. Because policing and lack of access to adequate health care intersect in low-income communities of color, this leads to more people living with HIV and also having to survive through sex work. This cycle leads to incarceration for people doing what they have to do to survive. Many of these issues are discussed in Sharmus Outlaw's final report, *Nothing about Us without Us*, which was completed before her passing in 2016 and was the first national report created by sex workers about the issue of HIV and policy.

CG and EH: *How might abolitionist organizing against the prison system make trans life livable in a time of HIV/AIDS?*

MJ: Prison abolitionists can help by sharing the real reasons that prisons are there. They are not there to rehabilitate and help people. They are there to criminalize everyday actions. Just like trans people were criminalized during the 1950s and 1960s for cross-dressing, now trans people are being criminalized for trying to survive in a world and country that does not want them to survive and exist. [The criminalization of cross-dressing also continues in prisons today.] Due to policies and laws that criminalize sex work and criminalize living with HIV, these issues intersect due to sustained attacks on harm reduction and Black lives. The consequence is incarceration. Incarceration can mean death for us. This system must end.

CG and EH: *Can you share more about your life and history of work against criminalization and Project ROSE, for those who have yet to see PJ Starr's film about your activism?*

MJ: For as long as I can remember, I have been working for change, and I am an organizer for the rights of trans people, low-income people, people of color, and sex workers. Because I am a Black trans woman with a disability, I face oppression on a daily basis, when I am walking on the street, going to a rally, traveling to the United Nations, and seeking education. Even though I am a committed organizer, I am still a human being who was arrested and harmed by a Phoenix-based sting operation known as Project ROSE. The fight against Project ROSE was a fight that had to happen, but there was an emotional toll. The casualty of Project ROSE was my education. My arrest happened while PJ Starr was filming *No Human Involved*, about the death of Marcia Powell, and it is mentioned in that film. The full story of what happened to me will be in the forthcoming film *Manifesting Monica Jones*, and we want to use the film to speak about the toll that I experienced. As activists we need to heal.

For those who have not seen the films, here is what happened. In 2013 I attended a rally to protest Project ROSE, which was a sting and antitrafficking program carried out by the Phoenix police, Arizona State University (ASU) School of Social Work, and other local service providers. The next day I was arrested under the sting myself as I was walking to a local gay bar in my neighborhood. I was taken to a church where I was told I had to accept diversion services or be charged with "manifesting the intent to prostitute" (which is basically being told that you look like a prostitute). I was taken to court and found guilty. I spent the next two years fighting the charges brought against me and bringing a constitutional challenge against the law. During that time, I was often unable to leave my apartment because police officers would station themselves outside, and I was followed by police constantly on the street. I had to keep attending the social work program at ASU, the same program that had been involved in my arrest, and my education was affected by the stress. Even though my conviction was vacated and Project ROSE was shut down, to this day I live with the knowledge that I could be arrested under the existing laws at any time. Other trans women and low-income women are still being arrested under these laws during COVID-19, and the laws are being used against undocumented people.

While I was fighting in the courts, I got to know Sharmus Outlaw through her research project she was doing at the time. When Sharmus died in 2016, I founded an organization named for her, the Outlaw Project, because I had learned that she was never able to fulfill her lifelong goal of starting her own organization. The Outlaw Project is based on the principles of intersectionality to prioritize the leadership of people of color, transgender women, nonbinary people, and migrants for sex worker rights.

Che Gossett is a PhD candidate in women's and gender studies and a graduate fellow at the Center for Cultural Analysis at Rutgers University–New Brunswick.

Eva Hayward is an associate professor in gender and women's studies at the University of Arizona.

Pose and HIV/AIDS

The Creation of a Trans-of-Color Past

LAURA STAMM

Abstract This article examines how the television series *Pose* (2018–) represents queer and trans people of color living with HIV/AIDS at the height of the crisis in 1987. While the series portrays an important part of transgender history, it also positions the AIDS crisis as something that is done and part of America's past. Despite the fact that rates of HIV infection remain at epidemic rates for trans women of color, *Pose*, like many other mainstream media representations, suggests that the AIDS crisis ended in 1995. The series brings trans women of color's experiences to a record number of viewers, but that representation comes with a certain cost—the cost of historicization.
Keywords *Pose*, HIV/AIDS

FX's *Pose* (2018–) takes place in 1987 New York City and follows the ballroom culture scene made up of black and Latinx queer, trans, and gender-nonconforming self-created families. The pilot episode begins with lead character Blanca (MJ Rodriguez) learning of her HIV+ status. Her status propels the narrative forward, as she seeks to create a house and a ballroom legacy to leave behind after her eventual death. Blanca works through her diagnosis with friend and ballroom emcee Pray Tell (Billy Porter), and they bond through their shared HIV+ status. The balls (fig. 1) become a way to celebrate the life they have left and to create an impact on the ballroom's children, who will carry on their history. The series itself seeks to give its audience a lesson on AIDS crisis history. Discussing the necessity of intersectional representations of people living with HIV, Elijah McKinnon states, "*Pose* is a very important period piece that showcases the impact of the HIV/AIDS epidemic on Black and brown LGBTQ-identified people in the ballroom community" (Feagins 2018). Despite the series's importance for teaching audiences about trans history, McKinnon's positioning of *Pose* as a period piece makes me wonder about the effects of making the AIDS crisis historical. When mainstream media has only one representation of trans women of color living with HIV, it is dangerous to put that representation in the past.

TSQ: Transgender Studies Quarterly ∗ Volume 7, Number 4 ∗ November 2020   **615**
DOI 10.1215/23289252-8665285   © 2020 Duke University Press

Figure 1. Angel (Indya Moore) performs in a ball as part of Blanca's (MJ Rodriguez) house for the royalty category in *Pose*.

Especially in light of recent 1980s nostalgia television series, such as *Glow* (Liz Flahive and Carly Mensch, 2017–) and *The Deuce* (George Pelecanos and David Simon, 2018–19), making trans HIV+ women part of a media trend reduces their very real existence in our present historical moment. When trans women, and trans women of color specifically, are continually left out of contemporary conversations about HIV/AIDS, representing their stories as past serves to further erase their need for treatment and activism in the present.

The series works to tell a history of HIV+ members of the ball community as not only involved in their self-fashioned community but also involved in broader queer politics. As Blanca's and Pray Tell's conditions worsen, Nurse Judy (Sandra Bernhard) encourages them to get involved with AIDS activism. In season 2, the series recreates the 1989 die-in at St. Patrick's Cathedral (set in 1990 in *Pose*'s diegetic world), which protested Cardinal John O'Connor's visit. O'Connor spoke out against the use of condoms at the height of the epidemic, an act demonstrating the Catholic Church's condemnation of the queer community. Pray Tell and Blanca encourage Blanca's house children—Angel (Indya Moore) and Damon (Ryan Jammal Swain)—to take part in the event and use their bodies and voices to support the queer community. When most historical narratives of the AIDS crisis focus on cisgender white gay men, putting trans women of color in this iconic moment of AIDS activism history is a radical gesture. Moreover, rather than write trans women out of this historical event, as accounts of events like Stonewall tend to do, this moment asserts that trans women were there putting their bodies on the line.[1]

Since the beginning of the AIDS crisis, mainstream film and television have rarely been able to capture the activism and experiences of affected marginalized communities. While New Queer Cinema filmmakers responded to the AIDS crisis with politically and aesthetically challenging films, these films rarely reached mainstream audiences.[2] Keegan argues that although the films were produced two decades apart, *Philadelphia* (Jonathan Demme, 1993) and *Dallas Buyers Club* (Jean-Marc Vallée, 2013) represent the only mainstream depictions of HIV/AIDS, both of which troublingly dequeer the AIDS crisis. *Philadelphia* features a straight actor (Tom Hanks) playing a gay man, whereas *Dallas Buyers Club* rewrites the Ron Woodruff story to feature a straight man who turns HIV/AIDS treatment into a business.[3] The film sidelines queer AIDS crisis activists who demanded HIV/AIDS research and treatment in order to portray Woodruff (Matthew McConaughey) as the Texan hero of the AIDS crisis. The only queer character shown in the film is Rayon (Jared Leto), a trans woman who becomes Woodruff's business partner. Not only is Rayon played by a cis male actor, but she is also frequently referred to as "he" throughout the film, undermining her status as a trans woman in the film.[4] Keegan uses Sarah Schulman's theory of aesthetic gentrification, along with the concept of disruptive innovation, to claim that queer and trans audiences are willing to accept mainstream representations of queerness, even if that means they come at a lower quality than independent productions produced by queer and trans filmmakers. Mainstream distribution, unfortunately, asks producers to consider what types of representation can be monetized, and that consideration leads to representations of queerness that do not challenge dominant culture's understandings of gender and sexuality.[5] Keegan (2016: 52) states, "Much like the rapidly gentrifying landscapes of New York City, Seattle, and San Francisco, these films are populated by white, bourgeois, straight, and cisgender bodies that then come to colonise the aesthetic spaces of the LTBQ cinematic archive as its representational subjects." I would add to Keegan's analysis Schulman's (2012) observation that most Americans believed the AIDS crisis had ended by 2001. AIDS crisis history becomes open to aesthetic gentrification because of the dominant culture's perceived temporal and affective distance from it. Put another way, when the AIDS crisis is assumed to be over, representations of HIV+ bodies become easier for film and television producers to monetize.

By positioning trans women of color's activism in the past, *Pose* suggests that trans women and the queer community no longer have something to protest. Recreations of these activist demonstrations seem to evoke a sense of longing for AIDS protest, a moment when the queer community was politically energized. This longing suggests that now is not a time for such protest when, in fact, many chapters of ACT UP are still active and thriving. The NYC chapter of ACT UP recently demonstrated (fig. 2) at the Whitney's exhibition of David Wojnarowicz's work, titled *History Keeps Me Awake at Night*. The chapter protested the exhibition's historicization of the AIDS crisis. More specifically, activists criticized the

Figure 2. ACT UP members stand in front of the exhibition's queer activist AIDS crisis media with information about current issues related to HIV/AIDS, including continued stigmatization and criminalization. Photograph by Michelle Wild.

way that the exhibition presented the AIDS crisis as something that is done and something that we can look back on as an object of study. While celebrating Wojnarowicz's legacy, the exhibition's placards and guided tours suggested that the AIDS crisis ended with his art production when he died of AIDS-related complications in 1992. This pastness, however, is not a reality, or at least the AIDS crisis is not a past for many marginalized members of the American population. ACT UP's nine weeks of demonstrations silently recaptioned Wojnarowicz's work by offering the public excerpts from current HIV/AIDS news media. For instance, ACT UP's (2018) alternative caption for the piece *Americans Can't Deal with Death* (1990) reads:

> A transgender Honduran woman died in ICE custody last Friday after coming to the US as part of a caravan of Central American migrants, including several dozen other transgender women fleeing persecution in their respective countries. Roxana Hernández reportedly died from HIV-related complications following an alleged five-day detention in what's known by immigrant rights groups as the "ice box"—ICE detention facilities notorious for their freezing temperatures.

The image, here, of a transgender Honduran woman dying in an "ice box" suggests the fate of HIV+ trans women of color in the United States; cast outside the dominant culture's field of vision, they are left in a metaphorical box to suffer alone. While this placard shares a compelling anecdote about HIV+ Latina trans women's vulnerability, the Whitney protest featured an overwhelming focus on queer black men's epidemic rates of infection. Without direct attention to the equally (if not more so) alarming rates of infection for black trans women, the demonstration risked repeating broader American culture's all-too-easy neglect of trans women's health.[6] Maybe Americans cannot "deal with" death, as Wojnarowicz suggests, but they seem to have no problem accepting death when it affects undesirable members of the population.

Critics have praised *Pose* over and over again for its diversity of representation; trans actors play trans characters, and Janet Mock works in production, making her the first trans woman of color to write and direct a television episode.[7] Moreover, out trans and HIV+ musician and writer Our Lady J serves as a writer and producer for the series. Billy Porter is the first out gay black man to win an Emmy for Outstanding Lead Actor in a Drama Series for his role in *Pose*. The possibilities opened up for queer and trans people of color in *Pose* has led critics to surmise that more opportunities for trans actors and actresses will open up in the broader media industry. During *Variety*'s "Transgender Actors Roundtable" (Setoodeh 2018), Jen Richards proclaimed that we are living in a post-*Pose* world, alluding to the seismic shifts it created for trans actors and producers in Hollywood.[8] The series has made trans women visible in new ways, including love scenes, a romance narrative, and ballroom scenes that show trans women celebrating themselves and each other. However, trans filmmakers and scholars, such as Sam Feder and Keegan, remind us that trans representation and visibility is never so simple.

HIV/AIDS activist Alex Juhasz's and trans filmmaker Sam Feder's (2016) conversation in *Jump Cut* reminds readers that visibility alone does not lead to progress. Too often, trans women are used to create a certain type of tragedy porn, a porn in which cis audiences are able to voyeuristically consume trans women's excessive suffering. Feder describes the appeal of this type of media: "Feeling bad reaffirms the audience member as a caring, ethical person. Emotional response gets the audience's attention and despair is the easiest emotion to evoke." Despair is not only the easiest emotion to evoke, but it is also the easiest emotion for the audience to experience; the audience feels bad for suffering trans women, but they do not have to feel implicated in that suffering. *Pose*, in many ways, performs many of these tropes, and by setting the series in the past, viewers do not have to feel implicated in (or even acknowledge) trans women's suffering and death in the present. I would argue that *Pose* thus becomes a safe way for audiences to learn about HIV+ trans women of color. By considering these experiences as part of the past, the series lets viewers off the hook; trans women of color living with HIV in the present remain outside their field of vision.

The ways that trans women become visible in mainstream media have severe consequences for the material lives of trans people. Laura Horak (2018: 203) states, "Even when representation is 'positive,' increased media attention to trans people correlates with higher rates of violence and political backlash. While some trans actors have new opportunities many trans women of color are at increased risk." Trans women of color become exposed to increased rates of violence with increased media representation, and, equally importantly, their unique set of concerns is often not addressed in mainstream media. Because the dominant culture (violently) excludes trans and queer people of color, they are left to invent their own culture and community. Jen Richards (2015) explains how ballroom culture depicted in *Pose* united disenfranchised trans women of color:

> Black, Latina, and Asian Pacific Islander trans women, along with some white artists and performers who came from gay male communities, found one another on city streets, in nightclubs, and at underground balls. The clear lines between what we now distinguish as transsexuals and queens didn't exist. *Total exclusion from mainstream society*, reliance on sex work and underground economies, and the necessity of sharing limited resources put a greater emphasis on groups than on individuals. (emphasis added)

Richards's piece predates *Pose*, and she goes on to discuss how *Paris Is Burning* (Jennie Livingston, 1990) represents the only portrait of queer ballroom community; and even then, she states, this portrait is produced by a cisgender director who exploited this community for her own profit. Despite many of its ethical and representational issues, *Paris Is Burning* became canonized as the best portrayal of Harlem ballroom culture, largely because it was the only one.[9]

The show's creators speak openly about using *Paris Is Burning* as *Pose*'s source material.[10] Series cocreator Steven Canals describes the series as "a history lesson" and has further talked about how Angel's story line drew inspiration from Venus Extravaganza's, but they changed the narrative to give trans sex workers more agency.[11] Agency in these terms would appear to mean not being murdered by a transphobic john, thus countering the "pathetic" trope of trans representation Julia Serano (2007) theorizes as central to dominant culture's understanding of trans women. However, one of the main characters, Candy (Angelica Ross), is killed off in exactly that way, with her body discovered in a hotel closet. The assumption that Venus Extravaganza lacked agency aside, Canal's explanation of *Pose* as a *Paris Is Burning* remake suggests a lack of creativity. It suggests an inability to imagine the history of Harlem's ballroom culture outside the lens of a white cisgender lesbian filmmaker's ethnographic lens. It additionally suggests an inability to imagine HIV+ trans women of color living in the present.

My criticisms of *Pose* presented here are less to do with its characters and story lines, many of which are groundbreaking and compelling, and more to do with the ways that mainstream media continues to position HIV/AIDS as something of the past. Treating the epidemic as a piece of history, moreover, does damage to the populations currently most vulnerable to HIV contraction. According to statistics provided by the Human Rights Campaign (n.d.), 21.6 percent of transgender women in the United States are living with HIV, and "HIV is three times more prevalent among black trans women than among white or Latina trans women." The invention of Truvada for PrEP and developments in anti-retroviral drugs have mitigated the risk of contracting HIV/AIDS for some members of the queer community, in terms of prevention and treatment. Yet the costs of medications and required doctor appointments make them inaccessible to those who are not upper-middle-class, white, and cisgendered. Assuming that trans women, and specifically trans women of color, do have financial access to HIV prevention and treatment measures, many trans people (understandably) avoid trips to the doctor out of fear of discrimination and mistreatment. PrEP may present the end of the AIDS crisis for a lucky few, but the drug is far from the utopic cure-all it has been billed to be. The combination of this perceived utopia and the sequestering of AIDS to the past makes *Pose* doubly dangerous.

I do not intend to diminish the cultural impact of *Pose*, specifically for transgender audiences who crave representation, but I also think we need to be critical about the effects of trans media representations when there are so few. *Pose* has aired contemporaneously with other series that place HIV/AIDS in the 1980s past, including Netflix's *Glow* and HBO's *Deuce*. Along with Ryan Murphy's *American Horror Story: 1984*, television right now seems to have a thing for 1980s nostalgia, which also means a nostalgia for AIDS.[12] In an interview with *Variety*, cocreator Murphy explains, "I thought [*Pose*] had a definite beginning, middle, and end." He continues on, "This show will end in 1995; it's going to end before AIDS drugs became available. So it really is about the rise and decimation of a world" (Framke 2019). Murphy's commentary suggests three endings, really. Explicitly, he discusses the end of *Pose*, but he also gestures toward the end of the AIDS crisis (with the invention of drugs) and the end of Harlem's queer ballroom community. Based on these statements, it appears the series is framed by the height of the AIDS crisis rather than the history of NYC ballrooms, which did begin long before the late 1980s. Murphy implies that members of ball culture did not survive past 1995 (fig. 3), and in doing so, he altogether ignores ballroom participants living with HIV in our present.[13]

Trans representation is always both a problem of visibility and invisibility. Representation is crucial, but the wrong kinds of representation are literally life threatening. When representations of trans women, not to mention HIV+ trans

Figure 3. Pray Tell (Billy Porter) and Blanca (MJ Rodriguez) visit Hart Island to mourn deceased friends and lovers in *Pose*.

women, are already so few, it makes the stakes for each representation that much higher. We might also recall the trans visibility dilemma Horak (2018) poses—the dilemma in which greater visibility leads to greater violence against trans women, and trans women of color in particular. I am not sure what types of trans representation Horak suggests correlate with increased violence against trans people. However, I can imagine what kinds of representations I think would lead to such violence, and representation that suggests that trans women of color are not part of our contemporary world could be one.[14] At the risk of producing a paranoid reading of the series, my fear is that *Pose* may be a less objectionable representation of trans women of color for mainstream audiences because the series is set thirty years in the past.[15] This temporal distance might provide a sort of safety valve for viewers who would otherwise not want to see HIV+ trans women on their prime-time channel lineup. Murphy's statement about *Pose*'s time line confirms my fear that Americans can watch and praise a series about HIV+ trans women of color, so long as they can be assured that they no longer exist.

Laura Stamm is visiting assistant professor of women's, gender, and sexuality studies at the University of Wisconsin–Eau Claire. She holds a PhD in film and media studies from the University of Pittsburgh, and her work appears in *Alphaville: Journal of Film and Screen Media* and *Spectator*. She is currently working on a book project that examines queer filmmakers' turn to the biopic film genre during the AIDS crisis.

Notes

1. Cáel M. Keegan (2016), in "History, Disrupted," discusses how Roland Emmerich's *Stonewall* (2015) explicitly and intentionally makes trans women of color disappear from the film's diegetic world. Instead, the film centers the character Danny (Jeremy Irvine), a fictional cis, white gay man.

2. A short list of such films includes *Poison* (Todd Haynes, 1991), *Zero Patience* (John Greyson, 1993), *Snow Job* (Barbara Hammer, 1986), and *Edward II* (Derek Jarman, 1991).

3. Those who knew Woodruff have asserted that he was an out bisexual man.

4. In addition to Keegan, see Copier and Steinbock 2018 for a thorough analysis of trans representation, or lack thereof, in *Dallas Buyers Club*.

5. As Feder puts it, "Entering the mainstream media means you've become a viable commodity" (Feder and Juhasz 2016).

6. ACT UP does not discuss trans women in their exhibition guide besides this one mention. However, during their demonstration in July 2018, they excerpted from the article "Infected and Invisible: South Florida's Housing Crunch and High HIV Rates Threaten Disaster for Its Transgender Population." In this news piece, Marcus (2018) discusses how lack of housing for trans women has led to an increase in HIV infection, with the rate of infection at 49 percent for trans women living in the Miami area.

7. *Pose* credits Janet Mock with writing seven episodes and directing three.

8. Ramin Setoodeh (2018) hosted a roundtable of trans actors to respond to the Scarlet Johansson *Rub and Tug* controversy, in addition to sparking conversation around the increase in trans representation with actresses like Laverne Cox. The roundtable included Jen Richards, Laverne Cox, Chaz Bono, Trace Lysette, Alexandra Billings, and Brian Michael.

9. See Butler 2011 and hooks 2012 for criticisms of *Paris Is Burning*.

10. In an interview with *NPR*, Janet Mock (2019) discusses how *Paris Is Burning* was the first representation of trans women she had ever seen and inspired her writing for *Pose*. Steven Canals discusses how *Paris Is Burning* served as the series's inspiration text in the documentary film *Queering the Script* (Gabrielle Zilkha, 2019).

11. Canals talks about Venus Extravaganza and the Angel story line parallels in *Queering the Script*.

12. We could also consider the 2018 Broadway revival of Tony Kushner's *Angels in America*.

13. Ironically, current house mother of the House of LaBeija, Kia LaBeija, was contacted to consult on the series. LaBeija is HIV+ and works to raise HIV/AIDS awareness in her art and activism.

14. *Pose* is not the first series to feature a trans woman of color lead; *Orange Is the New Black* (Jenji Kohan, 2013–19) featured Sophia Burset (Laverne Cox) from the beginning of the show. The film *Tangerine* (Sean Baker, 2015) also features a number of trans women of color and their stories. However, *Pose* is the first series to feature an ensemble cast of trans women of color.

15. I am thinking specifically here of Eve Kosofsky Sedgwick's (2002) theorization of paranoid versus reparative queer reading practices, as she outlines them in her book *Touching Feeling*. Her framework for queer paranoid readings begins with a discussion of the AIDS crisis and conspiracy theories surrounding the government's intentional spread of the HIV virus.

References

ACT UP. 2018. *A Companion Guide to David Wojnarowicz*. ACT UP NYC. actupny.com/wp
-content/uploads/2018/09/act-up-pamphlet.pdf.

Butler, Judith. 2011. *Bodies That Matter: On the Discursive Limits of Sex*. New York: Routledge.

Copier, Laura, and Eliza Steinbock. 2018. "On Not Really Being There: Trans* Presence/Absence in
Dallas Buyers Club." *Feminist Media Studies* 18, no. 5: 923–41.

Feagins, Raven. 2018. "HIV on TV: Why Representation Matters." AIDS Foundation of Chicago,
December 6. www.aidschicago.org/page/inside-story/hiv-on-tv-why-representation
-matters.

Feder, Sam, and Alex Juhasz. 2016. "Does Visibility Equal Progress? A Conversation on Trans Activist
Media." *Jump Cut*, no. 57. www.ejumpcut.org/archive/jc57.2016/-Feder-JuhaszTransActivism
/text.html.

Framke, Caroline. 2019. "'Pose' Season 2: Diving Deeper into One of LGBTQ History's Darkest
Chapters." *Variety*, June 6. variety.com/2019/tv/news/pose-season-2-preview-ryan
-murphy-1203232474/.

hooks, bell. 2012. *Reel to Real: Race, Sex, and Class at the Movies*. New York: Routledge.

Horak, Laura. 2018. "Trans Studies." *Feminist Media Histories* 4, no. 2: 201–6.

Human Rights Campaign. n.d. "Transgender People and HIV: What We Know." Human Rights
Campaign. www.hrc.org/resources/transgender-people-and-hiv-what-we-know (accessed August 25, 2020).

Keegan, Cáel M. 2016. "History, Disrupted: The Aesthetic Gentrification of Queer and Trans
Cinema." *Social Alternatives* 35, no. 3: 50–56.

Marcus, Noreen. 2018. "Infected and Invisible: South Florida's Housing Crunch and High HIV
Rates Threaten Disaster for Its Transgender Population." *US News*, April 11. www.usnews
.com/news/healthiest-communities/articles/2018-04-11/hiv-transgender-residents-hit-by
-south-florida-housing-crunch.

Mock, Janet. 2019. "On 'Pose,' Janet Mock Tells the Stories She Craved as a Young Trans Person."
Interview by Terri Gross. *NPR*, August 14. www.npr.org/2019/08/14/750931179/on-pose
-janet-mock-tells-the-stories-she-craved-as-a-young-trans-person.

Richards, Jen. 2015. "What Trans Movement?" *Advocate*, July 14. www.advocate.com/print-issue
/current-issue/2015/07/14/what-trans-movement.

Schulman, Sarah. 2012. *The Gentrification of the Mind: Witness to a Lost Imagination*. Berkeley:
University of California Press.

Sedgwick, Eve Kosofsky. 2002. *Touching Feeling: Affect, Pedagogy, Performatvity*. Durham, NC:
Duke University Press.

Serano, Julia. 2007. *Whipping Girl: A Transsexual Woman on Sexism and the Scapegoating of
Femininity*. New York: Seal.

Setoodeh, Ramin. 2018. "Transgender Actors Roundtable: Laverne Cox, Chaz Bono, and More on
Hollywood Discrimination." *Variety*, August 7. variety.com/2018/film/features/transgender
-roundtable-hollywood-trump-laverne-cox-trace-lysette-1202896142/.

Cecilia Gentili

An Interview

CHE GOSSETT and EVA HAYWARD

Abstract The following is an interview with performer, activist, and advocate Cecilia Gentili conducted by Che Gossett and Eva Hayward. Cecilia Gentili is a longtime trans activist in New York City.
Gentili has been involved in queer, trans, AIDS sex worker, and antiviolence organizing for decades.
In this interview Gentili discusses her recent performance *The Knife Cuts Both Ways*, the limits of trans
narratives and representation, and how she pushes at the thresholds of those limits such that they
seem to break, fold, and corrupt. Gentili refuses the liberal humanist narrative of proper citizenship,
for her trans cannot be incorporated, it is an excess, a story that does not claim redemption or
resolution. Instead, trans is antagonism.
Keywords Cecilia Gentili, *The Knife Cuts Both Ways*, HIV/AIDS

Gossett and Hayward: *In your stirring and hilarious 2018 show* The Knife Cuts
Both Ways, *staged at Dixon Place in New York City, you tell stories about sex,
migration, borders and state securitization, antitrans violence, trans women-of-
color resistance and resilience, survival and loss. How did you get comfortable using
comedy and humor as a political weapon, a knife that cuts? What are some of the ways
that you see your stand-up performance and storytelling as a form of narration? How
do you view the contemporary time of "trans visibility," and how might your own
performances trouble the narrative of visibility itself?*

Gentili: *The Knife Cuts Both Ways* is an artistic form born as the result of a
narrative that although true and intrinsically mine does feel designed to accom-
modate the morbidity of the general public about trans lives.

Besides the usual (extreme) interest in the dark and most painful parts
of my story by folks in general, I encountered a very specific need to craft my
narratives with a victimized lens: my asylum process.

After being handed to Immigration and Customs Enforcement from the
nice friends at Rikers and after being detained during a raid of a place where I was
being trafficked, I found myself facing deportation. Because of my trans identity,

Figure 1. Cecilia Gentili, in her one-woman show, *The Knife Cuts Both Ways*. Dixon Place Theater, New York, July 24–26, 2018. Styling and makeup by Gogo Graham. Photograph by Serena Jara. Courtesy of the artist.

the lack of accommodations, the issues encountered when cis women refused to share cells with me because of my genitalia (yes, cis women can also be awful to trans women), and the violent attacks from cis men in their detention center, I was let go with an ankle bracelet, which is still a terrible scarlet letter that lets everyone around you know that you are considered a criminal, but it somehow allows you to be in the world and not in a cell. I came out, and while accessing recovery services for a deep addiction to substances, I was told I could get asylum in this country (after living ten years in the United States), and I went for it.

I was optimistic from the beginning, but I did not anticipate how hard it would be not only to prove that I deserve it but also to relive the stories to make that case.

During that process I noticed that people had a hard time reacting to my history of misfortune. As I could see them being empathetic, I could also see them somehow grotesquely fascinated by it, and I could not find a reason to justify that. It was clear: people want to focus on the sad terrible realities of their trans peers, and I had no choice. I had to give it to them because my stay in this country, which after ten years felt more mine than Argentina, was on the line.

So, I talked of pain and I focused on the worst. Not only did that, but I made sure they got what they wanted. A narrative of gruesomeness without any sign of joy. A cruel reality that was truthful and unpleasant and lacking any signs of glee.

Rape? I got that!

Sexual abuse as a minor? Sure!

Beaten by strangers? Yes!

Family members? That too!

Discriminated at school? Of course!

Arrested for no reasons? Are you kidding me? Totally!

I talked about my pain nonstop for the whole year my asylum process took, to the point where I thought, why am I here if all I know is misery and disdain?

And then I realized happiness sometimes can be embedded in realities of torment. Maybe I wasn't fully happy, but sometimes I was!

I knew . . . even in those unhealthy moments I experienced sparks of jubilation.

I owned their desires about my experience. For that, I could not talk about the beauty of being a sex worker, I could not mention the fun of being dicked down by a stranger in a dirty bathroom of a fucked-up bar, and I did not mention that my abuser while abusing me was giving me the attention I craved at the time. And I got what I needed; I was allowed to stay in the country I called home already. And at the same time, I found myself miserable. My life was reduced to my pain, and I felt the most depressed I ever felt. Holding my work permit in my hand and suffocated by horribleness and terrible stories.

The Knife was a conscious reaction to that moment of my life. It was like a vomiting event where I say: yes, most of my life was terrible, but listen, in the heart of that terribleness I found joy too.

It is hard to be harassed by a police officer while whoring in the street, but let me tell you, it was this time when I beat them to that arrest, and it was fun. Let me bring to life the fact that my best friends were and still are "las mismas putas de la calle" . . . and while we were suffering at the hands of law enforcement, a system designed to bury the poor, and bad clients, as well as experiencing homelessness (in between so many other issues), we were able to be happy sometimes, and we laughed and we helped each other.

Let me tell you about the stories that are not empowering, the ones that will not motivate you to do better. Let me tell you about sucking dick in the alleyway without expecting to see the face attached to the cock. . . . Let me show you that sometimes when you see me victimized, I was also intoxicatingly strong . . .

And I started telling stories. Dixon Place gave me their small space in the bar to tell short stories and see how people reacted to it. To see if, when everyone expected misery, I could derail that expectation with laughter. And I did it. I felt folks shaping feelings; I saw them changing those expectations to my will, to my desire, and it was wonderful.

I've never written on a paper or document. The show lives only in my head; it feels like the deepest belonging to my being. If I ever owned something, it is this show, it is my narrative, and that narrative is untouched by the academic hand. It doesn't have a system that designs it as what we may understand as a more classic piece. It is what I want it to be, and it is the same all the time, being different all the time.

Come and listen to my story and don't wish for redemption. It is what it is. What is ugly is ugly and funny, and you have to respect my idea of fun.

Most of my career I have been seen as the epitome of redemption. Here it is, the trans, woman, of color, immigrant, undocumented, sex worker, survivor of violence, drugs, and incarceration being brilliant at legislation, rubbing elbows with elected officials, conquering the nonprofit world. She made it out and succeeded. And everyone decided to define success for me.

My show says, I was successful as a drug addict. I was the most resourceful slut and whore; I don't want to be defined by what they think is a testament to making it to a glorious platform out of the darkness of sex work because sex work is not dark all the time. I do not want to erase what I came from by saying it was a bad place. It was a place, and I will define it. Not you.

Gossett and Hayward: *You say, so brilliantly: "Come and listen to my story and don't wish for redemption. . . . I do not want to erase what I came from by saying it was a bad place. It was a place, and I will define it." Certain forms of trans visibility rely on polished and flattened versions of respectable trans people. This is something you refuse. How do you see your work in* The Knife Cuts Both Ways *as connected to struggles against trans and sex worker criminalization? How do you combat the idea that redemption happens through incarceration and that some people are innocent and redeemable and others are disposable?*

Gentili: The idea of redemption has followed me since I came out of treatment. And I do not reject it totally. It is fine. I did change things in my life in order to find a sense of security and wellness, but defining wellness is different for everybody. As a trans woman I feel I learn to live hand to hand with risk, and for that my idea of wellness is completely different from that of a cis person or a white person or a person born in the country. Wellness as risk is relative to who lives that life and for that, yes! I adjusted my life to a new idea of wholeness, and that idea is rooted in my past.

People love to see a polished trans woman who almost looks white, who almost can pass as cis, who can attest that it is possible to belong to their world, and they need to make a statement that involves rejection of her past. That is something I refuse to do.

Gossett and Hayward: *Can you talk about your own work in HIV/AIDS service organizations, and what are some of the contributions you've made and changes you've been a part of enacting in that work? What are some of the challenges that you feel as a trans woman of color in the field?*

Gentili: While introduced to the nonprofit world, I did not have many choices but to get a job in that industry.

My first job was as a patient navigator. I had to make sure patients living with HIV were taking their medications and support them in their daily lives. I thought they would all love me: gay men having a sister helping them. Sounds like a dream. NOT. I remember one of my first clients asked me to call him before meeting him and to wait for him around the corner. In the alley. He told me he had nothing against me, but he could not explain to his boss why he was meeting me. I thought he was worried about them knowing his status, but I learned that they knew. . . . He was ashamed to be seen with a "tranny" (his words). I was devastated. I realized it was going to be hard to work for the *L*, the *G*, and the *B* as a *T*, but I had no choice. I needed that paycheck.

I was fortunate to be given the opportunity to lead a trans clinic, and that is when I fell in love with services. These folks were not ashamed of me; they loved me, and I loved helping them with hormones or whatever else they needed.

Unfortunately, service is a hard job. Some people can do it and disconnect. Go home and have a life. I could not. How can I go home and eat dinner and go to bed knowing my sister, the one I just saw in the clinic, told me she is hungry and living under a bridge? If I have the money to pay for a meal for her, I cannot stop myself from doing it, and I knew I couldn't.

So, after four years in service I left. And while visiting my country after sixteen years, while experiencing the joy of seeing my friends and family with the pain of reliving bad stories while walking the same street where I was beaten by police officers, I got a call. GMHC (formerly Gay Men's Health Crisis) wanted to hire me. To do what? Whatever I wanted to! Still scared by my experiences providing services to gay men, I was doubtful, but I took a chance while they took a chance on me, and I went into policy.

I led their policy department, and I felt really empowered to make substantial change. I created the Trans Equity Coalition: a group of trans-led organizations doing trans work looking for funding that is not attached to HIV prevention. Services without offering pre-exposure prophylaxis (PrEP), unless you want PrEP. After so many years working in services, I learned that HIV funding is powerful, but sometimes the needs of the community are not just condoms. That services, unless managed by a hustler like me, are reductive to prevention, and prevention is much vaster than PrEP and condoms.

And we got almost $2 million to do the work we decided was needed, and we keep getting more with the years.

While working at GMHC I joined folks like Kiara St. James, who was already working on the passing of the Gender Expression Non-Discrimination Act (GENDA) for so many years, and I learned from her and was lucky enough to be included in the fight to finally get that legislation passed in 2019.

I was able to create another coalition: Decrim NY with the end goal of decriminalizing sex work in the state of New York. I was able to work with amazing people in drafting a bill with that finally proposing it to the assembly and senate. And I did all that as the dirty girl walking the street. With better clothes and better hair but the same.

In my show I talk about her and about how much love she had to give and how much love she got from whores. How much love she got from men and women and people while being as unholy as one can be . . .

It is a line in my show that never lands well, and I don't take it out: "He opened the door and left the bathroom after he fucked me and I stayed there with my legs shaking while cum traveled down to my ankles and found its way to my stiletto shoe." I can say: it is my favorite line. In the context of my fantasizing about having a relationship with this guy whom I know I will never see again, the whole dripping cum of my ass is cruel and funny. People hate it. It is gross, someone told me. Well, my life is gross. I was approached by someone who told me I should not celebrate unprotected sex with the actual situation around HIV infections and STIs. "You work in a place that promotes prevention," they said . . .

And I choose not to get into arguments, but I don't take it out. I love that line with all its unhealthiness and nasty components. I love that they pay to see me say that and that they can't do anything about it because it is my story.

And I love it.

Che Gossett is a PhD candidate in women's and gender studies and a graduate fellow at the Center for Cultural Analysis at Rutgers University–New Brunswick.

Eva Hayward is an associate professor in gender and women's studies at the University of Arizona.

Mattilda Bernstein Sycamore

An Interview

CHE GOSSETT and EVA HAYWARD

Abstract The following is an interview with author and activist Mattilda Bernstein Sycamore conducted by Che Gossett and Eva Hayward. Sycamore discusses how she uses fiction to work through historical traumas, inviting readers to imagine the AIDS pandemic as not simply memory but as continuing crisis that necessitates desiring into the archive so that we might begin to understand AIDS. Trauma cannot be historically rendered—this is the catastrophe of this experience, past and present are affectively collapsed—so we must be creative in how we refuse to forget a pandemic that remains ongoing.
Keywords Mattilda Bernstein Sycamore, HIV/AIDS, *Sketchtasy*, *The End of San Francisco*

CG and EH: *In* Sketchtasy *(2018), your protagonist is a trans sex worker living in Boston in the mid-1990s, also navigating a libidinal economy in which AIDS and desire are sutured and, as you say, "the trauma of growing up with AIDS suffusing your desires, and no way to imagine a way out." Your work explores these political emotions (Nussbaum 2013; see also Gould 2009). Can you talk about how your fiction is a space for you to work out these traumas and how they press upon the present?*

MS: When I started writing *Sketchtasy*, I knew I was writing about the pageantry and hypocrisy of Boston gay club culture in 1995, which was when I lived there, but I didn't know much else; I was just writing. But what happened pretty soon was that the trauma came through—the trauma of living in a city rabidly afraid of difference, the trauma of a gay culture that magnified all the worst aspects of straight complicity, and the trauma of AIDS in this particular time. Looking back historically from our current vantage point, we can see that something was about to change, that soon there would be medications that would make HIV into a manageable condition for many, but there is no way for the characters in the book to imagine this future. More people died of AIDS-related causes in 1995 than in any other year in the United States, and the characters in *Sketchtasy* only have this to imagine.

TSQ: Transgender Studies Quarterly ∗ Volume 7, Number 4 ∗ November 2020 **631**
DOI 10.1215/23289252-8665313   © 2020 Duke University Press

In *Sketchtasy*, the characters are mostly queens in their late teens and early twenties trying to figure out a way to cope with everyday violence—the homophobia and transphobia, racism and classism and misogyny of dominant straight and gay cultures. Instead of the nine-to-five reality, they try to live in the five-to-nine world, and while this does offer some shelter from the workaday world, it does not protect them from their own self-hatred or racism or misogyny or the violence of their peers. While *Sketchtasy* is about a particular moment in time, our cities are certainly more homogenized than ever, and gay culture is just as hypocritical. So I think the book speaks to the present as well as the past.

Also I think there is a kind of nostalgia for the 1990s that I really want to combat. Nostalgia always camouflages violence. And in the early 1990s, when I first entered the world as an avowedly queer person, it felt like everyone was dying—of AIDS, of drug addiction, of suicide. In 1992, when I moved to San Francisco, I went there in search of other queers trying to figure out a way to cope—direct action activists, hookers, sluts, vegans, anarchists, dropouts, druggies, freaks, and outcasts. I joined ACT UP soon after I arrived, and that was really my foundation as an activist. This was shortly after the heyday of ACT UP in San Francisco, after there was a split into two different groups over whether to focus on treatment activism alone, or to focus on fighting AIDS as a broader struggle. I was in the chapter that focused on the broader struggle, where it was assumed that we couldn't fight AIDS without fighting racism, classism, homophobia, and misogyny; everything was intertwined. So we focused on needle exchange, universal health care, women with HIV, prisoners with HIV, and alternative medicine. And it was incredible to be in a group that was so avowedly feminist and antiracist as part of being queer. And we operated by consensus. These were tools that I used in every other activist group I've ever been involved in, and also this intersectional analysis became a foundation for my life, and still is.

CG and EH: *When you say that "nostalgia always camouflages violence," do you see art around AIDS as nostalgic? Might this occlude and dissimulate violence? Can you speak to other political emotions in addition to shame and nostalgia that are important for your critical work?*

MS: To me, the opposite of nostalgia is truth. Truth is what I am after—work that speaks to all the complications in our lives, rather than packaging a lie for mass consumption. When someone wears a "Silence = Death" T-shirt as a fashion statement without even considering the meaning of the slogan, that is nostalgia without complication. Just something cute to impress your friends. But of course there is a middle ground. I've seen artists who died of AIDS represented in recent art shows where the work is as dead as the artists, and I've seen places where the work is still as moving as ever. Some work speaks to a particular time and is alive only then, and it becomes nothing more than a formal gesture when resuscitated.

And of course, no industry is better than the art world at commodifying death. And also I would say that when people are making art about AIDS now, this is crucial. So I don't want to make any generalizing statements, other than to say that I think nostalgia is the enemy of truth.

To go in a different direction, though, when I was in ACT UP in 1992, there were fags about five years older than I who would say, oh, I was in ACT UP, but it's over now. So you see, in 1992, it already wasn't trendy anymore. And when I was doing activism in the early 2000s, I remember a close activist friend saying something about how wasn't ACT UP just gay white men in the 1970s? But of course ACT UP didn't start until 1987, so this is how quickly historical memory in activist worlds ends. Now that ACT UP has reentered cultural memory and in some ways become commoditized—not the ACT UP chapters that still exist and are doing important work but ACT UP of the past—certainly the fact that people are talking about AIDS again in deep ways is important.

But when I hear people wishing that they were around in the early days of ACT UP, still I know this means they aren't really thinking about what that would mean, that everyone was dying, and that's where the rage came from. Or they haven't really thought about this in a deep way. And I think this is nostalgia—whenever we romanticize a golden age that never really existed, this prevents us from creating that possibility now. And for those of us who live in the dominant colonial power in the world, we are always living in a horrible time. Our lives are predicated on the destruction of the world—on colonialism, imperialism, endless war—and we have to challenge this and try to create something else anyway. In any time.

When you ask about emotions that are important for my critical work, I would say that this changes with every work. But probably I always write from a place of loss, of longing, of rage, of hopelessness, of impossibility, of desperation, of emergency, of emergence, of lack, of desire or at least a desire for desire, of brokenness, of brazenness, of trying to reach toward clarity and vulnerability and intimacy and accountability. If I say I write to stay alive, this is more than a rhetorical gesture, it's a strategy that has worked.

CG and EH: *You call your book* The End of San Francisco *(2013) "an exorcism." Why is that?*

MS: San Francisco is where I learned everything about how to be queer, how to be trans, how to create my own politics, culture, identities; how to challenge hypocrisy, demand accountability, create lust and love and intimacy and trust on my own terms; and how to find the people who could help me heal or give me hope or at least find ways to cope. I lived there for fourteen years, at three different times, starting when I was nineteen, and it's also the place that has let me down the most. But still I kept believing. I kept believing in these same queer dreams, even as I saw how corrupt queer could be. How the people with brilliant structural analysis, incisive ways of taking apart the status quo, these people, including some of my friends and lovers and fellow activists, would enact the same patterns of violence and abandonment as dominant straight or gay cultures. But they would do it by calling it accountability or mutual aid or self-preservation or just disappear and call it nothing at all, and it was the same hideous hypocrisy. And actually it hurt more. Because I didn't believe in straight people or mainstream gays, right? When the people you believe in let you down, I think it can be worse. I mean no one will ever harm me as much as my father who sexually abused me as a kid, but when the people and cultures and politics that I believed in so deeply—that I still believe in—when everything kept letting me down, over and over, eventually I had to write *The End of San Francisco* to map all my most formative moments, everything I kept believing in, and everything that kept letting me down. So that I could imagine something else.

But still, San Francisco is the only place where I've really felt like I had a home, and I wonder if I'll ever feel that way about anywhere again. When I moved to Seattle, people asked me if I was going to write *The End of Seattle* next, and I laughed, because I felt like this meant they didn't know what San Francisco meant to me. But my next book, *The Freezer Door*, is about Seattle, and this dream of the city as the place where you find everything you never imagined, and whether that possibility even exists anymore, in our gentrified cities.

Last time I was in San Francisco, when I was on tour for *Sketchtasy* in 2019, this was the first time when I really couldn't feel it at all. I was going on these long walks through neighborhoods I'd known, and even though they looked very similar structurally—most of the same buildings were there—there was none of the feeling that I belonged. I kept looking at people for that sense of recognition, that we are in this together, the weirdos and outsiders, but there was nothing. And then one night I was walking through South of Market, where I used to go out to clubs, and there was someone on the transfeminine spectrum wearing a giant red Afro wig trying to push her wheelchair up onto the curb, and she looked up at me, and her eyes got bright with euphoria as she opened her arms and said HELLO. And that was what I was looking for. That was what I used to feel all the time on the street, in certain neighborhoods. That was what made San Francisco feel like home. Not just the people I knew, but the people you recognize. And I realized, oh, now these people are not just on the fringe, they are literally living on the streets. And of course there has always been a crisis of homelessness in San Francisco, especially for people of color, for trans women and queer youth, for people living with HIV and AIDS, for runaways and escapees and people in drug culture or on the margins of anything, either intentionally or on purpose—I mean it's always been this way since I first arrived in 1992, when I was nineteen, but this time when I visited, it just felt like the people who have been pushed on to the streets were the only ones in the street whom I could relate to. Who related to me.

And all the energy has been emptied out—there are more people living in San Francisco than ever, but you walk around at nine at night and the streets are quiet. There isn't even any graffiti anymore, in most places. If people are on the way somewhere, they are looking at their phones, just like anywhere else. It doesn't feel like San Francisco anymore. And when I mentioned this at my readings, everyone just nodded yes. San Francisco has been emptied of the cross-pollination and outsider cultures that used to make it volatile and alive. The cultures are still there, but they are not visible. They are far less public. And of course this relentless gentrification works alongside never-ending structural racism and police brutality and ethnic cleansing. And this is happening in all of our gentrified US cities, but San Francisco is where I feel it the most because it's the place that has meant the most to me. And also, San Francisco is a place that has perfected the liberal ideology of tokenism without transformation, especially in terms of queer and trans people who oftentimes serve as window dressing for oppression. Sometimes willingly, and sometimes unintentionally.

CG and EH: *What are struggles for trans survival and resistance in a time of HIV/ AIDS that you imagine in the future or see emergent on the horizon? How have both the responses to the ongoing AIDS epidemic changed over time, and what are the contemporary struggles that trans politics can intervene in and combat at the moment?*

MS: I'm working on a new anthology called *Between Certain Death and a Possible Future: Queer Writing on Growing up with the AIDS Crisis.* I first thought of the idea when I realized that *Sketchtasy* was a generational novel about AIDS. So I'm starting with the premise that every queer person lives with the trauma of AIDS, and this plays out intergenerationally. Usually we hear about two generations—the first, coming of age in the era of gay liberation, and then watching entire circles of friends die of a mysterious illness as the government did nothing to intervene. And now we hear about a current generation growing up in an era offering effective treatment and prevention, and unable to comprehend the magnitude of the loss. But there is another generation between these two, a generation I belong to—one growing up in the midst of the epidemic, haunted by the specter of certain death, internalizing the trauma as part of becoming queer. So those are the personal stories I want to collect in this book.

One thing I'm learning is that there are so many queer and trans youth who are dying of AIDS now. Especially young trans women and young gay men. Especially people of color. I'm hearing about this from New York and Seattle and Los Angeles, and I'm sure it's happening everywhere. These are queer and trans youth with access to care. They are in the system. These have access to the treatment and prevention that is supposed to make HIV into a manageable condition, and yet, due to a wide range of issues that include homelessness, hopelessness, addiction, stigma, and trauma, as well as structural neglect, familial and societal homophobia/transphobia, and so many other challenges, this does not save them. I can't help thinking that if we had a cure for HIV, they would still be alive. But instead of fighting for a cure, most AIDS service organizations talk about "ending AIDS" through access to testing, treatment, pre-exposure prophylaxis (PrEP), and health care, without even mentioning a cure. I cannot stop thinking about this.

Sassafras Lowrey wrote a great piece for the book about coming of age as a homeless teen in Portland in the early 2000s, and then becoming the director of one of New York City's largest LGBTQ homeless youth drop-in and street out-reach programs, and, in the time Sassafras worked there, from 2010 to 2018, more and more youth were becoming positive. And Sassafras writes that the only way these youth could access services was to be HIV positive. And some of these kids, especially gay boys and trans women, were dealing with wasting syndrome and Kaposi sarcoma at a time when these conditions are not even supposed to exist in the United States. Some of these kids are dying of AIDS in their teens and twenties, just like in the 1980s. But do you hear anyone talking about this?

In terms of trans politics in general, perhaps never has trans visibility been greater, and at the same time trans women, especially trans women of color, are brutally murdered at an astounding rate. Trans people are routinely kicked out of our families of origin, harassed in school and at work, persecuted by religious leaders and politicians, and attacked on the street simply for daring to exist. Trans people are often denied access to basic services like health care and housing, fired from jobs or never hired in the first place, and forced to flee the places where we grew up, simply to survive. And then so many trans people arrive in cities, seeking refuge, and find themselves marginalized again—without housing, strung out on drugs, HIV positive. But the media story is one of progress.

Part of the media narrative involves a mainstreaming of trans identity, which is completely counter to the needs and desires of most trans people. The most obvious example of this is the fight for trans inclusion in the military. We are told that we don't need housing or health care, we just need the right to fight in unjust wars. So the notion is that fighting for the right to murder people of color around the world for corporate profit will solve the problem of our own bru-talization at home. But the US military is actually the problem—defund the military, and we could have everything we ever dreamed of—universal housing and health care and free, delicious, healthy food for everyone, a guaranteed minimum income, safe houses in every city and town for queer and trans kids to escape abusive homes, whatever we imagine, it would all become possible. But instead the issue is military inclusion. The same thing happened with gay inclusion in the military, starting in the early 1990s. But trans people don't even have a fraction of the power that gay people had twenty-five years ago, so how did this grotesque shift in priorities happen so fast?

I can tell you exactly how it happened. It all started with Jennifer Pritzker, described as the first trans billionaire, a member of a robber baron family with a fortune built on real estate speculation and insider trading—in 2014 she donated $1.35 million to the Palm Center to establish the Transgender Military Service Initiative. And suddenly trans inclusion in the US military became the next big thing on the LGBT agenda. So if you have $1.35 million lying around, you can shift the entire agenda of the so-called trans movement, that's how little power we have. And now military service is seen as a ticket to assimilation—what better way to prove that trans people are "healthy" and "fit for employment" than by participating in war for corporate profit? So, rather than calling attention to the structural conditions that make military service a tragic option for some people desperate to escape oppression, the so-called LGBT movement aggrandizes military service as the gold standard for bravery, furthering structural violence on a global scale.

For a long time, trans and queer activists have demanded that the *T* in LGBT stand for something more than window dressing, but now that the *T* has become more visible it's the same thing that happened with gay assimilation. You just add "gay" to any oppressive institution—gay cops, gays in the military, whatever—and it becomes a symbol of progress. Now that some gay people have fully assimilated into the power structure, it's even more progressive to talk about trans people in the military or the police or the fashion industry or whatever. But we don't need trans cops or trans soldiers or trans fashion models; we needed an end to the police, an end to the military, an end to the fashion industry—and every other horrifying institution. I don't want to live in a world where *trans* just stands for the *T* in LGBT; I want to live in a world where trans is an identity that challenges power, demands accountability, destroys binary gender, and creates new possibilities for self-determination for everyone. Is this too much to imagine?

Che Gossett is a PhD candidate in women's and gender studies and a graduate fellow at the Center for Cultural Analysis at Rutgers University–New Brunswick.

Eva Hayward is an associate professor in gender and women's studies at the University of Arizona.

References

Gould, Deborah B. 2009. *Moving Politics: Emotion and ACT UP's Fight against AIDS.* Chicago: University of Chicago Press.
Nussbaum, Martha C. 2013. *Political Emotions.* Cambridge, MA: Harvard University Press.
Sycamore, Mattilda Bernstein. 2013. *The End of San Francisco.* San Francisco: City Lights.
Sycamore, Mattilda Bernstein. 2018. *Sketchtasy.* Vancouver, BC: Arsenal Pulp.
Sycamore, Mattilda Bernstein. 2020. *The Freezer Door.* South Pasadena, CA: Semiotext(e).

Strategic Inessentialism

JULES GILL-PETERSON and GRACE LAVERY

Abstract The following introduction provides an overview to the Dossier on COVID-19, curated by Jules Gill-Peterson and Grace Lavery. This introduction explores how the pandemic has intensified the inessential denotation grafted onto trans people's material lives through health care, policing, incarceration, immigration, and racism. The ongoing crisis in academic labor and its uncertain pandemic futures are, similarly, an important place for trans studies to attend in this moment. **Keywords** COVID-19, pandemic, coronavirus, trans

We write from a moment when time and space are seemingly superseded every few days or weeks, and therefore when writing is more than usually conscious of its immanent irrelevance. Such a time and space of global pandemic is one in which trans people have real experience writing, practiced as we are in the arts of the inessential, the nonessential, and the wrongly essentialist. And so while we understand that the ideas gathered in this dossier will undoubtedly be read in a future whose form we cannot anticipate, we affirm that trans writing can make an affordance out of that condition of inessentiality to say something across the folds of pandemic time and space that ripple from us to you.

Although it is coincidental that this dossier on COVID-19 makes its home in this special issue of *TSQ* on HIV/AIDS, the shared space of these pages allows us to confront the many observed and disavowed points of interface between the two. Comparison, analogy, and allegory have been invoked time and time again between HIV/AIDS, as some form of precursor, and COVID-19, though such rhetorics fail when they presume that HIV/AIDS is already over, or precontemporary, or separable from this viral pandemic. As this special issue's coeditors Eva S. Hayward and Che Gossett importantly point out, HIV+ people have been placed under particular restriction and duress by this coronavirus. Individual and collective experiences with the state's investment in mass death may provide some lessons in activism and mutual aid, but the shape of COVID-19—its curve, however variably flat or peaked—is not the shape of HIV. They do not inhabit the same time and space.

TSQ: Transgender Studies Quarterly ∗ Volume 7, Number 4 ∗ November 2020
DOI 10.1215/23289252-8665327   © 2020 Duke University Press

Though that does not mean that they are unrelated, either. Far from a "great equalizer" because of its contagious spread through the air and surfaces, COVID-19 moves wildly unevenly and makes existing vectors of race, class, poverty, incarceration, ability, and citizenship into comorbidities. The fantasy that COVID-19 would compromise the immunity of the whole population as an act of egalitarianism, or make everyone into an immunocompromised subject, disavows the disproportionate impact of this pandemic on those who were already immunocompromised, where there is no equalization to be found, only intensification.

In a context of artificially restricted and market-driven health-care provision, trans people have had treatments deferred, delayed, or canceled on the grounds that they are—that we are—"nonessential." And for many more, being restricted to home effectively suspends forward movement in pursuing all manner of transition-related and gender-affirming plans, medical and otherwise. The further loss of income, financial security, and housing security many are facing only compounds those dynamics. In one sense, then, the state's admission that transgender and transsexual treatments are inessential dedramatizes the regime of medicalization under which trans people have been forced to live for decades, in which transition needed to be framed as urgent, irresistible, and its denial life threatening, before it could be accessible at all. To learn from that body of accumulated knowledge, as with the knowledge of the HIV+ and immunocompromised, rather than rail against our "new" position as inessentialized bodies, we want to ask what distinctive engagements might be enabled by a strategic inessentialism. The narrative drama that trans studies has lent to many of its accounts of oppression, transphobia, and necropolitics has perhaps diminished our attention to the bodies of knowledge that make possible the significant fact of living on and desiring otherwise, without the idealization that is often obliged to arrive at the exalted terrain of resistance we would imagine as successful. Though none of us has elected to dedramatize the conditions of contemporary trans life in this way—it was, after all, the state, in collusion with the pandemic, that did so—we nonetheless ask after its unexpected affordances.

Another way to say this is that we are worried about the widespread desire to be or become cops under the state of emergency, and for all that desire does to regenerate a biopolitics of comorbidity and racial capitalism. Our concern addresses the root biopolitical problem of "immunity" as a concept, which models a self-contained body and body politic that must be defended against the fantasized virus and/or invader. Yet to sustain that fantasy of an inside and outside, the body politic must likewise sustain an internal, constitutive violence: to kill and let die the life that has been deemed external to a healthy body despite already being inside it, or sacrificeable to preserve the integrity of the body/nation (Cohen 2009). Of course, viruses are unusual in that way, since they are not quite alive by conventional definitions, making them both disturbing in their indifferent actions on our bodies and eminently killable, en masse. Immunity metaphors therefore have immense purchase beyond all appeals to reason, or even shame: enter here the Republican Party's "kill your grandmas to save the economy" line, the line between reason and shame collapsing perhaps most spectacularly in the advice from a notoriously germophobe president that "it would be interesting" to consider "injecting" bleach into a living lung, to clean out whatever viral contamination dwells inside.

Yet these caricatured proposals from the usual suspects are not the only exercise of power that alarms us. We note the sheer patrolling of social participation that extends police powers to detain and interrogate, as well as to fine one's fellows, to every "good" and obeying subject in the realm, despite already ample evidence to suggest that police are deploying those very powers against people of color, immigrants, and sex workers, in typically violent manner. Here, to dedramatize the maneuvers of the pandemic affords us greater clarity with which to apprehend what forms of state power are actually being internalized under a moral-ethical framework of acting in the best interests of the social body. That imperative, of course, is not simply affirmative: it involves righteous punishment for those who do not live up to a monied, white scenography of social distancing while comfortably working from home, ordering delivery from local restaurants as a sort of moral practice of consumption. How much have certain elements of academia carried this banner in celebrating the heights of productivity possible while working from home; in exhorting feverish new value production for corporate universities as a form of self-sacrifice for the fantasized good of students; the displacement of teaching onto video-conferencing software, accelerating the convergence of teaching with surveillance technology distributed by profiteers; or, in the surprisingly inflexible approaches to students in distress who become unable to keep up with online learning, as so many social media tales relate? Has higher education not been a longtime laboratory for this sort of internalization of police power under the sign of benevolence? Isn't educability its progressive, but thoroughly governmental, mandate?

The form of ethical obligation supposedly entailed by pandemic conditions in which symptomaticity is not a requirement of viral communication, and recovery is no proof of immunity, is poised to satisfy as well as to reproduce the perfect form of isolation that neoliberalism has long sought to maintain. Distancing is an ethical obligation privatized solely in the individual subject, and it is, in principle, both interminable (without a knowable end) and limitless (without knowable exceptions). And that's exactly why it provides the perfect ideological cover for the traditional vehicles of state power, like the police, who are making the most of their new powers to harass, arrest, and detain people of color. It's why the vast majority of jails and prisons still have not been emptied out. Perhaps less spectacularly, it's also how regimes of state and corporate surveillance are already making use of the declared state of emergency to institute cellular, digital, and public modes of data capture and risk assessment that dovetail with, and greatly inoculate, policies that mere months ago were considered objectionable by many, such as "travel bans," or concentration camps on the border, precisely by subjecting the unmarked citizen to moderately less extreme forms of the same, and calling that a pretty good deal.

The securitization of the border, in particular, illustrates the outcome of a resurgent immunity concept regenerated from all sides, including those well-behaved and socially distant subjects. While militarized police presence has seen an observed uptick in places like the southwestern US states, we read that the detention and deportation of migrants have also increased significantly, as the emergency powers the federal administration has granted itself take advantage of the apparent legitimacy of public health to pursue once-contested plans with full-throated expediency. Not only is immigrant detention an incredibly dangerous place to be during a pandemic, but the deportation of so many people has itself played an observed causal role in Guatemala's COVID-19 outbreak, for instance (Martin 2020).

Anti-immigrant securitization is part of the racialization of virality and immunocompromised comorbidity. This manifests in the United States in the radically higher rates of COVID-19 mortality among Black patients, which has been characterized as an implication of institutional white supremacy, and for which the Surgeon General's claim that responsibility fell squarely on the shoulders of Black people's individual comportment led to rare public acknowledgment of its sheer absurdity (Sellers 2020). In the market, the hospital itself is part of racial capitalism's comorbidity, a space where risk is displaced onto already stigmatized bodies, while the heroic men and women in white coats are cheered, in their almost-comical absence, at seven in the evening. Meanwhile, considering that many nurses and low-wage health-care and senior-care workers are Black and immigrant women of color, particularly in the United Kingdom, their disproportionate deaths are also scrubbed from the balcony clapping for the National Health Service.

While the securitization of immunity and exhortations to individualize responsibility rely on exposing many groups of marginalized people to the vulnerability of being labeled inessential life, we note that inessentialism, then, is an axis of solidarity. Turning toward academia and trans studies, in which the inversion of our long-fought enemy "essentialism" is too rich to pass up, we would suggest that inessentialism puts the "contingency" in "contingent labor" and, even more so during the pandemic, the "adjunct" in "adjunctive treatment."

The crisis in academic labor has long felt like an event that destroys time and space for generations of scholars whose structural underemployment never measurably recovered from its supposed most recent cause in 2008, only to find that 2020 has now hit. Part of what has been so stark in the COVID-19 pandemic is the naked disaster capitalism of the most elite institutions, who set the stage for industry-wide adoption of contingent labor and other neoliberal practices, as was the case with the move to online teaching. Brown was among the first to announce a hiring freeze. Harvard, Princeton, and Yale, with a combined nearly $100 billion in endowments, have led the charge in refusing to extend contingent contracts while preemptively slashing the expectation of new employment for those who will lose their income and health insurance. Now we hear of public universities following suit by furloughing staff, slashing salaries, and making preemptive budgetary cuts.

Yet we might interject to say that the numbers don't quite check out, either: if you let all your adjuncts' contracts expire now, for one thing, there will be no one to provide the essential labor of the university later. Without contingent labor higher education would go belly-up. Indeed, contingent positions are being construed as inessential only because they exist under the university's fantasy that they are adjunctive treatments for prevailing economic conditions—which makes them, in fact, utterly essential because "cure" is not on the table. What we might rightly fear over the next several years, then, is not only that some existing contingent labor situations will disappear under mass layoffs but also that elite schools will pilot a much more aggressive adjunctification of the professoriate than we have already witnessed (though that scarcely feels possible). Perhaps this adjunctification will occur in concert with the collapse of smaller institutions of higher education that cannot withstand an economic downturn owing to their lack of multi-billion-dollar endowments to hoard, like community colleges. And so perhaps what we are now witnessing is the rapid acceleration of a process that has been ongoing for decades. The adjunct will be presented yet again as a stopgap for which we have no choice but to accept graciously, exactly as the Ivy League presented online teaching as a stopgap measure that we now expect to continue at least into the next academic year, as if this were not a flagrant and coercive shift in basic working conditions.

How do we say no? How do we make our strategic inessentialism a potent force for solidarity that generates action? Through labor organizing, for one thing. Jules writes fresh on the heels of a faculty organizing meeting held digitally, where an ongoing fight for a union has found newly expansive importance. While the faculty at the University of Pittsburgh have been obstructed by the administration at every turn, with a lengthy legal battle both pending and suspended by the pandemic, organizers have turned to solidarity and mutual aid to apply an important brake on administrative dictates, building collective energy to respond to radical shifts in policy and working conditions that were delivered in over sixty separate emails from university executives in March. Within departments, faculty have also reached out to colleagues in the spirit of affective solidarity and care. Jules can testify to the emotional relief that accompanied taking time to talk to her colleagues and share feelings of exhaustion, worry, and fear. This practice of care has countered the further individualization and isolation of labor that working from home intensifies and is made contingent on other assumptions (on a stable internet connection, a quiet room in which to work, and without other responsibilities for care work). And labor organizing builds strength to imagine better, more equitable working and learning conditions whose implementation would not require further individual Herculean effort, and that could include being cared for. The very inessentiality of taking time to refuse isolation and talk openly and vulnerably with colleagues prompts solidarity and nonessential care that can energize labor actions.

Grace, meanwhile, writes in the midst of a set of challenging conditions encountered by the wildcat strike called by graduate student laborers at the University of California, Berkeley, a vote for full work stoppage that passed on the same day as campus administrators suspended in-person instruction. Yet in addition to having the force of their collective actions blunted by the administration's response, grad student workers are now compelled to carry the affective weight of the present crisis, as frontline educators holding discussion sections and office hours—using software that, of course, makes surveillance all the easier. And, additionally, the fiction of an imminent rally of the academic labor market, a fiction with which campus administrators have busted unions and incentivized workers into unlivable conditions, has collapsed once and for all, and the work of ensuring that such workers can continue to live is one that now draws in more and more inhabitants of this collapsing institution.

The five short entries in this dossier on COVID-19 explore the zones of being, embodiment, knowledge, critique, and feeling that live in the trans inessential of pandemic space-time. We invited contributors to pursue genres that could move with their thoughts and capacities as they varied from day to day, or week to week, and so we are delighted to introduce several critical essayettes, a letter to the future, a reflection on contingent labor, and much that testifies to the specific feeling of writing now. This is writing generously offered without any expectation that the future in which that writing will appear, or in which it will be read, will resemble even the most recent past.

One axis of thought that travels through several contributions concerns what, exactly, constitutes this pandemic, and what sorts of critical knowledge formations take root in its midst. Gabriel N. Rosenberg explores the founding mytheme of zoonosis, an intimate contact between species (human and animal) that grounds the emergent historiography of COVID-19, as it continues to shape the way that HIV/AIDS is narrated and formulated into policy. Reading against the phobic response to intimacy that describes, for example, "wet markets" as racialized spaces of contamination and penetration rather than simply places where one buys produce, Rosenberg offers grounds for a conceptually robust engagement with zoonotic contact, in the name of developing new and newly porous ways of thinking about interspecies relation.

Kelly Sharron takes the COVID-19 pandemic as a powerful illustration of Karl Marx's understanding of wage labor as both the defining freedom of the free subject and, thereby, the sole freedom with which we are endowed by capital, whose interests have wholly subsumed any organs of governmentality in the US state. Sharron's analysis shows us how the very categories on which we engage with the present moment—of the (putatively antagonistic) difference between "economy" and "life"; the opposition of "freedom" and "health"—depend on the naturalization of capitalist logics whose death-dealing and freedom-limiting power is in forceful evidence.

A second axis of thinking across this dossier concerns the states of feeling that characterize writing from the scene of trans life, living on and, especially, working during a pandemic. Harlan Weaver writes a love letter to the future from a trans surgical team that has just completed major surgery on the present, a set of procedures for making whole chronic conditions that did not originate with COVID-19. Weaver writes from a future after the pandemic as it presently moves has shifted, from the perspective of the countless trans people who have long been engaged in vernacular sciences of survival and invention. In their name, Weaver asks after the collective expertise born of relegation to the nonessential rather than waiting for a crisis to end.

Julie Beaulieu digs further into the contradictions of surviving and suffering at the same time among the contingent: trans, academic, and teaching in the midst of registering the impact of what is happening to our workplaces, our students, and to us. Beaulieu sets trans pedagogy in a moving question about what it might mean "to teach students about topics as though they are happening to all of us." While a gentrifying university in a gentrifying city in a gentrifying world accelerates a loss of imagination about what it means to do more than get by, Beaulieu confronts a difficulty for so many queer and trans people in the academy: the brutal realities of contingent labor sit uneasily for many with a long-desired narrative of class escape. How does a pandemic enter this realm of academic laboring for queer and trans people, with its competing mandates to care for our students but to also "fail fabulously" at online teaching?

Since the beginning of the coronavirus crisis, governments have enacted or announced new restrictions on trans people in Poland, Hungary, the United Kingdom, and the United States, at both state and federal levels. The now dominant trans-antagonism, which positions trans bodies not as inessential but as positively undesirable, frames every expression of trans identity or desire as a metaphysics. A strategic inessentialism might help trip up these ever more certain philosophers as they frog-march us out of the toilet, out of the hospital, out of the clinic, out of the house, and out of the state. When we say "trans women are women," we are making a political claim rather than a metaphysical one: we are women because we are positioned by the capitalist cisheteropatriarchy as such. Our weak theory doesn't meet metaphysical charges of transphobia and violence with a more robust metaphysics but rather hews closer to an adaptability that mounts a political response to conditions of inessential life. If the ontology of the crisis is the logical grounds for ever more explosive and vicious implantations of disaster capitalism, perhaps strategic inessentialism can guide us toward what Morgan M. Page (pers. comm., April 2020) calls "disaster communism."

Jules Gill-Peterson is associate professor of English and gender, sexuality, and women's studies at the University of Pittsburgh and general coeditor of *TSQ*.

Grace Lavery is assistant professor of English at the University of California, Berkeley, and general coeditor of *TSQ*.

References

Cohen, Ed. 2009. *A Body Worth Defending: Immunity, Biopolitics, and the Apotheosis of the Modern Body*. Durham, NC: Duke University Press.

Martin, Maria. 2020. "Official Alleges That the U.S. Has Deported Many COVID-19 Positive Migrants to Guatemala." *NPR*, April 15. www.npr.org/sections/coronavirus-live-updates /2020/04/15/834999661/official-alleges-the-u-s-has-deported-many-covid-19-positive -migrants-to-guatema.

Sellers, Bakari. 2020. "What the Surgeon General Gets Wrong about African Americans and Covid-19." *CNN Opinion*, April 14. www.cnn.com/2020/04/14/opinions/surgeon-general -comments-covid-19-black-communities-sellers/index.html.

On the Scene of Zoonotic Intimacies
Jungle, Market, Pork Plant

GABRIEL N. ROSENBERG

Abstract COVID-19, like HIV/AIDS before it, is being allegorized as a cost of perverse intimacies with nature. This essay surveys three scenes of intimate zoonotic exchange—the jungle, the wet market, and the pork plant—and maps how each contributes to the operation of racial capitalism.
Keywords COVID-19, AIDS, animals, race, biopolitics

Zoonoses are a problem of intimacy, with germs and bacteria transgressing speciative boundaries willy-nilly in an orgy of unlicensed somatic exchange. To breed animals we must be intimate with them, and this intimacy always exchanges more than we had intended, more than we realized, and more than we can hope to control or contain.

Anyone who has ever had a messy roommate (or a twenty-something boyfriend) knows too well that sharing a *domos* means living in the detritus and filth of our intimates. The ancient Greek *domos* gives us domestication, which means literally to bring something into the home and to place it under the authority of the patriarch there. Animals are typically understood to be domesticated when they reliably reproduce "in the home" at the patriarch's direction. This foundational exercise of biopolitical imperatives, premised as it was on the inclusion of animals in the home subject to the entrainment of their reproductive capacities and subsequent multiplication, carried risk for all members of the household, patriarchs included. Archaeologists tell us that the proximity of domestic animals unlocked a variety of illnesses that may have driven down human life expectancy. Put differently, through the proximity of domestication, human bodies had increased contact with the vectors of animal illnesses: zoonoses. Political theorists such as James C. Scott (2017) ascribe world-historical significance to the intimacies of domestication: the ecological entanglements of humans, grain, and livestock—the orchestration of life and death across so many species we call

TSQ: Transgender Studies Quarterly ∗ Volume 7, Number 4 ∗ November 2020
DOI 10.1215/23289252-8665341 © 2020 Duke University Press

domestication—have ultimately rendered the reproduction of humans, plants, and animals alike as vital objects of governance (see also Hodder 1990).

The global COVID-19 pandemic concretizes the threat of zoonotic exchanges in ways that descend rapidly into allegory: of "nature" striking back at humanity's excesses and encroachments. The virus's posited origin in Chinese "wet markets" lends itself to this allegory, since the markets are allegedly organized around the sale and slaughter of "wild" animals for meat. These are animals an American audience will imagine belonging in a verdant forest or overgrown jungle and not in a soup pot. The fantasy image of wet markets is about problematic (and problematized) intimacy with animals, proximity and contact that leads to a fatal exchange of fluids and then viral seroconversion. My point is not about any positive transformative possibilities this intimacy with animals might offer— little, I would wager—but is, instead, about the selective narration of problematic interspecies intimacy. How does marking one interspecies intimate exchange as aberrant result in the normalization and immunization of other (arguably riskier) interspecies intimate exchanges? What is striking about the COVID-19 allegory, and what renders it continuous with the ongoing allegory of HIV/AIDS, is the way in which it marks some kinds of intimacy with animals as perverse and racialized, but, at once, it also normalizes other intimate contacts with animals that result in the accumulation of capital and are conducive to the reproduction of qualified white American life. In this essay, I survey three scenes of intimate zoonotic exchange and map how each contributes to the operation of racial capitalism.

1. HIV/AIDS: Man and Ape in the Jungle

Critical scholarship on the HIV/AIDS epidemic has shown that how we narrate epidemic illnesses shapes the political and social imaginaries that, in turn, constrain institutional and activist responses. These imaginaries include those centered on perverse relations with nature and animality. As Cindy Patton (1985: 28) argues, the designation of AIDS as a "gay disease" in the early years of the epidemic transformed a lethal medical condition into a morality play and reversed the conventional causal relationship between risk factors and symptoms: "Being homosexual somehow became a symptom of AIDS." Historian Jennifer Brier (2009) contends that the designation, by confusing sexual acts with sexual identities, also routed public health and activist responses through identitarian frameworks that, in turn, struggled to make inroads with at-risk people of color and, in particular, men who have sex with men who disidentifed with the gay community. Paula Treichler (1999) notes that, by the 1990s, narratives of HIV/AIDS pivoted toward understanding the trajectory of the illness outside the United States as an "African" problem overdetermined by the poverty, passivity, and bestial nature of "Africans." That narrative also contrasted a naturalized and indigenous "African

AIDS," transmitted by the natural hypersexuality of all Africans, with an unnatural American HIV/AIDS tied mostly to an immoral pathological minority (see also Patton 1990).

This contrast helped explain to the American public why AIDS could be "unnatural" in the American context, and therefore a problem eventually contained by forceful biomedical and state intervention. At the same time, it construed AIDS as a natural, if lamentable, fact of life in Africa about which there was little to be done (Farmer, Connors, and Simmons 1996). How else can we make sense of the fact that the lethality of the epidemic in the United States quickly waned after the introduction of effective antiretroviral treatments in the late 1990s, but that millions of people in sub-Saharan Africa perished from HIV/AIDS in the two decades after effective treatment was possible? Surely, the greed and rigidity of American and European pharmaceutical companies are partly to blame, but popular apathy was also rooted in the fact that, to the American public, an Africa ravaged by AIDS was indistinguishable from what many already assumed was Africa without AIDS.

These dominant public narratives were accompanied by a thicket of myths and conspiracy theories informed by the exotic othering of afflicted Africans (Gilman 1988). One long-standing myth is particularly striking in terms of zoonotic intimacy. Even in the 1980s, scientists studying AIDS recognized similarities between the disease and various immune disorders found in other primates. This gave rise to the theory that HIV/AIDS was a zoonotic illness likely transmitted from primates to humans somewhere in Central Africa during the early twentieth century. Subsequent epidemiological scholarship, based on gene sequencing and historical tissue sampling, supports this theory. Furthermore, this scholarship suggests that the specific context for zoonotic transfer was likely a hunter who was exposed to the blood of a chimpanzee infected with a simian immunodeficiency virus (SIV). In human hosts, SIV evolved into HIV-1, which, through sex workers and a colonial inoculation regime, spread rapidly in human populations (Pepin 2011). A pervasive vernacular myth, however, locates the viral "jump" from chimpanzee to human in an act of sexual intercourse between man and monkey. According to this theory, AIDS was the result of the prevalence of bestiality among African men, one of the many problematic relations Africans seemed to maintain with animals. As Treichler (1999: 114) writes, "Africans are said to have sexual contact with these monkeys, or eat them, or eat other animals they have infected (Haitian chickens?), or give their children dead monkeys as toys." Contemporary studies describe the AIDS "bestiality" myth as particularly "prevalent among US Whites," and, as recently as 2011, a Tennessee Republican state legislator publicly ascribed the origin of AIDS to "one guy screwing a monkey, if I recall correctly, and then having sex with men" (Heller 2015: 45; Signorile 2012).

As outlandish as the "bestiality" myth may strike the reader, it was animated by important assumptions about sexuality. Its assumptions about the prevalence of African bestiality dovetailed with American racial logics that portrayed black men as hypersexualized and animalistic, racial logics at least partially emerging from the violent extraction of sexual labor under slavery (Roberts 1998; Foster 2019). Less obvious, however, the bestiality myth also drew from a supposedly vanished premodern and nonidentitarian idea of sodomy inherited from Christian theology common in the early modern Atlantic World. This conceptualization collapsed homosexual sex into a broader category of nonprocreative sex acts that also included sex with animals (Murrin 1998; Godbeer 2002; Chauncey 2004; Tortorici 2012, 2016, 2018). That is, rather than linking the "gay disease" to a fixed and object-specific internal "gay desire," the bestiality myth placed it in continuity with a hypersexuality that was not object specific nor tied to a stable identity formation or interiority. This vision of sodomy reckoned the desire, instead, to be sparked by an opportunistic and fleeting encounter—that is, by the contingent environmental conditions that prompted the lure of bestial contacts.

This concept of the sodomitic was deeply interwoven with colonial violence in both the Americas and Africa, where colonized populations were presumed to be closer to nature and, therefore, in the grips of bestial lust and without the reason to restrain it (Tortorici 2018; Hagler 2019; Sigal 2000). Ecological transformation from wilderness to, first, settled agriculture and then urban modernity winnowed the opportunities for bestial contact while expanding the thick social relations necessary for complex interiority and stable, object-specific sexual identities. On the one hand, this is why metropolitan culture, in both the United States and Europe, has tended to understand bestiality as a sexual anachronism practiced almost exclusively in premodern societies or isolated rural quarters (Rosenberg 2020a). On the other hand, the sexology of the metropole also positioned indigenous "bestialists" and sodomites as the hypersexualized terrain that provided the specific contrast for the (white) identity formation of the homosexual. Simple as they were, bestialists did not possess an interiority or psychology; rather, they impulsively took whatever nature offered. Indeed, the reduction of colonized and indigenous subjects to mere instinct and impulse robbed them of the possibility of interiority and bestialized them, since animals were similarly considered to be incapable of the reflection and moral reasoning that fully human Europeans possessed. The "bestiality" myth, then, located the emergence of the global AIDS pandemic in an environment in which bestial men had too many opportunities to come into contact with sick apes. The narrative of the virus among American homosexuals, by contrast, revolved around a pathological interiority in which, in Leo Bersani's (1987: 212) memorable phrase, homosexuals were associated with the "intolerable image of a grown man, legs high in the air, unable to refuse the suicidal ecstasy of being a woman." Put simply, white Americans did not need a complex psychoanalytic account to make sense of African AIDS, since it fit perfectly with racist assumptions about the nature of bestial black sexuality.

2. COVID-19: Man and Bat in the Wet Market

Early efforts to narrativize COVID-19 have also rendered racialized interspecies intimacies as infectious. Although the epidemic imaginaries of AIDS and COVID-19 are quite different, both use the scene of interspecies intimacy to shore up the operation of racial capitalism. The image of the "wet market," in particular, now sets a different scene of intimacy across species, with the wetness of the market summoning the image of the slick kiss of fluid touching skin. In this mixing of skin, fluid, and viscera, the boundary of species gets soaked: the fluid of one animal enters the body of another.

President Donald Trump insists on calling the novel coronavirus the "Wuhan" or "Chinese" virus. Such scripting ascribes collective responsibility to China and exculpates American officials, Trump most of all, of criminal incompetence. But it also seeks to explain through racial designation the heightened virulence of the pathogen. That is, although the Chinese are said to have caused the virus, this narration also suggests that the virus itself shares an infectious character with the Chinese: that the virus is both racialized and racializing as Chinese.[1] This, in turn, draws from the history of racist tropes that characterized China and the Chinese as infectious, filthy, overpopulated, and riven by endemic illness. Turn-of-the-nineteenth-century white Americans frequently claimed that Chinese immigrants lived in unsanitary tenements because it accorded with their animalistic natures and their disregard of personal freedom and individuality. As historian Nayan Shah (2001) contends, white workers explicitly contrasted their own vision of dignified labor against the unfree "coolie," who resembled little more than a beast of burden. "The 'abjectness' of the Chinese 'mode of life' was manifested in the comparisons to farm animals," Shah writes, "feeding a perception not only of Chinese immigrants' inferiority but also of their inhumanity" (27). Contact with Chinese immigrants allegedly carried a heightened risk of contagion for white Americans precisely because it was an infectious bestial contact: contact between the fully human white American and a bestialized Chinese immigrant risked lowering the former to the status of the latter.

Diet tends to be one place where powerful lines of social exclusion and inclusion are drawn, since eating is a paradigmatic act that tests and constantly remaps the body/world boundary (Douglas 2003; Kristeva 1992). As such, diet is a frequent focus in racializing and bestializing discourses (Tompkins 2012). Inclusion in the category "fully human" entails following a diet defined by the protocols of one's species, gender, race, class, religion, nationality, and so on.

Divergence from culturally and historically specific dietary protocols sparks social revulsion, censure, and even punishment. Not surprisingly, images of Chinese immigrants as infectious agents dovetailed with widespread lurid fascination with strange diets that reaffirmed their bestial natures. Just as livestock subsisted on a monotonous diet of grain, the labor organizer Samuel Gompers (1908) famously claimed that the "Asiatic coolie" diet of rice was inadequate for a laboring "American manhood" that needed proper meat and bread to maintain his robust independence. But white publics have also long imagined Chinese diets to involve the regular consumption of taboo, forbidden, and exotic animals, a dietary pattern consistent with a bestial willingness to eat anything (Coe 2016; Kim 2015). White audiences were simultaneously intrigued and repulsed. By the early twentieth century, Chinese restaurants were increasingly popular as venues to consume what white audiences believed was an exotic, primitive cuisine. As Haiming Liu (2015) shows, this obsession with inappropriate meats has been a persistent and sensational component of anti-Chinese racism in the United States and continues into the present.

Given that history, it's predictable that the COVID-19 origin story has now narrowed to "bat soup" from "wet markets" as the dominant fantasy of zoonotic exchange and, indeed, as a vivid scene of racialized interspecies intimacy (Reid 2020). The strategic deployment of the term *wet market* itself does quite a bit of work, since it refers simply to markets where vendors sell fresh, as opposed to durable, goods. Wet markets are regular facets of daily life throughout much of the world and, in particular, in East and Southeast Asia where consumers frequent them instead of the Western-style grocery stores that offer both durable and fresh ingredients. Nevertheless, American and European media regularly conflate that general definition with a narrower set of "open-air markets where animals are bought live and then slaughtered on the spot for the customers," to quote philosophers Peter Singer and Paola Cavalieri (2020) in a recent essay calling for an international ban on wet markets. Their definition of wet markets is, of course, plainly wrong. Wet markets need be neither "open-air" (and so what if they are?) nor places where animals can be bought live and slaughtered on the spot. But they buttress this generalization with the sort of selective sensationalizing that is impossible to disentangle from the racist troping we've just reviewed. First, they list the menagerie of strange beasts available in these markets: "wolf cubs, snakes, turtles, guinea pigs, rats, otters, badgers, and civets." Next, they quote a vivid *NPR* report meant to illustrate the horrifying conditions of the market: "Live fish in open tubs splash water all over the floor. The countertops of the stalls are red with blood as fish are gutted and filleted right in front of the customers' eyes. Live turtles and crustaceans climb over each other in boxes. Melting ice adds to the slush on the floor. There's lots of water, blood, fish scales, and chicken guts."

Singer and Cavalieri are vocal proponents of vegetarianism, but surely one or the other has been to an American seafood restaurant with live lobster tanks. "Wet markets, indeed," they then add. Wet is the tactile sensation of fluid touching skin. What makes the market wet is wild animal fluids making contact with human flesh and unlocking an infectious intimacy.

3. Impossible Intimacies: Man and Pig in the Pork Plant

Industrial animal agriculture fails to lend itself to similar allegories about the intimate. In late 2019, "African swine fever" swept through China, killing an estimated 300 to 400 million pigs (Charles 2019). At the time of this writing, farmers in South Carolina are battling a strain of avian flu that, during a similar 2015 outbreak, killed some 50 million poultry in the United States (Pitt 2020). Both diseases have dramatic zoonotic potential, and it is mostly just simple chance that the "big one" happens to be linked to (some) wet markets rather than to the vast zoonotic exchanges that occur in the context of industrial animal agriculture. The grisly slaughter of wild charismatic megafauna in wet markets dramatizes the tragedy of human encroachment on pristine wilderness, and it lends itself immediately to an allegorical narrative of COVID-19 as "wild nature strikes back." The death of millions of livestock from veterinary illness does not. It can hardly be understood as a tragedy, since those millions of pigs were bred only to die anyway. Swine fever hastened deaths that most American consumers think of as positive contributions to their qualified "good lives." When pigs die, humans usually eat well, and, for humans to eat well, pigs must usually die. If their deaths are reckoned tragic, it is only because their deaths were financially wasted. It is a tragedy, then, for human farmers, but not for the pigs or for an abstract nature.

Our collective comfort with this scene, despite its loudly heralded and well-documented possibility for zoonotic exchange, may partly lie in our inability to see domestication and animal agriculture as a scene of sociality and intimacy (Wallace 2016). Indeed, we are accustomed to collapsing the horrors of animal agriculture into the scene of killing: the slaughterhouse is an especially evocative symbol of modernity's capacity to produce mass death. In this, we see the slaughterhouse as the apotheosis of the nonrelational, driven by the cruel absence of attachment to animals by the slaughterer and the impossibility of real contact. Yet empirical work on the labor of animal agriculture suggests that livestock agriculture is also the sight of abundant, if often harrowing sociality among and between animals and humans alike. Alexander Blanchette's (2020) ground-breaking ethnography of industrial pork production, for example, shows that animal agriculture produces and ultimately relies on affective relations, somatic contact, and sensual proximities between workers and pigs. These entangle-ments span the deep emotional attachments workers forge with runty piglets they bottle-feed to the arousal and impregnation of sows during artificial insemination.[2] Blanchette resists the tendency to overread those social spaces as merely those in which the speciesist domination of pigs by humans is enacted. Instead Blanchette notes that the pork plant remakes the social relations of all its workers, humans and porcine, and that the decisive divide is between racialized labor and capital, not human and animal.

COVID-19 has also laid bare the fact that agricultural workers in both China and the United States share something quite important with the animals they labor alongside. Livestock facilities are extremely dangerous places to work without infectious disease, but workers there also face the heightened risk of exposure to zoonoses and subsequent illness as a result of their intimate interactions with animals. Low wages and dangerous working conditions are par for the course in low-margin, high-volume industries like meat. In China, as in the United States, the rapid consolidation of the pork industry has been partially driven by the availability of cheap grains for feed (Schneider 2014). The growing need for farmlands to sustain the grain-meat complex, in turn, causes agricultural encroachment into wildlife areas, heightening the risk of zoonotic exchange between previously secluded ecologies and highly susceptible industrial monocultures. It has also pushed small farmers out of the pork market and into one of the few remaining niche agricultural markets: the exotic game market. Due to competition from huge multinational agribusinesses, some Chinese farmers must farm civets and wolf cubs, not pigs (Lynteris and Fearnley 2020). Rather than seeing wet markets where wild game are slaughtered as the characteristic of a perverse and racialized "Chinese" appetite, then, we should see them as an intimate form produced through the ecological transformations of global capitalism. Workers in those wet markets and pork plants both enact a dangerous intimacy with animals. Americans see the one form of intimacy as barbaric, and the other they do not see at all. Capital orchestrates both, just as it orchestrates the exposure to zoonotic exchange workers in both locations bear.

COVID-19, like HIV/AIDS before it, is being allegorized as a cost of perverse intimacies with nature. Yet these allegories work primarily to dramatize the danger of bestial humans, bestialization that has long been interwoven with the racialization of nonwhite and colonized peoples (Rosenberg 2016, 2020b; Heyward and Gossett 2017; Pergadia 2018; Jackson 2020; Amin 2020). Even as inappropriate intercourse with wild nature becomes a site of anxiety, these allegories immunize the human-animal interactions of industrial agriculture, in which slaughter is not reckoned as intimate. Indeed, the public largely misapprehends interactions in animal agriculture as fundamentally nonrelational and, therefore, unlikely to carry the same threat of zoonotic contagion. This, in turn, reinforces the commonsense terms of the "anthropocene" allegory: we live in a time when humans have conquered nature; nature is victim and humanity the perpetrator. We should resist this allegory, but not because we should be indifferent to the current ecological catastrophe or deny its reality. We should be skeptical of how the sole axis of difference that structures this allegory—humans versus nature—elides the unequal access many humans have to the category of "human," the economic system of racial capitalism that drives that inequality, and the vital possibilities for the more-than-human solidarity that may be needed to resist it.

Gabriel N. Rosenberg is associate professor of gender, sexuality, and feminist studies and history at Duke University. He is the author of *The 4-H Harvest: Sexuality and the State in Rural America* (2016).

Notes

1.   On the complex racialization of the nonhuman, see Chen 2012.
2.   On the somatic intimacy of livestock breeding, see Rosenberg 2017.

References

Amin, Kadji. 2020. "Trans* Plasticity and the Ontology of Race and Species." *Social Text*, no. 143: 49–71.

Bersani, Leo. 1987. "Is the Rectum a Grave?" In "AIDS: Cultural Analysis/Cultural Activism," edited by Douglas Crimp. Special issue, *October*, no. 43: 197–222.

Blanchette, Alexander. 2020. *Porkopolis: American Animality, Standardized Life, and the Factory Farm*. Durham, NC: Duke University Press.

Brier, Jennifer. 2009. *Infectious Ideas: U.S. Political Responses to the AIDS Crisis*. Chapel Hill: University of North Carolina Press.

Charles, Dan. 2019. "Swine Fever Is Killing Vast Numbers of Pigs in China." *Morning Edition*, August 19. www.npr.org/sections/thesalt/2019/08/15/751090633/swine-fever-is-killing-vast -numbers-of-pigs-in-china.

Chauncey, George. 2004. "'What Gay Studies Taught the Court': The Historians' Amicus Brief in *Lawrence v. Texas*." *GLQ* 10, no. 3: 509–38.

Chen, Mel Y. 2012. *Animacies: Biopolitics, Racial Mattering, and Queer Affect*. Durham, NC: Duke University Press.

Coe, Andrew. 2016. *Chop Suey: A Cultural History of Chinese Food in the United States*. New York: Oxford University Press.

Douglas, Mary. 2003. *Purity and Danger: An Analysis of Concepts of Pollution and Taboo*. New York: Routledge.

Farmer, Paul, Margaret Connors, and Janie Simmons, eds. 1996. *Women, Poverty, and AIDS: Sex, Drugs, and Structural Violence*. Monroe, ME: Common Courage.

Foster, Thomas. 2019. *Rethinking Rufus: Sexual Violations of Enslaved Men*. Athens: University of Georgia Press.

Gilman, Sander L. 1988. *Disease and Representation: Images of Illness from Madness to AIDS*. Ithaca, NY: Cornell University Press.

Godbeer, Richard. 2002. *Sexual Revolution in Early America*. Baltimore: Johns Hopkins University Press.

Gompers, Samuel. 1908. *Meat vs. Rice: American Manhood against Asiatic Coolieism. Which Shall Survive?* San Francisco: Asiatic Exclusion League.

Hagler, Anderson. 2019. "Archival Epistemology: Honor, Sodomy, and Indians in Eighteenth-Century New Mexico." *Ethnohistory* 66, no. 3: 515–35.

Heller, Jacob. 2015. "Rumors and Realities: Making Sense of HIV/AIDS Conspiracy Narratives and Contemporary Legends." *American Journal of Public Health* 105, no. 1: e43–50.

Hayward, Eva, and Che Gossett. 2017. "Impossibility of *That*." *Angelaki* 22, no. 2: 15–24.

Hodder, Ian. 1990. *The Domestication of Europe*. Oxford: Basil Blackwell.

Jackson, Zakiyyah Iman. 2020. *Becoming Human: Matter and Meaning in an Antiblack World*. New York: New York University Press.

Kim, Claire Jean. 2015. *Dangerous Crossings: Race, Species, and Nature in a Multicultural Age*. New York: Cambridge University Press.

Kristeva, Julia. 1992. *Powers of Horror: An Essay on Abjection*. New York: Columbia University Press.

Liu, Haiming. 2015. *From Canton Restaurant to Panda Express: A History of Chinese Food in the United States*. New Brunswick, NJ: Rutgers University Press.

Lynteris, Christos, and Lyle Fearnley. 2020. "Why Shutting Down Chinese 'Wet Markets' Could Be a Terrible Mistake." *Conversation*, January 31. theconversation.com/why-shutting-down -chinese-wet-markets-could-be-a-terrible-mistake-130625.

Murrin, John. 1998. "'Things Fearful to Name': Bestiality in Early America." In "Explorations in Early American Culture." *Pennsylvania History* 65, supplement: 8–43.

Patton, Cindy. 1985. *Sex and Germs: The Politics of AIDS*. Boston: South End.

Patton, Cindy. 1990. *Inventing AIDS*. New York: Routledge.

Pepin, Jacques. 2011. *The Origins of AIDS*. Cambridge: Cambridge University Press.

Pergadia, Samantha. 2018. "Like an Animal: Genres of the Nonhuman in the Neo-Slave Novel." *African American Review* 51, no. 4: 289–304.

Pitt, David. 2020. "Industry Scrambles to Stop Fatal Bird Flu in South Carolina." Associated Press, April 10. apnews.com/article/7e284ee45dae602841d246f933fae6ec.

Reid, Claire. 2020. "Scientists Say Bats Could Be Linked to Coronavirus as Videos of Bat Soup Appear Online." *Lad Bible*, January 23. www.ladbible.com/news/news-scientists-say-bats -could-be-linked-to-coronavirus-20200123.

Roberts, Dorothy E. 1998. *Killing the Black Body: Race, Reproduction, and the Meaning of Liberty*. New York: Vintage.

Rosenberg, Gabriel N. 2016. "A Race Suicide among the Hogs: The Biopolitics of Pork in the United States, 1865–1930." *American Quarterly* 68, no. 1: 49–73.

Rosenberg, Gabriel N. 2017. "How Meat Changed Sex: The Law of Interspecies Intimacy after Industrial Reproduction." *GLQ* 23, no. 4: 473–507.

Rosenberg, Gabriel N. 2020a. "Animals." In *The Routledge History of American Sexuality*, edited by Kevin P. Murphy, Jason Ruiz, and David Serlin, 32–41. New York: Routledge.

Rosenberg, Gabriel N. 2020b. "No Scrubs: Livestock Breeding, Eugenics, and the State in the Early Twentieth Century United States." *Journal of American History* 107, no 2: 362–87.

Schneider, Mindi. 2014. "Developing the Meat Grab." *Journal of Peasant Studies* 41, no. 4: 613–33.

Scott, James C. 2017. *Against the Grain: A Deep History of the Earliest States*. New Haven, CT: Yale University Press.

Shah, Nayan. 2001. *Contagious Divides: Epidemics and Race in San Francisco's Chinatown*. Berkeley: University of California Press.

Sigal, Peter. 2000. *From Moon Goddesses to Virgins: The Colonization of Yucatecan Maya Sexual Desire*. Austin: University of Texas Press.

Signorile, Michelangelo. 2012. "Stacey Campfield, Tennessee Senator behind 'Don't Say Gay' Bill, on Bullying, AIDS, and Homosexual 'Glorification.'" *Huffington Post*, January 26. www .huffpost.com/entry/stacey-campfield-tennessee-senator-dont-say-gay-bill_n_1233697.

Singer, Peter, and Paola Cavalieri. 2020. "The Two Dark Sides of COVID-19." *Project Syndicate*, March 2. www.project-syndicate.org/commentary/wet-markets-breeding-ground-for-new -coronavirus-by-peter-singer-and-paola-cavalieri-2020-03.

Tompkins, Kyla Wazana. 2012. *Racial Indigestion: Eating Bodies in the Nineteenth Century*. New York: New York University Press.

Tortorici, Zeb. 2012. "Against Nature: Sodomy and Homosexuality in Colonial Latin America." *History Compass* 10, no. 2: 161–78.

Tortorici, Zeb, ed. 2016. *Sexuality and the Unnatural in Colonial Latin America*. Oakland: University of California Press.

Tortorici, Zeb. 2018. *Sins against Nature: Sex and Archives in Colonial New Spain*. Durham, NC: Duke University Press.

Treichler, Paula. 1999. *How to Have Theory in an Epidemic: Cultural Chronicles of AIDS*. Durham, NC: Duke University Press.

Wallace, Rob. 2016. *Big Farms Make Big Flu: Dispatches on Infectious Disease, Agribusiness, and the Nature of Science*. New York: Monthly Review Press.

Viral Capital and the Limits of Freedom

KELLY SHARRON

Abstract This article considers the strained conditions of freedom under capitalism that are further inflected by COVID-19. Taking seriously the calls to reopen the economy as necessary steps to survival, the larger relationships of production must be called into question. Just as capitalism can ensure basic needs for some, it has always ensured the death of many. When spaces of production become both necessary for the working class and rampant with risk, Marx's "double bind of freedom," as well as the cyclical crises and contradictions of capital warrant heightened attention and contextualization.
Keywords capitalism, Marxism, pandemic, public health, COVID-19

C OVID-19 has laid bare some of the central tenets of capitalism, namely, the focus on the health of value, business, and markets over the physical health and well-being of people. COVID-19 has been spurred and spread through global capital—a pandemic of an increasingly connected world, a world connected by its markets. Nevertheless, we are also told that the market can be the cure, or that many more will be affected by market slowdown than the virus itself, making clear the ever-perilous relationship to capitalism—it is necessary for us to live but causes us to be unwell. Moreover, this dangerous relationship to capital is unevenly distributed. For some, pandemics and crises represent an opportunity to consolidate wealth and power (Klein 2020). For others, this has exacerbated precariousness: high-risk groups and people with HIV have been forced to halt daily life; trans* people and others have been forced to delay medical attention and surgeries deemed "inessential"; and incarcerated people remain structurally at risk while producing hand sanitizer to be shipped out. The distribution of risk and care illustrates the disparities essential to capitalism, demonstrating how discriminatory viruses can be.

Karl Marx (1977) describes this paradox through freedom: workers are free to sell their labor, and labor is their only means of exchange. With what Saidiya

TSQ: Transgender Studies Quarterly ∗ Volume 7, Number 4 ∗ November 2020   **657**
DOI 10.1215/23289252-8665355   © 2020 Duke University Press

Hartman (1997) calls "dark humor," Marx (1977: 272–73) describes freedom under capitalism as "free in the double sense, that as a free man he can dispose of his labour-power as his own commodity, and that on the other hand he has no other commodity for sale, is short of everything necessary for the realisation of his labour-power." Capitalism requires a working class for whom labor is their only commodity, and who must continually "freely" exchange that commodity to subsist. This article explores that relationship through the market and government responses to COVID-19: that one must work to continue to live, even as work endangers one's life. While this relationship between labor and capital is persistent and omnipresent, our current political moment structured by COVID-19 allows for a moment of pause at the nexus of marginalized populations, care, and capitalism to think about how to organize life in resistance to the deadly and endangering relationship to wage labor.

The central class struggle of capitalism, and its underlying tensions, are exacerbated only through external pressures. COVID-19 has made clear that Marx's analysis of capital is still very much relevant to contemporary conditions: living labor is necessary to value, capitalism's most essential workforce is underpaid, and compounding growth is a fiction. Capitalism is punctured by its crises, which offer a moment to either reveal its impossibility or concentrate wealth and power. The particularities of COVID-19 are its expressions of two foundational contradictions of capitalism, the tyranny of exchange value over use value and the expression of free will in laboring.

David Harvey (2014) explains the contradiction of use vs. exchange values through the example of housing. Houses provide a use value, but they also to a greater extent have exchange value. In other words, houses are not just a means for living, but they also become a means for savings and profiteering. The larger the gap between use and exchange values, the more likely an economic crisis. The "use" value of home ownership has shifted away from shelter and toward savings and profit. In 2008 speculative capital caused a bubble in the housing market, which then reorganized exchange values, causing many to be unable to afford shelter. Harvey asks pivotal questions post-2008: Why do we organize basic needs through a capitalist system of exchange? Why prioritize exchange values over use values?

Similarly, there have been calls to rethink the organization of use and exchange amid COVID-19 and shifting and shaky markets. While we have not lost the ability to make or produce exchange values and basic needs, speculative capital has shaken financial markets built off exchange value. Andrew Liu (2020) explores this contradiction:

Such dynamics expose a basic absurdity at the heart of our global society. It is not a system aimed at satisfying our desires and needs, at providing humans with greater amounts of physical utility. It is instead governed by impersonal pressures to turn goods into value, to constantly make, sell, buy, and consume commodities in an endless spiral. Unlike an earthquake or famine, the coronavirus outbreak has not destroyed our capacity to make *things*; indeed, it has resulted in perhaps the greatest ever accumulation of two of the most useful substances known to humanity, oil and steel. But several weeks of quarantining have decimated their value, tanking currencies, stock market indexes, and personal savings. Instead of enriching us and relieving us of natural wants, this glut of goods is only making us poorer. Given this irrational social system of organizing wealth and value, it is no wonder that so many societies have found it impossible to contain the coronavirus by asking citizens to limit commercial activity.

The virus has not short-circuited our ability to live, produce, meet society's needs, and create use value. Instead it has altered the system of exchange values, which relies on the premise of persistent and compounding growth and constant circuits of consumption and production. The calls to limit commercial activity have spurred a domino effect of lost jobs, unemployment, and closing businesses. We can't simply pause the economy, because capitalism has been structured so that we all depend on its ongoing circulation.

These underlying problems of capital are shouldered by the working class, particularly in times of hardship. In the last few months, the responsibility to keep small businesses and restaurants afloat has demanded that individuals shop online and order takeout. The particularly crafty among us can make masks and personal protective equipment for frontline workers. And, to receive any benefits from the tattered social safety net left by neoliberalism and buoyed from stimulus packages, we must be persistent as systems are overrun with requests. As the market looks more and more grim, personal responsibility, not mutual aid, has filled the gulf left by capitalism.

Neoliberalism has conflated the interests of the government and capitalism so that they are indistinguishable in moments of hardship. Elected leaders acted swiftly based on stock market collapse, and they measure their success based on how markets respond to political action, day by day, hour by hour. Moreover, there are ongoing questions about the divisions between state and capital as allegations of insider trading and a stimulus "slush fund" fill our headlines. Austerity and privatized, for-profit health care are structured on the premise that worthiness among people is based on their market share and productivity. These systems are being stretched to their logical end, making clear what the original stakes have always been, and what kinds of lives are considered worthy, productive, and valuable. The promises of success are individualized, while the comforts of neoliberalism are privatized. The responsibility to uphold societal norms, protection, and mutual aid depend on the strength of nongovernmental networks.

COVID-19 is a particularly capitalist crisis. It was brought to many nations through markets, trade, and a globalized traveling business class. While the flu of 1918 was a wartime pandemic, coronavirus is a capitalist one. Each nation's response has often depended on how quickly and thoroughly countries can halt production and provide relief and basic needs to its citizens and workers. But the United States is "not built for this," as President Trump continues to remind us. We are not built to shutter or halt capital because the lives of the workers depend on low-wage labor that produces, at best, barely enough to live. This pandemic has exposed that most people cannot go a month, or even two weeks, without a paycheck. While this is in some ways devastating, and surprising, given the ongoing concentration and production of wealth, it is also what Marx saw as foundational to capitalism. For wage labor to function, the laboring class must depend on work every day; it is the limit to freedom under capitalism. Many workers are forced to confront this in new ways as their low-paying jobs in the gig economy, at retailers, or in the caring economy force them to reckon with a level of exposure that is increasingly risky. Yet, the options are thus: to be exposed in order to work, or to go without pay. For many, losing a paycheck is worse than the risk of contracting the virus. Marx's double freedom takes a dark turn: one is free to risk their lives at work, or to risk their access to housing and food by not working. To be deemed a nonessential worker is to lose pay, and to be deemed essential is to be at risk.

As news of COVID-19 spread, and before widescale public health measures, including social distancing and shelter-in-place orders, the population was immediately split into those at high risk (immunocompromised, older, and those with existing respiratory illnesses) and those who were potential carriers but not at risk for long-term effects. As knowledge and cases rise hand in hand, these distinctions have become more porous, yet the organizing principle stands. Some bodies are deemed "higher risk" than others and told to act accordingly, while others are told to act with the public's best health interest in mind. For many (particularly in the United States), HIV/AIDS is the most recent cultural and historical touchstone to consider the language and response of a "pandemic." Yet the current pandemic is the first time many people outside targeted populations are being told that their bodies may contain a contagion that can be unknowingly and easily transmitted and can cause others severe harm. Much has also been made about what or who the "Rock Hudson" of COVID-19 is (with answers ranging from the National Basketball Association to Tom Hanks), meaning the person/case that spurs public action and recognition of the severity of the pandemic. These comparisons to HIV illustrate two things: first, there is a limit to care and response in the face of harm to unknown others; and second, COVID-19, much like HIV, exploits preexisting socioeconomic conditions. Under capitalism, economic security is necessary for health.

COVID-19 has differentiated not only the at-risk among the population but also essential from nonessential kinds of medical care. This affects a number of people that require medical care for noncoronavirus conditions, including mental health and trans-related health care. It becomes evident not only what kinds of care are essential, but also who. Again the pandemic exposes already existing conditions and societal values. Not only are there newfound barriers to health care but also disparities in conditions that exacerbate the virus—diabetes, smoking, heart conditions; violence at home; and low-paying jobs that require ongoing labor—that disproportionately affect marginalized people. Thus it is no coincidence that the death rates are unevenly distributed by race and class.

The pandemic, and other instances of disaster, create a moment to foster a critical relationship to the structures of power that limit and demarcate our responses. The cure for the virus does not stand apart from our needs in other times: economic, racial, and environmental justice. The terms of freedom have been manipulated by capital. As Malcolm Harris (2020) writes, "If employees in essential industries had agreed to their job contracts freely, because they were fair deals, then except those with unusual loyalty or love for their work, and barring large raises, all of them would have quit. Their working conditions just got much, much worse, to the point of mortal danger, and yet there haven't been many walkouts or strikes yet." Some workers must work to the point of exposure to a deadly and unknown virus, while the capitalist class structurally withholds systems of care and mutual aid. The working class must exist after the virus, and for that to happen, people must depend on wage labor. Our response must question the underlying assumptions about the terms on which we enter the labor market: free to work, and free of anything but the capacity to work. These conditions will always only make us sick.

Kelly Sharron is lecturer in the Department of Women's, Gender, and Sexuality Studies at California State University, Long Beach. Sharron completed her PhD in gender and women's studies at the University of Arizona in 2019. Her current project, "The Caring State: The Politics of Contradiction in Ferguson, Missouri," considers the multiple state tactics at play in police brutality, including the extension of a feminist ethic of care in producing violent effects.

References

Harris, Malcolm. 2020. "Take Care." *Commune*, April 1. communemag.com/take-care/.

Hartman, Saidiya. 1997. *Scenes of Subjection*. Oxford: Oxford University Press.

Harvey, David. 2014. *Seventeen Contradictions and the End of Capitalism*. Oxford: Oxford University Press.

Klein, Naomi. 2020. "Coronavirus Capitalism—And How to Beat It." *Intercept*, March 16. theintercept.com/2020/03/16/coronavirus-capitalism/.

Liu, Andrew. 2020. "Chinese Virus, World Market." *n+1*, March 20. nplusonemag.com/online-only/online-only/chinese-virus-world-market/.

Marx, Karl. 1977. *Capital*. Vol. 1. New York: Vintage.

A Love Letter to the Future (from the Surgical Team of the Trans Sciences Collective)

HARLAN WEAVER

Abstract "A Love Letter to the Future" speculatively fabulates a future that has undergone a (the?) surgery at the hands of a team of trans scientists. Explicating the how and why of decisions to remove organs of oppression, systems that engender violence, and individual nodules of violence, the letter details the scientists' work in remaking the future into a space and place where trans thrives. The letter also delineates how the trans sciences that unite the collective—experiments in building and reworking the self/body through (re-)mappings of community, ways of being in the world, and networks of care that challenge larger social orders—involve unique temporal and geographical expertise. The letter details how this unique expertise, which emerges through ongoing labors challenging the construction of trans - "modern," identifying the work of quick and slow systemic violences, and mapping community and connectivity well outside understandings that join family with blood with the domestic, led to the collective's nomination for the surgery in the first place. Finally, the letter details processes necessary to the future's recovery and also extends love to this future, the multitudes it contains, and its emergent connectivities between trans and justice.
Keywords trans sciences, speculative fabulation, futurity, temporality, geography

Dear Future,

I'll admit that with the onset of the COVID-19 pandemic, I was worried about the present. We all were: the prognosis was grim, the comorbidities were extensive, and, frankly, it was looking like soon there wouldn't even be a you! No one was quite sure what to do. However, as trans scientists, we are expert in listening to what people tell us about their bodies and needs, and what we heard during our conferences, rounds, and fieldwork enabled us to shift our approach. The tipping point was when we learned that trans-related health care was deemed "nonessential"; this knowledge transmuted our worry, shifting and sharpening it until we were able to grab and hone it into a tool we could wield: rage. Of course, rage was not all we had to work with, for as trans scientists we already worked

TSQ: Transgender Studies Quarterly ∗ Volume 7, Number 4 ∗ November 2020
DOI 10.1215/23289252-8665369 © 2020 Duke University Press

extensively with care, and, fortuitously, care's collectivist strands flourished under the pandemic, making it possible for us to not only use its fibers to stitch you together but also ferment and distill it into the daily doses you have been taking as you heal. I'm guessing you are (understandably!) bewildered by this information. Yet your surgical team deemed it necessary to give you these details, for even as we are confident in your results, your temporal incisions proved particularly challenging, such that we thought it best for you to be aware of what to watch for in the unlikely event that you need a revision. And so I write you this letter, which serves as an explanation of your surgery, an addition to your medical records, and, crucially, an infusion of love to facilitate the absorption of your care doses.

I will begin with our scalpel: rage. When trans-related care was deemed nonessential, it felt to us like a bad joke. I remember thinking: isn't all trans health care supposedly nonessential? I mean, isn't that why most US insurance companies refuse coverage? And then there was the positioning of *trans* and *health care* together; if I were to describe it in the scientific terms you likely expect from us, holding *trans* in proximity to *health care* seemed, then, like trying to hold two magnets with their repelling poles aimed at each other. Put differently, the being of trans in its more formal sense—routed through the state and medico-juridical formations indexed through "transgender" and "transsexual"—happened, then, only through a coerced consent into pathology. Trans people had to agree to be diseased, dis-eased really, if we wanted or needed formal recognition; crucially, this was a recognition that we, in many ways, could "not not want" if we desired, even in a small way, to thrive (Spivak 1994: 278).[1] And then there was the nigh necessity of having to use a system to craft ourselves that was fundamentally structured to deny our existence—virtually no doctor's office even had entries other than *m/f* on their intake forms! Further, the landmark achievements of this system had been to contain our existence through a past and present of deeply racialized and colonialist abuse and trauma, with some sprinklings of exceedingly normative gains.[2] The pandemic's arrival made us recognize that such a system hardly merited the descriptor *health care*; galvanized, we transmuted our fear into a knife we wielded with and through transformative fury.

The linkage between *trans* and *nonessential* was, of course, a key facet of your surgery, and given our reconstructive work in excising that *non-*, you are undoubtedly confused by my last paragraph. Let me explain. The present's joining of *trans*, *nonessential*, and *health care* rested on what we trans scientists term disavowal; trans was in fact essential, but it was denied. *Trans*, and more specifically *transgender* and *transsexual*, were critical to the present and past's stabilization of a white-normative male/female binary rooted in Western and northern settler-colonial, imperial, and anti-Black discourses that had been promulgated the world over through LGBTQ* activisms.[3] In addition, those activisms, which served only the most normative trans and queer subjects, frequently engaged in a necropolitics—for example, arguing for increases in and expansions of hate crime laws—made possible through the appropriation of the deaths of mostly transfeminine people of color, many of whom came to be regarded as trans in the first place through such politics (Snorton and Haritaworn 2013; Lamble 2008). Indeed, on the subject of politics, *trans* was essential as a stand-in for the deviance formerly allocated to queer in its most pejorative sense. The fact that the governor of the US state of Idaho signed two antitrans bills into law the very week that the pandemic was anticipated to enter its initial peak in the United States reveals this labor; *trans* acted as a locus of deviance crucial to the bait and switch of public attention away from literal cum moral failures of governance. Finally, there was all that fucking queer theory in which trans bodies, but very rarely trans voices or lives, provided the basis for transcendental (but, really, let's call it trans-incidental) claims about what gender and sex supposedly really are. *Trans* was undeniably essential, but as a figuration and absent presence whose denial was vital to the work of destructively normative systems that ravaged the present and past. And so a key element of your surgery was the excision of *trans* and our cultivation of it into the new cell lines whose vitality sustains key elements of your being now.

Of course, the systems that relied on and disavowed *trans* extended well beyond the above concerns, for the production of gender and sexuality as white-normative, "modern," and discrete entities that yielded *trans* as both distinct from homosexual and disavowable was central to an array of structures whose extensive interweavings the pandemic laid bare. Indeed, we had long sought to identify and remove nodules of what are called structural violences—violences caused by systems that rendered some more than others vulnerable to the predation of disease, as with the transnational colonialist and anti-Black forces weighted with the history of slavery that made people in Haiti susceptible to a range of epidemics (Farmer et al. 2006). And when the pandemic made some but not others not only dead but disposable, we were able to identify, at great cost, the reach of those nodules and their interrelations by tracing the violences of those murders, often couched in language such as "preexisting conditions," back to the connective tissues among the structures (spanning the past and present!) that created them. And, fortuitously, as we carefully excised those nodes, we ruptured the hierarchical orderings of their interconnections, allowing us to extract the logics that incubated them through various organs of oppression. Indeed, being able to identify and remove those organs was a highlight of your surgery for us! For your medical records, I do want to note that in removing those nodules, logics, and organs, we were also able to cut out some structures entirely, such as capitalism. However, we left some structures in place, such as race, in the hopes that our careful sutures might facilitate the formation of new tissues through which alternate logics might flourish.

With regard to your connective tissues, I want to draw your attention to your temporal scars in particular. To begin, the pandemic quickened what had been slow violences. Years, rather than weeks, of food insecurity entwined with systemic racisms, including those endemic to medicine, augmented and hastened the labor of the structures and violences the virus exposed. Further, the ecological devastation wrought by the systems we extracted—that which is most commonly referenced through the terminology of slow violence—bears mentioning here, for the very peoples whose lives were most at risk from the destructions of capitalist global climate change were among those most likely to be killed and maimed by COVID-19. In this regard, our labors in cutting out and removing systems and nodules of violence entailed a reworking of your temporality. However, our work extended beyond these extractive measures into a larger temporal reconstruction. This is because, put simply, the pandemic intensified what can be described as colonial time, which operated by consigning to the past the violent machinations of colonization, even as, for example, transnational capitalist formations deprived wildlife of habitats and organized the deliberate killing of indigenous leaders seeking to protect the earth. Notably, this intensification retrenched the norms of your gender systems in marking as deviant and less-than-"modern" many non-white, non-Western/northern, and non-Anglo doings of gender and sexuality. In this regard, our temporal work diverged from simple removal, for we not only carefully cut out such norms as organs of oppression but also stitched the holes they left so that they would scar into apertures of accountability, through which we wove new bands of recognition and continuity that now thread the past into you. We need you to carefully monitor these scars and weavings, and if you encounter any problems in using the dilators we provided to maintain these apertures, please call us right away!

Of course, we were by no means the only members of your surgical team, but as you have probably guessed, it was our expertise with temporality that led to our selection. As Jacob Lau (2016: 2) brilliantly notes, the more normative time in which many of us are made to live is a cisnormative or "cis time," one that "presumes a kind of linear coherence to and with white supremacist capitalist heteropatriarchy's super-structures in order for the trans (and particularly the trans-of-color) subject to be understood as a coherent, not-impossible subject." For Lau, such a time contrasts with "trans temporality," a time that exists "within and beside" cis time, one that "understands trans embodiment, narratives, and livability as possible branching alternative temporalities to state bio- and necropolitical practices" (2). Lau's trans temporality will, I hope, give you a good understanding of why we were chosen to be part of your surgical team, for as trans people invested in identifying how gender and sexuality operate as colonial and racial projects—thinking that emerges in and through trans-of-color critiques such as Lau's—we were uniquely attuned to a different time than that of the present, which allowed us to suture together the alternate connectivities that now shape you.

I should note that, while we were recruited for our temporal knowledge, our geographical skills were also central to your operation. As I know you remember (because of your apertures of accountability!), mappings of self and other were transformed (or, perhaps, trans-formed?) the world over through the pandemic. Concepts that had rested on claims to blood—both metaphorical and literal—such as family, kinship, and the nation, came undone. Indeed, the very idea of the domestic as a space where only family might reside and through which ties to the nation become articulated was upended (see, e.g., Berlant and Warner 1998). I know this may seem counterintuitive, given that the pandemic seemingly cemented the domestic as a space of refuge, but I encourage you to rethink this. Put plainly, rather than reifying blood/family/the domestic as forms of proximity, the pandemic brought into relief intimacies crafted through distance, including air. Further, the affective labor supposedly contained in the concatenation of family/blood/the domestic shifted loci entirely, such that care, for example, came to be expressed not through the space of "home" but rather through practices extended both at a distance and toward imagined others whom the carer(s)— both individual and collective—often would never come to meet. Such mappings and concomitant ways of knowing are central to our work as trans scientists, which, in conjunction with our temporal expertise, made us such critical members of your surgical team.

In naming our work as trans scientists, I want to highlight our positioning in the larger field of what we term trans sciences. With trans sciences we index the many ways that trans folks—in experimenting with, building, and reworking senses of self; mappings of community, networks of care, ways of moving and being in and through the world; and challenges to larger social orders—engage in sciences that are unique to the claiming, being, defining, and doing of trans. For some, trans sciences may look like the repeated experiments undertaken in attempts at passing, efforts to reduce friction in a social order that wishes us harm and even death. For others, trans sciences are those repeated experiments that aim to increase certain worldly frictions and even augment the pleasure they give, projects that can also be described as deliberative deviances or, perhaps more loosely, rage-filled fuck-you's that emerge in reworkings of bodies/selves as they interface with the social. Crucially, trans sciences exist and have always existed, much like Lau's trans temporality, alongside, within, outside, and even counter to medical and medico-juridical renderings. For example, even as we consult medical doctors and proffer particular narratives in an effort to obtain access to hormones, questions about what to expect from their use in terms of bodily and affective changes are almost always directed at other trans folks in a range of spaces and mappings of intimacies, many of which work through not proximity but distance. Further, trans sciences are by no means delimited to what might be considered more technically as medical, for trans sciences encompass practices of sharing hormones and other injectable materials, getting advice from trans elders, finding and befriending knowledgeable strangers through the internet and friends of friends, contributing knowledge and sometimes capital to others' journeys, and learning to understand what trans means on an individual level through an array of practices and doings that form intimacies through distance. In this sense, COVID-19's remapping of relationality extended mappings of sociality with which we trans scientists were intimately familiar, such that we were uniquely positioned to help you become differently than the present had planned.

In closing, I want to note while this letter has served as an explanation of how and why we were chosen to perform your surgery, along with the provision of certain medical details that I hope clarify the ways we chose to reshape you, it has also been a means to convey love. Indeed, writing on behalf of your surgical team, I hope you will come to see how we have made you, the future, beautiful. You are a gift, and I hope that you will come to appreciate how our rage-sharpened scalpels' removal of specific systems, nodes, and organs made room for the implantation of cultures that only we could grow, such that your structure of gender, for example, now vibrates with trans at its core, reconnected with systems such as sexuality that have been deracinated of connections with colonialism and white-normative racialization, which in turn can now be located only through your (hopefully well-dilated!) apertures of accountability. You contain multitudes, as you always have, but only now are those multitudes positioned to collectively thrive. And, of course, as trans scientists, we are particularly delighted to see the transformations (trans-formations?) in your politics of health and the ways that our care-ful stitches have scarred into permanent joins between health and justice. We love the new you, and we look forward to seeing you flourish!

Sincerely,

Dr. Futurestein, on behalf of the Trans Sciences Collective

Harlan Weaver is associate professor of gender, women, and sexuality studies at Kansas State University. Their book, *Bad Dog: Pit Bull Politics and Multispecies Justice*, is forthcoming.

Notes

1. Here I am also in conversation with Toby Beauchamp's *Going Stealth* (2019).
2. Jules Gill-Peterson's *Histories of the Transgender Child* (2018) and Amanda Lock-Swarr's *Sex in Transition* (2012) are some standouts in related literatures.

3.   See Towle and Morgan 2006 and Yv Nay's wonderful "The Atmosphere of Trans* Politics in the Global North and West" (2019). Notably, these discourses are uneven and can and do often work alongside other renderings of self in relation to gender and sexuality, as Fadi Saleh's wonderful "Transgender as a Humanitarian Category: The Case of Syrian Queer and Gender-Variant Refugees in Turkey" (2020) demonstrates.

References

Beauchamp, Toby. 2019. *Going Stealth*. Durham, NC: Duke University Press.

Berlant, Lauren, and Michael Warner. 1998. "Sex in Public." *Critical Inquiry* 24, no. 2: 547–66.

Farmer, Paul, Bruce Nizeye, Sara Stulac, and Salmaan Keshavjee. 2006. "Structural Violence and Clinical Medicine." *PLoS Medicine* 3, no. 10: 1686–91.

Gill-Peterson, Jules. 2018. *Histories of the Transgender Child*. Minneapolis: Minnesota University Press.

Lamble, Sarah. 2008. "Retelling Racialized Violence, Remaking White Innocence: The Politics of Interlocking Oppressions in Transgender Day of Remembrance." *Sexuality Research and Social Policy* 5, no. 24: 24–42.

Lau, Jacob Roberts. 2016. "Between the Times: Trans-Temporality and Historical Representation." PhD diss., University of California, Los Angeles.

Lock-Swarr, Amanda. 2012. *Sex in Transition: Remaking Gender and Race in South Africa*. New York: State University of New York Press.

Nay, Yv. 2019. "The Atmosphere of Trans* Politics in the Global North and West." *TSQ* 6, no. 1: 64–69.

Saleh, Fadi. 2020. "Transgender as a Humanitarian Category: The Case of Syrian Queer and Gender-Variant Refugees in Turkey." *TSQ* 7, no. 1: 37–55.

Snorton, C. Riley, and Jin Haritaworn. 2013. "Trans Necropolitics: A Transnational Reflection on Violence, Death, and the Trans of Color Afterlife." In *The Transgender Studies Reader 2*, edited by Susan Stryker and Aren Aizura, 66–76. New York: Routledge.

Spivak, Gayatri. 1994. "Bonding in Difference." In *An Other Tongue: Nation and Ethnicity in the Linguistic Borderlands*, edited by Alfred Arteaga, 273–86. Durham, NC: Duke University Press.

Towle, Evan B., and Lynn M. Morgan. 2006. "Romancing the Transgender Native." In *The Transgender Studies Reader*, edited by Susan Stryker, 666–68. New York: Routledge.

Turning toward Pedagogy in a Crisis

JULIE BEAULIEU

Abstract This essay considers the complex emotions of COVID-19 and the different horizons of expectation that are a by-product of US structural inequality. It also considers the experience of teaching in a pandemic, the labor of teaching, and the politics of survivor's guilt.
Keywords emotion, class, pedagogy, survivor's guilt

As I write this, I can hear the sound of concrete being tossed into a construction dumpster. Living in a gentrifying neighborhood means living with the sound of constant development. I have to tune it out. I am intensely aware of the privilege of this, the choice and ability to tune out a dull, constant sound, my attempt to prevent it from acting on me, the privilege to temporarily forget what it means. This privilege does not bring guilt, this tuning out or turning away, not nearly as much as it should; the sound of development is also the sound of removal, a forcing out. I know that as I am turning away from the sound of displacement, others are tuning out sirens in COVID-19 hot spots, and there are others that do not have the choice to tune anything out. In choosing to turn away, with or without guilt, we might convince ourselves that we can, in fact, prevent something from acting on us. In so doing, we have inhibited our capacity to apprehend the ways something *is* acting on us, no matter our ability to turn away. This misapprehension—the belief that we can turn away and survive untouched—precludes us from seeing ourselves as part of a collective, a belongingness forged out of enduring and surviving. This is a critical loss, this thwarted belongingness. *They* survived COVID-19. *They* survived HIV. *They* survived a trans childhood. What happens when we are convinced that something is not really happening to us? We might not know how to feel.

Scholars in gender and sexuality studies have turned to emotion to stress how affect directs us toward and away from objects, to document how public cultures are forged from collective, nonnormative feelings, and to theorize our attachments to particular lives and values. Affect is tied to precarity, insecurity, and contingency in ways that directly impact our feelings, but our individual expectations can shape our experience of insecurity and, by extension, our identification or disidentification with a socioeconomic class. More directly, you might not feel insecure if you never expected to be where you are today, and you might not feel like a member of the gentrifying class if you still spend most days surprised that you own a home. You can "make it" in the eyes of your people, but others might remind you that you deserve more. Like other sensibilities, socioeconomic class creates a set of normative feelings and a horizon of expectations that structure our sense of entitlement and, more generally, our sense of "making it" or "surviving."

Class-escape stories are central to navigating the complex affects of so-called social mobility and our responses to collective trauma. The queerly classed, like the queerly gendered, might find familiar feelings in a text, as I did when I first read Allan Bérubé's (1996) powerful consideration of how class shapes not only our desires but also our sense of home in "Intellectual Desire." Bérubé writes: "Class escape stories tell what happens when you get out of the class you grew up in and enter one of higher status. They reveal unresolved conflicts about what you have lost and gained. They expose the anguish of leaving a home you can't return to while not belonging where you've ended up" (140). In "Queers Read What Now?" Martin Joseph Ponce (2018: 317) writes, "Gay and lesbian readers frequently attest to the pivotal role that reading for representations of same-sex desire has played in facilitating sexual self-understanding and alleviating a sense of isolation." However, Ponce continues, queer and trans people of color "often remark on the absence or scarcity of representation, thus implying that the canonical traditions remain inadequate, if not hostile, to their needs" (320). For white scholars, racial privilege creates a similar horizon of expectation such that one might consider themselves "represented" even if the existing archive is far from representative.

I offer these speculations to make some intimate links between precarity and positionality, and to explore the impact of normative feelings in a time of crisis. We might be most familiar with the subject that turns away to neglect, or to avoid, the kind of person that uses the classic us/them dualism in an attempt to minimize violence against and/or the death of others (as an example, and one that deserves much more than this parenthetical, the "only them" rhetoric of early HIV public health—only gay men, only IV drug users, only people of color, only sex workers). We might be familiar, in other words, with those who turn away because they think they have something to gain or nothing to lose. I turn instead to different subjects, those who might identify and disidentify with both surviving and suffering. We might simplify this as being in limbo, unable to see the self as surviving or suffering, and at times haunted (presumably inadvertently, but certainly not always) by the many very certain subjects that walk among us, whose knowingness about the self does not produce doubt in others' self-perception (well, certainly sometimes it does) so much as it causes a deepening feeling of indeterminacy for those not-so-sure subjects, those who cannot say for sure what they are or are not enduring. (Another example that deserves more than a note in passing: the tyranny of "trans enough" politics, which suspends many trans folks in a similar space.)

When in limbo it might feel like surviving and suffering are always on the horizon, but also, being in limbo—characterized here as having a mixed-class sensibility, a trans identity that gets more-or-less trans depending on the decade, or being a homeowner with a traumatic relationship to home—might make it impossible to know where we stand as subjects of a collective feeling and history. Held outside because there is a "real" subject that rightfully belongs there, we might not even be able to see the self as experiencing something (a pandemic, trans violence, traumas of our past, exploitation) merely because we have, or we imagine that we have, fared better or differently. This is often the case, but in a global pandemic we might be more likely to experience this, more likely to turn away from the impacts on the self, and not only in the spirit of self-care, but out of an ethical obligation—particularly, if it is not really happening to us, not in the way we imagine or know it is happening to others (if it is not yet as bad as it could be). This survivor's guilt speaks directly to horizons of expectation; we presume we will survive, so it feels unethical to consider how we might suffer. To further complicate the affect of indeterminacy, some of us have a real problem with the real.

This might be a feeling familiar to those who cannot say if they are surviving or suffering academic labor—perhaps most notably, the middling sort. Such indeterminacy is predictably shaped by expectation and entitlement. For those of us who never expected to be here in the university (like those who never expected to be homeowners, who might surely appear grossly apologist about their position in the system of gentrification), a steadfast sense of amazement about the privilege to do academic work in queer and trans studies (not to mention, to be working and relatively safe now in that labor) can undermine the capacity to take in collective affects and politics around labor issues. Even further, survivor's guilt can ensure a steady stream of gratitude from above, but also persistent apologies for and public grievances over differences in structural support, which can sometimes make the work less bearable, however vital these interventions are. Work that feels "good enough" and often deeply meaningful can transform into exploited labor in these encounters. If the only appropriate response to praise with apology is to reassure those with survivor's guilt that you do, in fact, have an excellent job, these encounters create new forms of affective labor, structured by the needs of those with security. It is very likely, under all these conditions, that one might not really know how to feel about labor, or whether to turn toward it, or turn away from it.

Such feelings are heightened now, since COVID-19 contingency plans and the move to online teaching came with ethical calls to fail fabulously at online teaching, to set the bar low—something we might intentionally or unintentionally do. Public feelings about productivity in the wake of COVID-19 have predominantly included calls to be of use or to redefine use. We are also reminded to take the labor of online teaching seriously, to downplay any ease we might find, and to recognize research and practice in online pedagogy. COVID-19 contingency has also raised key questions about accessibility policies that exclude students with disabilities. The debate over whether we should show our students our "true selves" in a time of crisis applies a range of speculative theories about fostering resiliency, creating a fascinating archive of what we think our students need.

Demands to turn away seem to forget the reality of contingent labor and our students. Most of us want to be of use to our students. For historically minoritized teachers, who might also expect teaching and service to feel reparative, the question of what students need and being of use cannot be neatly separated from our histories, our desires, or our sense of value. The opening questions in this inquiry, however, raise different questions about teaching. What would it mean to teach students about topics as though they are happening to all of us? How can we hold onto an ethics of intersectional analysis without perpetuating a diminished capacity to understand the broader loss or impact of historical violence? In *The Gentrification of the Mind: Witness to a Lost Imagination*, Sarah Schulman (2013: 14) makes connections between "literal gentrification" and "a diminished consciousness" to create a broader framework for understanding "the unexplored consequences of AIDS." What are the consequences of a lost imagination? This is the question that invites us to turn toward, to see ourselves as subjects of events, as people who have also lost something, even when, or especially when, we cannot yet articulate or imagine that loss.

Julie Beaulieu is lecturer in the Gender, Sexuality, and Women's Studies Program at the University of Pittsburgh, with a research and teaching focus in LGBTQ studies and the history of sexuality.

References

Bérubé, Allan. 1996. "Intellectual Desire." *GLQ* 3, no. 1: 139–57.

Ponce, Martin Joseph. 2018. "Queers Read What Now?" *GLQ* 24, nos. 2–3: 315–41.

Schulman, Sarah. 2013. *The Gentrification of the Mind: Witness to a Lost Imagination*. Berkeley: University of California Press.

"I've Never Seen You When You Weren't Pregnant"

Trans Reproductivity against AIDS

NICHOLAS C. MORGAN

Abstract This essay posits in Vaginal Davis's 1987 video *That Fertile Feeling* a strategy of resistance to HIV/AIDS rooted in the dynamic of transfeminine pregnancy and fertility, arguing that Davis develops a range of aesthetic strategies for undermining, inverting, and appropriating mainstream discourses of reproduction as they intersect with legal strictures and cultural scripts around normative understandings of embodiment, health, and the notion of morality embedded in the period's dominant set of "family values." AIDS is not, on the surface of things, a central referent in *That Fertile Feeling*, but the author shows how precisely this submerged status of the crisis as a signifier in the video allows Davis to visualize a broad biopolitical field and situate the epidemic within that field to address the interrelated, mutually supporting injustices perpetuated at its peak in Los Angeles. The figure of the excessively fertile trans woman emerges as useful for theorizing this oblique yet radiant approach to developing a coalitional ethos to confront both the politics around the AIDS crisis in LA at the time and its material and psychic impact.
Keywords Vaginal Davis, *That Fertile Feeling*, AIDS

The 1987 video *That Fertile Feeling* opens with Vaginal Davis, doyenne of Los Angeles's artistic underground, reading and watching TV alongside her friend, Fertile LaToyah Jackson. Suddenly, Fertile's water breaks and, after a desperate drive to a hospital where they are turned away for lack of health insurance, the two make their way to Fertile's boyfriend's apartment. There, Davis delivers Fertile's eleven new children before Fertile speeds away via skateboard, leaving Davis to care for the many newborns. That all this plays out in under ten minutes—accompanied, at times, by an infectious disco beat—speaks to the video's intensely heightened and comedic affect.

Though Davis looms large in accounts of trans artistic practice since the 1980s, and though she was close with a number of HIV+ artists such as Ron Athey (who was falsely said to have thrown buckets of his blood at spectators in a live

TSQ: Transgender Studies Quarterly ★ Volume 7, Number 4 ★ November 2020
DOI 10.1215/23289252-8665411 © 2020 Duke University Press

performance at the Walker Art Center in 1994, igniting one of many battles in the culture wars), her work has not been much discussed in relation to AIDS—perhaps because it rarely thematizes the crisis directly. But in *That Fertile Feeling*, AIDS—especially as it intersects with trans, Black, and Latinx life—shows up in subtle, sometimes barely perceptible ways. To register its presence requires reading between the lines. This nonsensationalist, even submerged mode of engaging AIDS offers a useful opening onto the problem of visibility in relation to the epidemic. Representing AIDS only latently, the tape produces a space in which subjects excluded from mainstream (and even most subcultural) narratives of the epidemic could formulate alternative political strategies for addressing its practical, psychic, and bodily impacts. In this sense, Davis departs from theorizations of AIDS art that emphasize the ways that virality can be appropriated as an aesthetic strategy and turned against the epidemic (e.g., Bordowitz 2010: 65), proposing insemination more than infection, and impregnation rather than contamination. Engaging AIDS as a labile, mobile signifier was a viable strategy (and remains so) for dismantling its totalizing association with white gay men, and for instead limning a broader biopolitical field within which, the tape insists, the crisis must be understood. This field includes HIV/AIDS as well as inequitable distribution of health-care access, reproductive rights, and racist discourses around reproduction. Asking us to read between the lines, Davis proposes AIDS as an object that can be read only between the lines, as something occurring between, in, and around plastic bodies whose borders it violated and whose boundaries it was also used to secure. Instead of foregrounding virality or dramatizing the epidemic, it presents an alternative mode of propagation: the mutable fertility of the pregnant trans woman.

Cyrus Grace Dunham (2015) suggests several possible readings of *That Fertile Feeling*:

> Fertile's delivery is an ambiguous miracle: both because of the large quantity of babies, and how Davis and Fertile perform an uncertain womanhood. Are they mocking the fact that they have bodies that may not be able to give birth . . . ? Or are they mocking a cultural fixation on pregnancy as the marker of womanhood? Either way, the two artists parody an entire epoch of divine births. Maybe Mary was a virgin; just as possible, perhaps, is that she was trans.

The video gives ample evidence for both satires. However, the nearly instantaneous ontogenesis of Fertile's newborns is not quite the product of an immaculate conception: in the opening scene, as Fertile and Davis sit on a couch in front of a television, Davis channel flips, eventually stumbling on a "porno movie" she "loves." Fertile, playing coy, protests that she doesn't want to watch porn, asking why such an explicit video is even on television. Davis replies that it is a VHS cassette. Fertile quickly fesses up to "maybe" wanting to actually watch the tape, and as they bicker the two clap and undulate on the couch, drawing attention to the deeply embodied responses that, as Linda Williams (1989) notes, porn is, like horror film, designed to elicit. A problem, Davis tells Fertile, is that "I know you like seeing those big penises but if you get too close to one you wind up pregnant." And indeed, a few beats later, Fertile's water breaks. The tape thus relays a concept of impregnation through representation. Watching porn hasn't turned Davis into a pervert or made her palms hairy, lending the tape a sex-positive vibe. But the notion that erotic imagery has literally impregnated Fertile nevertheless suggests a satiric proximity to the conservative notion of representation (porn, especially, but really any images of nonnormative bodies) as materially infectious, a hallmark of the AIDS-phobic discourses operative in the late 1980s (Watney 1987). Here, it is coupled with a satire of the fin de siècle pathology of female hysteria, evoked when the two share an extended convulsive reaction to the tape, clapping and writhing.

In this scene, the rise of pornography viewable in private domestic settings situates the viewer in relation to Reagan-era neoliberalism. Davis tells Fertile, "You're a rich Black girl honey, now you can afford to have a VCR." The video also cites the 1970s: Davis is reading *Vaginal Politics* by Ellen Frankfort (1972), a volume advising women to seize control over information about their bodies, assume an agential role in interactions with medical institutions, and question the illusion of scientific objectivity central to their doctors' authority. The chapter Davis is reading—shortly before the water breaks, she paraphrases it to Fertile—focuses on Bionx, a little-known male birth control technology undergoing clinical trials at the time, in which a small valve would block the sperm duct (47–54). Technological interventions into the body are central to Frankfort's book in a way that complicates its otherwise straightforward relationship to second-wave feminism, as when another chapter focuses on menstrual extraction devices (homemade apparatuses ostensibly meant to extract menstrual fluid but which actually induced abortions, sidestepping legal barriers). *Vaginal Politics* frames the body as something that can be intervened in and on through technological modifications. Porn, and the VCR allowing for home viewing of erotica, are other such technologies operating on the body. Meanwhile, Fertile flips through *Brides' Book* magazine, suggesting her immersion in a comparatively normative world of monogamous heterosexuality, echoed by her initial aversion to porn.

After Fertile's water breaks, Davis drives her to the hospital, but as the car careens and veers, she confesses she does not know how to drive because she never took driver's education. While in the first scene Davis refers to Fertile as a "rich Black girl," when they arrive at a hospital Fertile is turned away for lack of health insurance. In an establishing shot, the Clinica de Las Americas is obviously closed, with security bars over its door and blind-covered windows, visualizing how Fertile and Davis are cut off from medical care, even from what looks like a small, community-focused clinic. That structural imbalances in health insurance subtended the epidemic's spread was one of AIDS activism's crucial insights. Universal health care was the goal of a contingent of ACT UP members who, from the outset, looked beyond the immediate project of getting drugs into bodies and concentrated on "issues related to racism, sexism and poverty" (Gould 2009: 353). Davis uses screwball comedy to draw attention to the ways these inequities impact Black and Latinx trans subjects in particular. Health care was a central concern for ACT UP/LA, founded in late 1987 (the same year Davis's tape was made), with early actions focused on demanding a dedicated AIDS ward at the LA County+USC Medical Center. The group protested at the hospital in 1988 and mounted a weeklong vigil there (staging a theatricalized ward just outside its entrance) in 1989. According to Benita Roth (2017: 101–2), the organization was internally fractured from the start by a perceived divide between its lesbian and feminist members and its male cohort. Less visible to its core membership was the way it overlooked the concerns of people of color. Trans folk evidently had little visibility within the group, with the significant exception of Connie Norman, who participated in a number of actions, was a prominent member of the group's Women's Caucus, and hosted radio and television programs and staged theatrical performances (81). Preferring the moniker "AIDS Diva" to a more official title as activist or organizer, Norman employed a strategy similar to Davis's in its embrace of the dramatic and pop culture as tools for combatting AIDS.

After they are spurned by the medical establishment, Davis and Fertile make their way to Fertile's boyfriend's apartment. Called only "Nude Husband" or "Nude Boyfriend," the man greets them in an apron-like toga that leaves his buttocks exposed. He tidies the apartment as Fertile prepares to give birth, wielding a feather duster that codes him as a gay stand-in for a traditional housewife; his sedate performance of male femininity contrasts with the vibrant presence of the two gender-nonconforming heroines. As Davis urges Fertile to push, he does push-ups, now wearing a little white thong, occasionally glancing over between reps. Utterly passive in the face of a medical crisis, Nude Boyfriend functions largely as an object of aesthetic appreciation, and it is hard not to think of him as a stand-in for the white, gay male bodies routinely presented by the mainstream media, but also by many artists and writers (and ACT UP/LA's leadership), as the exclusive bearers of HIV/AIDS. His lack of affect contrasts sharply with the vivid animation characterizing Fertile and Davis, an opposition that points to how what Sianne Ngai (2005: chap. 2) describes as rhetorics of the excessive animatedness of people of color are deployed in official HIV/AIDS narratives, and also how those narratives occlude gender plasticity.

As Fertile gives birth, we do not see her offspring; the frame lingers on her contorted face, framed against a window opening onto the bright LA light, the cheap camcorder's autoexposure pulsating between blowing out Fertile and underexposing her face in favor of the exterior street, echoing her contractions and lending the tape an embodied-feeling, homemade aesthetic. After the first two babies, Davis exclaims, "Oh my god, there's more in there!" But the shock value of Fertility's extreme fertility diminishes after the fourth or fifth baby, and Davis's tone shifts from pseudo-hysteria to disinterest. Finally, she announces, "Fertile, you have eleven-tuplets!" As Dunham points out, this exaggerated performance of childbearing and the overloaded quality of Fertile's fertility parody the cultural script that Frankfort (1972: xxxiv) described as the way "women have been taught to equate their whole sense of self with childbearing." Fertile banalizes reproduction by repeating it ad nauseum. Davis undermines the scientific scripts undergirding the normative logic linking pregnancy and womanhood with her word choice, foregoing proper Latin nomenclature for the simpler "eleven-tuplets." And she assumes the role of an amateur but effective, perhaps self-trained midwife, evoking (especially given her namesake, Angela Davis) the community-based health clinics established by the Black Panthers from the late 1960s (Nelson 2013: 183–84). A homegrown, nonscientistic form of health care is being pictured. The particular oppositional stakes of this alternative modality of reproductive institutions are clarified by Fertile's impossible superabundance: she is said to already have twelve children, and so by tape's end has twenty-three; she also abandons her offspring, becoming an absent mother. Clearly, then, one local target of the tape's satire is the discourse of the "welfare queen" trumpeted by the conservative right throughout the 1980s, a discourse drawing on long-standing stereotypes to present women of color as irresponsible drains on public resources, rooted in a racist troping of their inherently excessive sexuality (Davis 2009). In the tape, excess surfaces not only in Fertile's fertility but also in the superabundance of affect in Davis's and Fertile's performances: the video's emotional valences are as "fertile" as the character.

That Fertile Feeling raises the notion of excessiveness inherent in welfare queen discourse to an all-permeating aesthetic principle in a way that reveals the underlying absurdity of that rhetoric. That the escalation of welfare queen rhetoric coincided with the rise of phobias brought to light amidst the AIDS epidemic was not coincidental: as Melinda Cooper (2017: chap. 5) argues, 1980s neoliberalism's emphasis on the family precipitated a rise in acceptance of nontraditional family configurations (culminating in the legalization of gay marriage), but only on the condition that those families be self-sustaining and with the proviso that the medical coverage they were able to purchase for themselves would cover morally acceptable conditions alone. The single mother operating outside a sta-bilized nuclear dynamic, as well as the HIV+ (whose serostatus was attributed to moral failure), not to mention trans folk in need of hormones or surgeries that insurance providers refused to cover, were equally marginalized by neoliberal-ism's prioritization of the economically autonomous family unit. In this light, the lyrics to one of the catchiest songs by Davis's contemporaneous band Cholita! (of which Fertile was also a member) read as a striking repudiation of normative notions of lines of descent and familial pride: "I hate your mother, your father, your sister, your brother / I hate your fuckin' family tree."

Is the absurdity of Fertile's "eleven-tuplets" lessened by the emergence, in the decades following, of figures such as Nadya Suleman, known as "Octomom," who in 2009 delivered eight babies at once? The obsessive media coverage of Suleman reflected anxieties around the technological capabilities and potential missuses of assisted reproductive technology (ART)—and, implicitly, around technologically mediated forms of reproduction opposed to the classic humanist notion of an uncorrupted, authentic body. As Suleman's case demonstrates, ART was celebrated when linked with white, heteronormative fertility and demonized when connected with the reproduction of women of color and/or economically disadvantaged mothers, perpetuating the welfare queen discourse (Davis 2009). For Mel Y. Chen (2012: 134–35) Suleman is an ambivalent figure of the "monstrous humanimal," at once materializing the possibilities of the body's extensive capacity for change, animation, and stretching and on the other hand exacer-bating the cultural obsession with reproduction.

The nonnormative quality of Fertile's motherhood partly stems from the fact that she rejects the nuclear family paradigm, but also from the plasticity of her body and the indeterminate way she figures her gender. If the tape uncannily anticipates "Octomom," this is because the intertwined discourses it satirizes— including cisgender-oriented health care, the fear of plastic or animated bodies, and the discourse of the welfare queen—remained largely intact in 2009. Weaving this and other threads—Nude Boyfriend's whiteness, inaccessible health care, a prehistory of Black and, later, LGBT alternative medical networks—together into one plot that centers trans bodies of color, the tape predicts the coalitional approach Cathy Cohen (1997) advocated in her influential article of ten years later, an approach that understands the struggles of women of color, LGBT folk, and the seropositive as shared. In light of Cooper's argument, Davis's coalitional ethos should be understood as imagining a different kind of family dynamic, and a different relationship to reproduction, amidst the crisis. It does so by fore-grounding the bodies of those subjects most overlooked during the epidemic (and in the histories of its art), skewering the discourses central to maintaining that invisibility while imagining their own reproductive capabilities. The overloaded mathematics of Fertile's motherhood (eleven plus twelve), for example, subverts the algorithmic logic—one that posits ends and means and calculates outcomes according to quantifiable decision-making processes—organizing pro- and antireproduction arguments alike, from pro-choice debates to queer anti-futurist positions (Deutscher 2017: chap. 2). The tape moves instead in favor of a more anarchic, undetermined relation to a future—one particularly apt for combatting the AIDS crisis's impacts.

The plasticity and animatedness at play in *That Fertile Feeling* sends up racializing tropes while also suggesting revisions of and resistances to dominant understandings of materiality and embodiment. That Fertile's newborns (which the viewer never sees) "look like puppies," as Davis announces, is important: far from the monstrous, here animality is figured through an aesthetic of cuteness that levels the adorability of the animal and that of the child. Hallmark gone haywire, this comic vision frames the body as something animal yet endearing. The tape severs any presumed connection inhering between reproductive organs, gender, and reproductive agency, a point brought home by one shot in this scene, when Fertile asks "sure there's no more?" and the camera tracks up and toward her skirt, revealing that she is still fully clad in many layers of clothing. *That Fertile Feeling* embraces a plastic and flexible notion of embodiment, one in which reproduction is not so much elided as differently imagined, fusing two of the trans representational strategies Jack Halberstam (2018: 96) posits: "the representation of the body as inherently unstable and contradictory" and "the representation of the body as an absurd site that eludes linguistic and visual codes." That is, Davis melds the rhetorical register of Frankfort's proto-cyborgian polemic with a lowbrow register, suggested by *Bride's Book*, that embraces some aspects of normative gender. Her tape insistently imagines the trans woman's ability to reproduce in a biologically normative way, even as it undermines the cultural scripts that place such an emphasis on that ability to reproduce by ridiculing the cultural obsession with fertility.

In keeping with Davis's dedramatized approach, the specter of the "AIDS baby" feels distant. Instead, the tape represents a future forged through non–biologically determined reproduction. Davis was not alone in envisioning alternative modes of reproduction as a tactic for trans artistic intervention into the AIDS epidemic: Greer Lankton, for example, often posed for photographs cradling her sculptural dolls as one would an infant. The lighthearted aesthetic of Chloe Dzubilo's drawings, which encode a range of trans strategies for living with HIV and for caregiving, could also be productively compared with Davis's approach. But what is so striking in *That Fertile Feeling* is the way in which the materiality of the offspring remains in flux, not determining of its status or import, much as their mother's reproductive organs are a bracketed nonissue. Robustly envisioning precisely the sort of future neoliberal family values would ban from its utopic imaginary—one in which trans women give birth on a massive scale—the tape ends with the pleasurable tautology of Fertile's loop de loops as she flees by skateboard. Rather than run away into the night, she circles the parking lot across the street from Nude Boyfriend's apartment: without a destination, she wants to revel in the pleasure of pushing and gliding herself circularly around a contained space outside—but only just outside—the home.

That Fertile Feeling reframes neoliberal understandings of the productively reproductive subject by imagining a future that is not leveraged against the procreative economics of the present, and by articulating a vision of what happens when that reproductive logic is "fertilized" to an excessive degree. What results is a picture of a space of resistance to the medical imperatives targeting the HIV+, those at risk of seroconversion, and the many other overlapping groups impacted by mutually supporting routinized exclusions, and a joyous visualizing of a trans revaluation of family values.

Nicholas C. Morgan is a postdoctoral core lecturer in art history at Columbia University. His research focuses on questions of identity in visual art of the 1980s and 1990s and on art of the AIDS crisis considered through a transnational lens. Recent articles have appeared in *ART-Margins* and *QED: A Journal in GLBTQ Worldmaking*.

References

Bordowitz, Gregg. 2010. *Imagevirus*. London: Afterall.

Chen, Mel Y. 2012. *Animacies: Biopolitics, Racial Mattering, and Queer Affect*. Durham, NC: Duke University Press.

Cohen, Cathy J. 1997. "Punks, Bulldaggers, and Welfare Queens: The Radical Potential of Queer Politics?" *GLQ* 3, no. 4: 437–65.

Cooper, Melinda. 2017. *Family Values: Between Neoliberalism and the New Social Conservatism*. New York: Zone.

Davis, Dana-Ain. 2009. "The Politics of Reproduction: The Troubling Case of Nadya Suleman and Assisted Reproductive Technology." *Transforming Anthropology* 17, no. 2: 105–16.

Deutscher, Penelope. 2017. *Foucault's Futures: A Critique of Reproductive Reason*. New York: Columbia University Press.

Dunham, Cyrus Grace. 2015. "The 'Terrorist Drag' of Vaginal Davis." *New Yorker*, December 12. www.newyorker.com/culture/culture-desk/terrorist-drag-vaginal-davis.

Frankfort, Ellen. 1972. *Vaginal Politics*. New York: Quadrangle.

Gould, Deborah B. 2009. *Moving Politics: Emotion and ACT UP's Fight against AIDS*. Chicago: University of Chicago Press.

Halberstam, Jack. 2018. *Trans*: A Quick and Quirky Account of Gender Variability*. Berkeley: University of California Press.

Nelson, Alondra. 2013. *Body and Soul: The Black Panther Party and the Fight against Medical Discrimination*. Minneapolis: University of Minnesota Press.

Ngai, Sianne. 2005. *Ugly Feelings*. Cambridge, MA: Harvard University Press.

Roth, Benita. 2017. *The Life and Death of ACT UP/LA: Anti-AIDS Activism in Los Angeles from the 1980s to the 2000s*. Cambridge: Cambridge University Press.

Watney, Simon. 1987. *Policing Desire: Pornography, AIDS, and the Media*. London: Methuen.

Williams, Linda. 1989. *Hard Core: Power, Pleasure, and the "Frenzy of the Visible."* Berkeley: University of California Press.

Erratum for Jules Joanne Gleeson, "Are Jokes Going to Cut It? Concerning Andrea Long Chu's *Females*," *TSQ* 7, no. 3 (2020): 332–44.

Kay Gabriel's name was misspelled as "Kaye" on pp. 332, 343, and 344.

DOI 10.1215/23289252-8955609

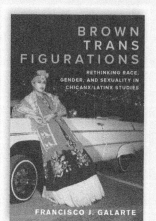

Keep up to date on new scholarship

Issue alerts are a great way to stay current on all the cutting-edge scholarship from your favorite Duke University Press journals. This free service delivers tables of contents directly to your inbox, informing you of the latest groundbreaking work as soon as it is published.

To sign up for issue alerts:

1. Visit **dukeu.press/register** and register for an account. You do not need to provide a customer number.

2. After registering, visit **dukeu.press/alerts**.

3. Go to "Latest Issue Alerts" and click on "Add Alerts."

4. Select as many publications as you would like from the pop-up window and click "Add Alerts."

read.dukeupress.edu/journals

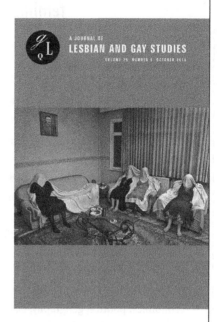

Printed and bound by CPI Group (UK) Ltd, Croydon, CR0 4YY

13/04/2025

14656484-0004